ALLEN CARR

The
LITTLE
BOOK *of*
QUITTING

Sterling Publishing Co., Inc.
New York

Published by Sterling Publishing Co., Inc.
387 Park Avenue South, New York, NY 10016

© 2000, 2005 by Allen Carr's Easyway (International) Ltd.

Allen Carr's Easyway and **Easyway** are trademarks of
Allen Carr's Easyway (International) Ltd.

ISBN 1-4027-3132-9

Library of Congress Cataloging-in-Publication Data
available upon request

3 5 7 9 8 6 4

Manufactured in the United States of America

IMPORTANT WARNING!

Unless you have already quit, do not attempt to do so, or even to cut down, before you have read and understood the whole book.

INTRODUCTION BY THE AUTHOR

Imagine a drug that causes the premature death of one in every two users, costs the average addict $100,000 in a lifetime, makes you feel insecure, bored, and tense, tastes foul, ruins your confidence, impedes your concentration, and has no advantages whatsoever.

Can you believe that at one time over 90% of the adult population of Western society was addicted to this drug?

Can you imagine yourself becoming addicted to such a drug? If you are a smoker, casual or otherwise, you already are an addict. The drug is nicotine.

Suppose I, being a former chain-smoker for thirty-three years, could convince you that the facts about smoking are exactly as I have described above and, furthermore, that any smoker can find it easy to quit

IMMEDIATELY AND PERMANENTLY
WITHOUT USING WILLPOWER,
GIMMICKS, OR SUBSTITUTES, AND
WITHOUT PUTTING ON WEIGHT.

What if I could further convince you that you won't miss smoking, that you'll enjoy social occasions more, and be better able to cope with stressful situations? Would you quit? Then read on. I have nothing but good news for you.

WHEN DID YOU DECIDE
TO BE A SMOKER?

No. I don't mean what was the occasion of your first cigarette, but when did you decide to smoke every day?

Or did you just drift into it like every other smoker on the planet?

WILL YOU ALWAYS BE A SMOKER?

So when will you quit?

> After you've spent the $100,000?
> When you've crippled your health?
> When the time is right?

How many years have you smoked?

Do you ever wonder why it never seems like the right time to quit?

WHY DO YOU SMOKE?

Because it tastes good?

> *Do you eat it?*

For something to do with your hands?

> *Try a ballpoint pen.*

For oral satisfaction?

> *Use a pacifier.*

To relieve boredom and stress, and aid relaxation and concentration?

> *Surely, boredom and concentration are opposites.*
>
> *So are stress and relaxation.*

WHAT ARE YOUR FAVORITE CIGARETTES?

First one in the morning? *Isn't that the one that tastes the worst?*

After a meal or with a drink, when answering the phone or during stress? *How can the identical cigarette out of the same pack taste different than, or have the complete opposite effect from, the one smoked an hour earlier?*

Do You Wish Your Children Smoked?

If the answer is no, it means that you wish you were a non-smoker! So why aren't you? *Because smoking is a habit and habits are difficult to break?*

Are they? In England people are in the habit of driving on the left. If they drive in the United States, they break the habit immediately, without difficulty.

SO WHY DO SMOKERS CONTINUE TO SMOKE?

For one reason and one reason only—they have fallen into the most subtle, ingenious trap that man and nature have combined to lay:

THEY ARE ADDICTED TO NICOTINE!

THE MOST POWERFUL DRUG IN THE WORLD!

Nicotine is the most powerful addictive drug known to mankind. Just one cigarette can hook you, particularly if you have been addicted previously.

A POWERFUL POISON!

The nicotine content of just one cigarette injected directly into a vein would kill you. Please don't try it. This is why those first cigarettes make you feel dizzy and sick.

THE NATURE OF THE TRAP

When the nicotine from the first cigarette leaves your body, it creates a feeling of emptiness and insecurity—the feeling that smokers know as "needing a cigarette" or "something to do with their hands."

TIGHT SHOES!

When you light the next cigarette, the nicotine is replaced, and the empty, insecure feeling immediately disappears. This is the feeling that smokers describe as a satisfaction or pleasure.

It's like wearing tight shoes just to get the pleasure of removing them!

THE LIFETIME'S CHAIN

When you extinguish the next cigarette, the nicotine leaves and the empty, insecure feeling returns. Now you need another cigarette, and another, ad infinitum, until death do you part!

THE LITTLE MONSTER

Think of that empty feeling as a tapeworm inside your body that feeds on nicotine. The true reason that any smoker continues to smoke is to feed that little nicotine monster.

YOU ARE ABOUT TO STARVE IT TO DEATH!

WHY ISN'T IT OBVIOUS?

Because it works back to front. It's when you aren't smoking that you suffer the craving. The moment you light up, it's relieved. Your brain is fooled into believing you receive a genuine pleasure or crutch.

What you are really enjoying is getting back to the state you had permanently before you lit the first cigarette.

In fact, you are simply trying to feel as relaxed as a non-smoker!

YOU NEVER GET THERE

Unless you quit. When you learn to smoke, you are merely teaching your body to become immune to a powerful poison. After a short period you only partially relieve the empty feeling. This is why the tendency is to smoke more and more.

DRUG ADDICTION OR GENUINE PLEASURE?

Genuine pleasures, like a nice vacation, create no feeling of guilt. We are pleased to boast about them and, while we would like to enjoy the pleasure more often, we do not feel deprived or miserable when not partaking of the pleasure; whereas all smokers brag how little they smoke, and even the thought of being without cigarettes creates panic.

PICTURE A HEROIN ADDICT

That terrible panic when he has no heroin and the wonderful feeling of "pleasure" when he plunges that hypodermic into a vein. Non-heroin addicts don't suffer that panicked feeling. Heroin doesn't relieve it. IT CAUSES IT! Non-smokers don't suffer the panic feeling of needing a cigarette. Neither did you before you became addicted to nicotine.

THE INCREDIBLE IRONY OF IT ALL

The only reason you or any other smoker needs or wants a cigarette is to try to get rid of your nicotine withdrawal. But it is only smokers who suffer nicotine withdrawal. Non-smokers do not. So all you are trying to do whenever you light a cigarette is feel like a non-smoker!

CHECK IT OUT

Light up now. Take six deep drags and ask yourself what it is that you are actually enjoying.

Isn't it true that it's not so much that you enjoy inhaling toxic fumes into your lungs as that you can't enjoy social occasions or cope with stress without them?

But Drugs Are Difficult To Kick

Only if you believe you get some genuine pleasure or benefit from them. Once you realize that not only does smoking destroy your health and wealth but that it actually destroys your nerves and confidence, you—or any smoker—can genuinely enjoy the process of quitting

IMMEDIATELY AND PERMANENTLY!

WHAT ABOUT THE WITHDRAWAL PANGS?

Although nicotine is the world's most powerful drug in the speed with which it hooks smokers, you are never badly hooked.

The actual physical withdrawal from nicotine is so slight that smokers only know the feeling as

I WANT A CIGARETTE!

IDENTICAL TO FOOD

Nicotine withdrawal is identical to the hunger for food. In both cases you feel irritable and empty when unable to relieve the craving, and feel confident, content, and relaxed once you satisfy the hunger or craving.

THE COMPLETE OPPOSITE
OF HUNGER

Good food genuinely tastes good, tobacco tastes foul. Food is survival, tobacco is death. Food genuinely satisfies hunger, tobacco creates the craving. Eating is a genuine pleasure we can enjoy throughout our lives. Smoking is an illusion of pleasure, an ingenious confidence trick that enslaves us for life.

I Enjoy the Taste

Most smokers can remember how foul those first cigarettes tasted, and how hard they had to work to inhale. Ask a smoker: "If you can't get your own brand, do you abstain?" A smoker would rather smoke old rope! It's like working on a pig farm. After a while you become immune to the smell. Smokers become immune to the smell of stale tobacco.

INTRODUCING
THE BIG MONSTER

From birth we are subjected to a massive, daily bombardment telling us that cigarettes relieve boredom and stress, and aid concentration and relaxation. In movies, when someone is about to be executed, his last request is always a cancer stick. In TV dramas, a husband chain-smokes outside the maternity ward. When the baby is born, cigars are handed around in celebration.

THE BRAINWASHING

This is the "Big Monster" in the mind and the real reason we find it difficult to quit. It doesn't affect us before we become hooked, because the beautiful truth is that our lives were complete before we tried those first experimental cigarettes.

But once we do, the "Little Monster" confirms the brainwashing or, more accurately, fools our brains into believing it.

THE VOID

Our children all seem to be searching for some magical elixir or prop, as if the incredible intelligence that created us (be it God or three million years of natural selection) has omitted some vital ingredient essential to our enjoyment of life or to our ability to survive.

THE INCREDIBLE MACHINE

The human body is the most sophisticated survival machine on the planet. It is complete. But children and teenagers have yet to mature. They feel insecure and vulnerable. Little wonder they turn to illusory props that guarantee they will never mature, unless and until they are free from both monsters.

Like Claustrophobia

Try forcing a claustrophobic into a confined space and he will panic. He won't suffocate, but if he believes he will, it amounts to the same thing. If you believe that you can't enjoy life or handle stress without a cigarette, you will feel miserable and insecure without one.

THE ITCH

Think of the "Little Monster" as an almost imperceptible itch that you can partially and temporarily relieve by lighting up. Like tight shoes, the longer you suffer, the greater the relief. This is why the so-called "special" cigarettes follow a period of abstinence: after a meal, exercise, sex, or whatever.

THE FIRST OF THE DAY

The one that makes us cough our lungs up, but ironically a favorite for many smokers. That's because we've gone eight hours without nicotine. When we awake, we relieve a series of aggravations: our bladders, our thirst, etc. A non-smoker will relieve his hunger. A smoker is more likely to light a cigarette.

FOOD OR NICOTINE

Although the empty feelings are indistinguishable, nicotine will not relieve the hunger for food or vice versa. This is why I became a chain-smoker. After that first cigarette of the day, I still had the empty feeling, which was hunger for food. But to my confused brain it meant: I need another cigarette and another.

THE TUG-OF-WAR

All smokers suffer from a permanent tug-of-war:

On the one side —
It's filthy and disgusting slavery, destroying my health and wealth.

On the other side —
It's my friend, my pleasure, my crutch.

THE REALITY

It's a tug-of-war of fear. There is no genuine pleasure or crutch. The other side is also fear. The reality is: *How can I enjoy life or cope with life without cigarettes?* Both sets of fear are caused by nicotine. Non-smokers don't suffer from either.

NEITHER WILL YOU,
ONCE YOU ARE FREE!

I Wish I Were a Happy Casual Smoker

There is no such thing. With a permanent itch, the natural tendency is to scratch it continuously. The natural tendency for a smoker is to become a chain-smoker. So why aren't all smokers chain-smokers? Because the effect on our health, wealth, and self-respect makes us try to control our intake of poison.

SMOKE LESS–HOOKED MORE!

The less you smoke, the less it affects your health and wealth, and the less your desire to quit. The longer you go before scratching the itch, the greater the illusion of crutch or pleasure, and the greater your desire to continue smoking.

I Can Go a Week
Without Smoking

If there is genuine pleasure, why would you want to? If there is none, why smoke at all?

I can go a week without carrots, but feel no need to boast about it. Perhaps I would boast if I'd had to discipline myself and deprive myself for a whole week. If we are proud of how little we smoke, just think how great it will feel to be free!

ALL SMOKERS LIE
TO THEMSELVES

Why? Because we sense that we've fallen into a trap and feel stupid and weak-willed because we've failed to escape from it. So we give phony reasons to justify our stupidity in order to retain some semblance of self-respect. No way do we deceive non-smokers. We don't even deceive ourselves.

I Only Enjoy Two a Day

So why do you smoke the others?

In fact, you never enjoy any.

This is why the vast majority of cigarettes are smoked subconsciously. If every time you lit a cigarette you had to be aware of that $100,000, the filth in your lungs, and that this might just be the one to trigger lung cancer, even the illusion of enjoyment would go.

WHY SMOKERS FIND IT HARD TO QUIT

Because the two monsters have fooled them into believing that they are making a genuine sacrifice, that a meal will never be as enjoyable, that they won't be able to handle stress, that they have to go through a transitional period of misery, and that, even if they succeed, they will have to resist temptation for the rest of their lives.

THE ADDITIONAL
BRAINWASHING

The umpteen smokers who quit for ten years then started again or are still moping about how they miss them. Ex-smokers who tell you how great they feel and who next time you see them are puffing away again. Smokers who are clearly killing themselves yet still smoke. And the misery of your own failed attempts when using willpower.

THE WILLPOWER METHOD

Something triggers an attempt to quit. The smoker forces himself into a self-imposed tantrum, like a child being deprived of candy, hoping that if he has the willpower to resist the temptation long enough, one day he will wake up with the feeling

EUREKA! I'M FREE!!!

WHY HE NEVER ACHIEVES IT

After a few days the congestion goes, you have more money, no longer despise yourself, and have that wonderful holier-than-thou feeling of no longer being a slave. All the reasons that made you decide to quit are rapidly disappearing. Meanwhile, the "Little Monster" hasn't had his fix—your brain is saying:

"I WANT A CIGARETTE!"

The Confusion

For some mysterious reason you still want a cigarette but aren't allowed to have one. You start to feel deprived and miserable. This is one of the occasions your brain has been programmed to light a cigarette, so you feel even more miserable. Soon your whole life is dominated by the misery of not being allowed to smoke.

EVENTUALLY YOUR WILLPOWER RUNS OUT

You get fed up with always feeling miserable. You start searching for reasons to have just one cigarette, and eventually you find one. The longer you have abstained, the weirder that first cigarette tastes. The longer you have suffered the misery of feeling deprived, the greater the illusion of pleasure. You are soon back to where you started.

Absence Makes the Heart Grow Fonder

If you believe there is some genuine pleasure in smoking, why should that belief ever go? The "Little Monster" is identical to normal hunger and normal stress. So, long after the "Little Monster" has died, during times of normal hunger or stress, the ex-smoker's brain is still fooled into believing that a cigarette will help.

It's Conflict, Not Lack of Willpower

At our clinics we ask smokers who think they are weak-willed: "If you ran out late at night, how far would you walk for a pack of cigarettes?"

A smoker would swim the English Channel for a pack. A strong-willed child will keep his tantrum going forever. It takes a strong-willed person to block his mind to the terrible health risks and continue to smoke.

I Knew That
I Was Strong-Willed

I couldn't understand why no one and nothing else in my life controlled me, yet I was completely dominated by something I loathed. Or why my friends could smoke ten cigarettes a day and I had to chain-smoke. It never occurred to me that they couldn't afford to chain-smoke, or that their lungs couldn't cope with the poison.

NATIONAL NO-SMOKING DAY

According to the media, that's the day every smoker attempts to quit. In reality, it's the day every smoker smokes twice as many and twice as blatantly, because smokers don't like being told what to do by people who don't understand. It takes a strong-willed person to resist the massive antisocial pressures that smokers are subjected to nowadays.

CHECK OUT YOUR SMOKING FRIENDS

The main illusion about smoking is that it relieves stress. It is physical and mentally dominant people who tend to take up highly responsible professions. You'll find that your acquaintances who are still heavy smokers are strong-willed in other ways. We are about to remove this conflict of wills.

How Does
"Easyway" Work?

By simply removing the confusion and misconceptions that make it difficult to quit. Smokers try to "give up" smoking. This implies a genuine sacrifice. For the reasons I have already explained, there is absolutely nothing to give up.

The two monsters create the illusion of pleasure or crutch. The reality is the complete opposite.

THE ADVANTAGES OF BEING A SMOKER

There aren't any. I don't mean the disadvantages outweigh them. I mean there is no pleasure or crutch whatsoever. On the contrary, smoking destroys your nerves and confidence and creates boredom, restlessness, and dissatisfaction. Far from being your friend, it would be difficult to imagine a worse enemy.

IT'S FEAR THAT KEEPS
US SMOKING

A subtlety of the nicotine trap is to keep its victims trapped for life.

You might feel that I'm taking away and giving nothing back. You might be tempted to stop reading or to abandon your attempt. Please don't fall for the trap. Like me, ex-smokers who used my method found it to be the most rewarding experience of their lives.

SNUFF-TAKING

Sniffing dried tobacco is a form of nicotine addiction. Like smoking, it was regarded as a habit. Addicts used similar gimmicks, such as silver snuff-boxes, to disguise the filth. Do heroin addicts enjoy injections? Do cocaine sniffers enjoy sniffing for sniffing's sake? Or are these just the rather disgusting methods we use to administer the drug?

I ENJOY THE RITUAL

Smokers believe that there is an actual pleasure in smoking, and that the health risks and expense are merely hazards that interfere with that pleasure. If that were true, smokers would enjoy herbal cigarettes. They never do. Smoking is merely a more dangerous and disgusting form of nicotine addiction.

A MOMENT TO REFLECT

If you are not yet convinced that there is nothing to give up and that the pleasure or crutch from smoking is merely an ingenious confidence trick, it is essential that you stop reading at this stage, go back to the beginning, and start again. Remember, I have nothing but good news for you, provided you follow my instructions.

WHAT ARE YOU
TRYING TO ACHIEVE?

Never to smoke again? No. This is what smokers who use willpower do. They go through the rest of their lives hoping they'll never smoke again. Which means they don't achieve their object until they die. This means they never know whether or not they succeeded.

WHEN DO YOU BECOME
A NON-SMOKER?

It is important that you reflect on this question. Typical answers are:

When I stop thinking about smoking.

How do you stop thinking about it?

When I can enjoy a meal or answer the phone, etc., without craving a cigarette.

How long will that be?

When I've quit for a year.

Why wait a year? Why not longer?

It's all so vague and indecisive.

WHAT ARE YOU TRYING TO ACHIEVE!

The real difference between a smoker and a non-smoker is not that the latter doesn't smoke but that he has no desire to smoke. If you have no desire to smoke, there is no temptation to smoke and therefore no need for willpower to resist the temptation.

62

A FRAME OF MIND

What you are trying to achieve is a frame of mind, so that when you extinguish the final cigarette, for the next few days and for the rest of your life, whenever you think about smoking, instead of thinking, "I'd love a cigarette" or "When will I be free?", you say to yourself:

> "EUREKA! I'M ALREADY FREE!
> I'M ALREADY A NON-SMOKER!"

HOW WILL YOU KNOW
THAT YOU ARE FREE?

By clearing up all the doubts and confusion before you extinguish the final cigarette. By realizing that there is no such thing as a special or occasional cigarette, only a lifetime's chain of misery. By realizing that you are giving up absolutely nothing. On the contrary, you are receiving marvelous positive gains.

THOSE MARVELOUS POSITIVE GAINS

I knew I was literally burning my hard-earned money and risking terrible diseases. The chain reaction was like a time bomb ticking away inside my body, never knowing the length of the fuse, hoping I would quit before it went off. It's great to be free of the fear and self-loathing, but there were even greater, unexpected gains.

THE LETHARGY

I knew the coughing and congestion were due to smoking, but I thought the lack of energy was due to old age. I struggled to get up in the morning, and fell asleep each evening watching TV. It's great to wake up full of energy and feeling that you've had a good night's rest, actually wanting to exercise and feeling like a young boy again.

THE FEAR

As a youth, I enjoyed physicals, believing I was indestructible. As a smoker, I hated them. I even hated visiting other people in hospitals. The mere thought of chest x-rays would create panic. I was convinced that cigarettes gave me courage. It's so great to feel strong again, able to enjoy the good times and being fully equipped to cope with the bad.

THE SLAVERY

So intent was I on resisting all the attempts of the do-gooders who were trying to inform me of what I already knew—SMOKERS ARE FOOLS—it never occurred to me that I spent half my life feeling miserable because I wasn't allowed to smoke and the other half miserable because I did.

IT'S SO LOVELY BEING FREE!

A Sociable Pastime?

It's about as sociable as farting in an elevator! In the old days you could visit a strange office or a friend's house and ask, "Do you mind if I smoke?" It was really a polite way of asking for an ashtray. Ask for an ashtray nowadays and people look at you as if you are requesting some relic of the distant past. Smokers regard themselves as social pariahs.

THE SINISTER BLACK SHADOW

All our lives the fear of quitting makes us block our minds to the bad effects of smoking. It's like an ever-increasing black shadow forming in our subconscious. Strong people hate being controlled by something they loathe. The greatest gain is to be free of this dark cloud and self-loathing and to genuinely pity rather than envy smokers.

THE FIRST POWERFUL INFLUENCE

Before I started smoking, life was exciting. I could enjoy the highs and handle the stresses. When I finally discovered the "EASYWAY" to quit, it was like waking from a nightmare, escaping from a black-and-white world of fear and depression into a sunshine world of health, confidence, and freedom. I still can't get over the euphoria.

THE SECOND POWERFUL INFLUENCE

All creatures on this planet instinctively know the difference between food and poison. Even before that first experimental cigarette, we know that there is something evil and unnatural about breathing lethal fumes into our lungs. To have to do it all day, every day, because of the influence of a subtle, sinister drug, is not only evil but unthinkable.

THE CORRECT DECISION

Some decisions are difficult to make. How can you be certain that a particular car or TV is the best value for you? There is one decision in your life, however, that is easy to make: whether to spend the rest of your life as a smoker or a non-smoker. Smoking provides no advantages whatsoever and horrendous disadvantages.

IF YOU HESITATE

It's not because you are too stupid to see the obvious—you don't even need me to tell you the correct decision—it's because of FEAR! The greatest gain is to be free of that fear, which is caused by the drug. You never decided to become a smoker, but fell into an ingenious trap that is designed to enslave you for life.

THE INGENUITY OF THE TRAP

We are fooled into believing that we smoke because of some genuine pleasure or crutch. Therefore, we don't decide to quit until we have stress in our lives, such as a money shortage or bad health. But these are exactly the times we most need our little *"friend."* If we quit, the reasons why we quit soon disappear, so we start smoking again.

WHY THE TIME WILL NEVER BE RIGHT

Because the times you most need to quit are the times you most need your little *"friend."* Because there will always be some occasion coming up shortly in your life, be it social or stressful, that will enable you to put off the evil day. That's part of the ingenuity of the trap. Be aware of it! Don't fall for it!

SOME SMOKERS JUST DRIFT OUT OF IT

Rather like they drifted into it. I waited thirty-three years, hoping that would happen to me. Believe me, it will no more happen than you would drift out of a bear trap. You will only escape if you make a positive effort to do so, and the first step is to make the decision to make that attempt. I want you to do that now.

IT TAKES COURAGE

And I want you to have the courage to make that decision now. I'm not asking you to smoke your final cigarette now—I'll advise you when to do that—but merely to make the decision that you'll go for it. If you have the courage to do that and follow my instructions to the letter, you will not only find it easy but enjoyable.

A Feeling of
Doom and Gloom

If you have such a feeling, dismiss it now. You are about to achieve something marvelous, something that every smoker on the planet would love to achieve: TO BE FREE! It's a no-lose proposition. If you don't succeed, you are no worse off. But let's not even think of failure. After all, it was you Americans who taught the rest of the world not just to reach for the moon, but to actually land on it! Start right now with a feeling of excitement, challenge, and elation.

How Do I Cope With the Withdrawal?

The actual physical withdrawal from nicotine is no worse when you quit than throughout your smoking life. Although nicotine is the world's most powerful drug in the speed with which it hooks you, the good news is that you are never badly hooked. Smokers experience physical withdrawal from nicotine their whole smoking lives. If a smoker sleeps for six hours a night, when he wakes he is 97% nicotine-free. He has been going through withdrawal the entire night, but it's so mild that it doesn't even wake him up!

SO WHY DO SMOKERS GET SO IRRITABLE?

For exactly the same reason they get into a panic when they run out of cigarettes. Smokers don't wake up in a panic, even though they've gone eight hours without nicotine. Most smokers nowadays will leave the bedroom or eat breakfast before they light their first cigarette. Others will wait till they arrive at work.

THAT PANICKED FEELING

It can start even before you run out. You're at a party and ration your cigarettes, saving one for bedtime and one for the morning. Some joker says: "Do you mind if I have one of yours?" As you meekly hand it over, you're thinking: *"Mind? Of course I mind! I'd rather give you a pint of blood or even donate a kidney!"*

ADDICTION IS MENTAL, NOT PHYSICAL

The almost imperceptible physical discomfort created by the "Little Monster" acts as a catalyst that triggers the "Big Monster." It's the "Big Monster" that creates the fear and panic—the belief that we cannot enjoy or cope with life without nicotine. Fortunately, we can remove the illusion, fear, and panic, prior to the final cigarette.

BE AWARE OF THE "LITTLE MONSTER"

For a few days after quitting, the "Little Monster" will live on. You might be aware of a feeling of insecurity or merely think: *"I want a cigarette."* This is when ex-smokers get confused and miserable because they can't have one. They believe they are being deprived of a genuine pleasure or crutch.

BE PREPARED FOR
THAT FEELING

But don't worry about it. Recognize it for what it is. Say to yourself, *"It's what smokers feel throughout their smoking lives and what keeps them miserable, poor, lethargic, unhealthy slaves!"*

Rejoice in the fact that you have already escaped from the prison. Revel in the death throes of the "Little Monster"!

ESCAPED OR TRYING TO ESCAPE?

You become a non-smoker the moment you extinguish your final cigarette. *But how do you know it is your final cigarette?* Simply by removing all doubt and uncertainty first. If you have doubts, you are merely hoping not to smoke again. How will you ever know? You'll be waiting for nothing to happen, and like so many ex-smokers, will do so the rest of your life.

But How Can You Ever Be Certain?

Would you take up a pastime that gave you no pleasure or advantages whatsoever, that cost you a fortune, shortened your life, and made you feel nervous, lethargic, unclean, stupid, and miserable? The biggest idiot on earth wouldn't! Having made what you know to be the correct decision, never punish yourself by ever doubting it!

OH, I'D LOVE A CIGARETTE!

How often do you hear ex-smokers, whether they have quit for a few hours, days, or even years, make similar statements? It is these whining stoppers who make existing smokers frightened to even make the attempt—they perpetuate the belief that once a smoker always a smoker, that once addicted you can never be completely free!

IT'S ABSOLUTE NONSENSE!!!

HOW STUPID CAN YOU GET?

Why do otherwise intelligent people decide to quit, then spend the rest of their lives bemoaning the fact that they can't smoke the occasional cigarette? It's because they doubt their decision, they believe that they have made a genuine sacrifice, that they actually received some genuine pleasure or crutch from smoking.

In Reality, It's Even More Stupid!

What they are moping for never actually existed. For example, the favorite cigarettes, such as the one after a meal. Can you ever actually remember thinking: *"This really tastes marvelous"*?

Isn't it true that it's not so much that we enjoy smoking cigarettes, but that we assume we do, because we are miserable without them?

REMEMBER THOSE STRESSFUL SITUATIONS

When your car broke down in the pouring rain in the middle of nowhere, and you were soaking wet and covered in grease, can you remember lighting up and thinking: *"I'm late for the most important appointment of my life. But who cares? I've got this gorgeous pack of cigarettes!"*?

Did they make you happy and cheerful?

I CAN'T ANSWER THE PHONE
WITHOUT ONE

A common plea of the many powerful business executives who attend our clinics. What's so stressful about the phone? It won't blow up or bite you. It's that little itch that's causing the stress. That's also why smokers find it difficult to concentrate without first removing the distraction. Non-smokers don't seem to suffer from the problem.

BUT IT DEFINITELY
RELIEVES BOREDOM

Does it? Boredom is a frame of mind. When you smoke a cigarette, do you sit there thinking: *"Oh, how mind-absorbing and fascinating this is"*? Can you think of anything more boring than chain-smoking cigarette after cigarette, day in, day out, for thirty-three years, as I once did? We smoke when bored, because there is nothing to distract us from the itch.

NEVER DOUBT YOUR DECISION

It's the uncertainty that makes it difficult to quit. Having made what you know to be the correct decision, never punish yourself by questioning that decision. If you see one cigarette as a pleasure or crutch, you'll see a million cigarettes that way. By craving one, you'll be miserable because you can't have it, and even more miserable if you do!

THE GREATEST MISTAKE

Smokers make when they try to quit is to try not to think about smoking. This merely creates a phobia. Remember that something marvelous is happening. It's what you are thinking that's important. If it's: *"I can't have one"* or *"when will I be free?"* you'll be doubting your decision. Instead always think:

YIPPEE! I'M A NON-SMOKER!!!

"THE MOMENT OF REVELATION"

If you follow the instructions, after just a few days you'll have a moment—it might be in a social or stressful situation, one of those times that you thought you could never enjoy or handle without a cigarette—when not only did you enjoy or handle it, but you never even thought about smoking. That's when you know you are free!

Don't Wait For It To Happen

If you try to force "The Moment of Revelation," it will be like worrying about not being able to sleep— you'll merely ensure it won't happen. You become a non-smoker the moment you cut off the supply of nicotine. Just get on with your life. Accept that you'll have good days and bad, just as smokers do.

DON'T CHANGE
YOUR LIFESTYLE

Just because you've quit smoking: things such as avoiding your smoking friends. If you do, you'll be miserable. Remember you aren't giving up living. You aren't giving up anything. On the contrary, as your energy level and confidence improve, you'll find both your capacity to enjoy life and to handle stress will increase.

IT ALL HAPPENS SO SLOWLY

Another ingenuity of the nicotine trap is that our slide down into the pit is so gradual that we aren't even aware of the increasing debilitation of our physical and mental health. The problem is that when we quit, the recovery is also gradual, and if we are using the willpower method and feeling miserable and deprived, we tend to be blind to the immense gains.

"It Takes Seven Years to Clear The Gunk"

Or, "Every cigarette you smoke takes five minutes off your life." Such statements are true, but only if you contract one of the killer diseases. If you quit now, your health can recover up to 99%, as if you'd never been a smoker, and the bulk of the gunk goes away during the first few days and weeks.

USE YOUR IMAGINATION

If it were possible to project any smoker three weeks ahead to give him a direct comparison of how he would feel as a non-smoker, not just physically but in terms of confidence, he would have no hesitation in quitting cheerfully and immediately. I can't do that, but you can:

JUST USE YOUR IMAGINATION!

TIME IS ON YOUR SIDE

Provided that you've first removed the brainwashing, once you've cut off the supply of nicotine, nothing can prevent you from being free. You will already be a non-smoker, and it is essential that you think of yourself as one immediately. If you wait for it to happen, it will be like sowing seeds, then watching the ground until they grow.

EXPECT SOME DISORIENTATION

Even changes for the better, like a new job, house, or car, involve a period of adjustment. If you do feel somewhat strange at first, that will soon go, provided that you don't start worrying about it. Remember, any slight aggravation you might suffer is not because you've quit but because you started in the first place. Non-smokers don't suffer from withdrawal.

I KEEP FORGETTING I'VE QUIT

Don't worry! It's quite normal and a good sign. It means that already your mind isn't completely obsessed. But these are the times when those who've stopped through willpower start to doubt and mope. Train yourself to reverse the moment immediately. Remind yourself how lucky you are to be free, or just think: YIPPEE! I'M A NON-SMOKER! That way those moments become pleasurable.

I Can't Get Up Without a Cigarette

When you extinguish that final cigarette, look forward to being free the rest of the day. Lie in bed, reflecting that you have already achieved the most difficult part—making the start and anticipating the exciting challenge of proving you can not only survive but actually enjoy a whole day, from dawn to dusk, FREE!!!

IT HAPPENS ON SOCIAL OCCASIONS

You're chatting away, oblivious. The cigarettes are handed around. You find yourself subconsciously taking one. Your friend smirks, "I thought you'd given them up!" You feel stupid. Don't just stand there. Instead say, "I'd quite forgotten." (Which is all that happened.) "I can't tell you how lovely it is to be free. You should try it!" The situation is reversed.

NEVER ENVY SMOKERS

There is a constant battle between smokers and ex-smokers. As more and more smokers leave the sinking ship, those left on it feel more stupid, insecure, and isolated. This fear can cause even people who love you to try to get you hooked again. Never forget that the ex-smoker holds all the aces, and the smoker doesn't even have a pair of twos!

ATTEND SOCIAL FUNCTIONS IMMEDIATELY

Even if you are the only non-smoker present (usually the reverse now), always be aware that every one of those smokers would love to be like you. They will expect you to be miserable. When they see you happy and cheerful, they'll think you are a Superman or Superwoman.

The important point is:

> YOU'LL FEEL LIKE ONE!
> ENJOY YOUR ESCAPE!

WHEN WILL THE CRAVING GO?

The "Little Monster" causes the physical itch to your body. But it is only your brain that is capable of craving a cigarette. For a few days the "Little Monster" might continue to trigger the thought: "I want a cigarette." Your brain has the choice of craving one or recognizing the feeling for what it is and thinking:

"YIPPEE! I'M A NON-SMOKER!!!"

When a Friend or Relative Dies

You have to go through a period of mourning. Eventually, time partially heals the wound and life goes on. It's the same with people who stop smoking through willpower. If they can suffer the misery long enough, life goes on. But they still believe they've given up a genuine pleasure or crutch. Come a trauma in their lives, smoke one cigarette, and they're back in the trap!

WHEN AN ENEMY DIES

You don't have to go through a mourning process. You can rejoice immediately and for the rest of your life. The cigarette was never a friend. It was the worst disease you'll ever suffer from. You have it in your control. You have the choice of spending the next few days moping for an illusion or rejoicing:

"YIPPEE! I'M A NON-SMOKER!!!"

I NEED A SUBSTITUTE

I presume that you are searching for some elixir that will have contradictory effects like relieving boredom and helping concentration, relieving stress and improving relaxation, and which at the same time won't destroy your health and wealth. If you ever find it, please let me know. By the way, do you search for Aladdin's lamp?

DO NOT USE SUBSTITUTES

By even searching for one, you are confirming that you are making a sacrifice: "There is a void in my life. I need something to take its place." When you get rid of a bout of the flu, do you search for a substitute disease? Nicotine created the void. You didn't need to smoke before you became hooked. Substitutes merely prolong the feeling of a void.

WILL I PUT ON WEIGHT?

Only if you substitute candy or gum, or start picking between meals. If you do, not only will you get fat and miserable, but you won't even satisfy the empty feeling and will prolong your search for illusory rewards. If you put on a couple of pounds due to a better appetite at main meals, don't worry. When you've kicked smoking, you can control anything, and will soon be able to lose them.

WILL NICOTINE GUM OR PATCHES HELP?

NO! In theory, while you are breaking the habit, they ease the terrible physical withdrawal pains, and when you've broken the habit, you wean yourself off the nicotine substitute. In fact, the physical withdrawal is almost imperceptible, and it's not habit but addiction. They keep the "Little Monster" alive and the "Big Monster" craving!

ENJOY HAVING A NON-SMOKE

If you cannot visualize certain activities without smoking, break the association from the start. Have your drink, do your crossword puzzle, whatever. Enjoy being a non-smoker. Enjoy not only removing the gunk from your body but also proving that you can enjoy life without smoking. It's only smokers who can't enjoy life without nicotine.

I'll Have To Give Up Golf

In fact, you will not have to give up anything. I couldn't visualize even wanting to play golf without smoking. In fact, I couldn't visualize life without cigarettes. Now I can't visualize that I was once a nicotine slave. Soon, you'll find it difficult to understand why you ever felt the need to smoke, and wonder why you can't make other smokers appreciate just how nice it is to be free!

Observe Casual Smokers at Parties

They almost chain-smoke! Notice how agitated they are when not smoking. Watch the obvious relief when they light up. Observe how quickly the cigarette burns and watch the increasing agitation when the nicotine leaves. Remember, the next day they have to continue the chain, ad infinitum, for life!

OBSERVE SMOKERS GENERALLY

W atch young girls smoking in the street, drivers in a traffic jam, office workers outside a non-smoking office, vacationers whose flight has been delayed, or lone smokers at a social function. Notice they don't even seem to be aware that they are smoking, or, if they are, how uncomfortable they look, and how even more miserable they are, when not allowed to smoke.

TIMING

The natural tendency is to pick a period when you feel you least need a cigarette. Like practically every other aspect about smoking, the correct course is the complete opposite. Start at a time you consider to be the most difficult, prove straight away that you can enjoy the social occasion or handle the stress, and the rest is easy.

A DEGENERATIVE DISEASE

With a disease that gets worse and worse, it doesn't take a Sherlock Holmes to deduce that the quicker you get rid of it the better. If you had Alzheimer's or Parkinson's disease and there were a simple cure, would you delay a single day? Smoking is the Number One killer disease in society. Fortunately, there is a simple cure:

DO IT NOW!

THE FINAL PREPARATION

You should now be like a dog straining at the leash to smoke that final cigarette. If not, there can only be two reasons: that you do not believe that smoking conveys no advantages whatsoever—if so, read back from the beginning—or that you believe but still have a feeling of doom and gloom. In which case, stop being stupid and trust me.

THE FINAL CIGARETTE

I want you to smoke it, not with a feeling of doom and gloom but with a feeling of elation. Did you decide to fall into the trap? Just think how great the Count of Monte Cristo felt when he finally escaped from that prison. Don't extinguish that final cigarette thinking: *"I must never smoke again."* Rather:

> *"ISN'T IT MARVELOUS —*
> *I DON'T EVER NEED TO!"*

NEVER ENVY SMOKERS

You are not being deprived. If you see someone smoking, no matter what the occasion, be aware that they are not smoking because they choose to. They are being deprived of their money, health, energy, relaxation, self-respect, and freedom. All that, to achieve what? Nothing! Just trying to feel like a non-smoker. Smokers are drug addicts, and like all drug addiction — it'll just get worse and worse.

HELP THEM!

Poison Pen

A FORENSIC HANDWRITING MYSTERY

SHEILA LOWE

AN OBSIDIAN MYSTERY

OBSIDIAN
Published by New American Library, a division of
Penguin Group (USA) Inc., 375 Hudson Street,
New York, New York 10014, USA
Penguin Group (Canada), 90 Eglinton Avenue East, Suite 700, Toronto,
Ontario M4P 2Y3, Canada (a division of Pearson Penguin Canada Inc.)
Penguin Books Ltd., 80 Strand, London WC2R 0RL, England
Penguin Ireland, 25 St. Stephen's Green, Dublin 2,
Ireland (a division of Penguin Books Ltd.)
Penguin Group (Australia), 250 Camberwell Road, Camberwell, Victoria 3124,
Australia (a division of Pearson Australia Group Pty. Ltd.)
Penguin Books India Pvt. Ltd., 11 Community Centre, Panchsheel Park,
New Delhi - 110 017, India
Penguin Group (NZ), 67 Apollo Drive, Rosedale, North Shore 0632,
New Zealand (a division of Pearson New Zealand Ltd.)
Penguin Books (South Africa) (Pty.) Ltd., 24 Sturdee Avenue,
Rosebank, Johannesburg 2196, South Africa

Penguin Books Ltd., Registered Offices:
80 Strand, London WC2R 0RL, England

Published by Obsidian, an imprint of New American Library, a division of
Penguin Group (USA) Inc. This is an authorized reprint of an edition published
by Capital Crime Press. For information address: Capital Crime Press; P.O. Box
272904; Fort Collins, CO 80527

First Obsidian Printing, April 2008
10 9 8 7 6 5 4 3 2 1

This book is dedicated to my brother and friend, Rick Taylor, for being such an excellent writer himself that he inspired me to return to my earliest wish   to write a mystery.

Acknowledgments

Over the long period of time that this book was in development, I asked a lot of questions of a lot of people. I appreciate so much the valuable input of professionals in various fields. Thanks are due my law enforcement buds for their advice on procedure: Kenny Brown, Jeff Hazer, and Scott Young; to Suzanne Bank, feng shui master extraordinaire, for helping with interiors.

Tanya Radic and Doctor John Quinn helped with medical info. Extra special thanks to my dear friend and first editor, Bob Joseph, who freely gave a tremendous amount of time and energy over several drafts, and to editor Ellen Larson, whose (thankfully) brutally honest comments made such a difference in the final polish. Finally of great importance was the input of the Santa Clarita Valley Mystery Writers—you know who you are, and I love you all.

Chapter I

"*No,* girlfrien'." The woman gave an emphatic shake of her head that set elaborately beaded braids swirling. "Dat was *not* her way. Not sui*cide*."

Claudia Rose figured her for around thirty. High cheekbones in a strikingly handsome face, café au lait skin, athletic frame in a casually elegant Chanel suit. The lilt in her voice suggested West Indies.

Her companion was Wal-Mart Goth. A girl about eighteen in tight, low-slung jeans and a brief top that showed off a pierced navel. Unnaturally black hair cut short and spiky. A tattoo decorated her upper chest: seven daggers thrust into a bloody heart. In the dry-eyed designer-clad crowd, she stood out like a dot of spaghetti sauce on a white dress, weeping into a soggy tissue as though her heart were broken.

"Stop your cryin'." The beaded woman's order had a sharp edge to it.

"But I'm *scared,*" the girl said, dashing Claudia's sympathetic assumption that her tears were for Lindsey Alexander, the woman they had come to bury.

"You *should* be scared, girlfrien'!"

"The cops said she killed herself."

"De *cops*! I am tellin' *you,* girl, before she come to dis earth, dat one make a pac' with God how she will go out, and it is not like *dis.*"

"But it could have been an accident . . . couldn't it?"

"An acci-*dent*?" The older woman's tone echoed scornful

disbelief. "I say someone *do her in*. Now you stop it, girl! You are makin' a scene."

A muddy trail of mascara dribbled down ashy pale cheeks. The tissue shredded and the girl switched to the back of her bare arm.

Claudia dug a clean tissue from her purse and leaned forward to offer it. The girl turned, snatched the tissue while eyeing Claudia with the suspicious glare of a feral cat, and wadded it against the one in her hand. She blew her nose with a loud, wet snuffle, pushed the waterlogged mess into her Levis pocket, then hurried off without a word. Flicking an annoyed glance at Claudia, the older woman followed.

Claudia lifted a brow at her friend, Kelly Brennan, who had also observed the exchange with interest. "Think she could be right?"

"What, that someone killed Lindsey?" Kelly snorted rudely. "Why not? I wanted to kill her myself. Not only me. *Everyone* hated her."

"That's cold, Kel. I don't think anyone hated her enough to *kill* her."

There was a short silence. "*I* did," Kelly said, so softly that Claudia almost didn't hear it.

"You did what? Hate her enough to kill her? There's a pretty big leap to actually doing it, which is what those women were talking about. Anyway, there was a suicide note, remember?"

Kelly shrugged. "I guess that was good enough for the cops. I wish *you* could've taken a look at it."

Claudia pursed her lips, nodding agreement. Yes, she would definitely have liked to see the note that had been recovered from the floor beside Lindsey's bathroom Jacuzzi. What handwriting analyst wouldn't?

Handwriting had been Claudia's passion since childhood, her career for more years than she cared to count. And it had created the bond between Claudia and Lindsey in college. Both psychology majors, they had opted to specialize in handwriting analysis. Kelly, who had been Claudia's best friend since the first day of kindergarten, had started out with them, but had gone on to Southwestern and now practiced family law.

It seemed a lifetime ago. They had been close friends, Claudia, Kelly, and Lindsey. Until Lindsey seduced one of Kelly's boyfriends. The first time, she had seemed genuinely contrite. But over the years, the backstabbing escalated, until finally, her acts of treachery went beyond the point of forgiveness and tore the friendship apart.

What kind of hypocrite am I? Attending the funeral of someone I no longer liked nor respected. What the hell am I doing here?

Exhuming memories better left buried.

Claudia turned to view the fans and paparazzi waiting at the bottom of the hill, an unruly mob decked out in bright T-shirts and shorts, floppy hats, and sunshades, crowded around the largest pair of wrought-iron gates in the world.

Forest Lawn Memorial Park. A stately convoy of limousines made the turn into the wide driveway, and the mob overflowed onto Glendale Avenue, calling out to their favorite stars, hoping for a glimpse through darkened windows.

"This whole damn thing is a Hollywood cliché," Claudia muttered, leaning close to Kelly's ear so that no one else might hear.

Kelly made a sound that might have been agreement. "So, where else would you expect Lindsey to be buried?"

"Good point."

Forest Lawn, where burial plots had names like Babyland, Graceland, and Sweet Memories. Where reproductions of famous statues and other works of art were offered for sale. Where more Hollywood celebrities were buried than anywhere else in the world.

Not that Lindsey Alexander herself had been a celebrity, of course. Having dropped out of handwriting analysis after a few years, she had turned to the public relations field, where she could be nearer the limelight. After reaching the height of her career as a publicist, she'd been content to make her famous clients the main attraction.

Kelly stared over the tops of her Gabbana shades at the platoon of CHiPs in golden helmets and jackboots handling crowd control. Petite, girlish for her thirty-nine years, Kelly had eyes the special blue of a summer sky, fringed by artificially long, dark lashes. Her hair was a cap of curls, currently blonde, trimmed a half-inch from her head. She was wearing a little black number that Claudia had last seen on her at a nightclub.

Kelly's eyes went to a limo easing to the curb fifteen feet away from them. Six matching hunks climbed out, their movements as practiced as if they had rehearsed for a major production. "*Ho-ly shit*," she breathed. "Talk about star-*studded.*"

Every last one of Lindsey's pallbearers was *GQ* cover material. Gathering behind the hearse, they lifted the satin-rubbed mahogany casket to their shoulders, well-toned abs flexing beneath coats designed by Armani, Canali, and Zegna.

Funeral as screen test?

Claudia glanced down at her friend, who was half a head shorter than her own five-seven. "They must be melting in those suits. It's hot as hell out here," she said.

Kelly's smile became a smirk. "Well, that's fitting, don't you think?"

Claudia chose to ignore the remark and began fanning herself with the prayer card she'd picked up in the chapel. The flimsy bit of cardboard had no effect on air as dry and still as the bones beneath the sod. Ninety-eight degrees by noon, the mercury was still rising.

"I could be home right now, working," Claudia grumbled, wishing she were in her car, the air conditioner cooling her skin, as she drove toward Playa del Reina, the small beach community where she lived.

"It's Saturday afternoon, for crying out loud. What's so pressing that you have to kick your own ass for taking time off for a funeral?"

"I have a court-ordered handwriting analysis to do. They're using it in a custody issue. A six-year-old kid."

"Abusive parents?"

"The mother claims the ex-husband takes the little girl in the shower with him."

Kelly's face twisted into a grimace. "Well, I know what I'd do with him. I'd give him the knife."

Claudia gave her an eye roll. "You *would*. Thank god, all I have to do is describe his behavior."

They fell into step with the well-heeled coterie of mourners, picking their way around the graves. So many deaths represented by the bronze and granite monuments, so many tears.

Claudia's own inability to dredge up the slightest hint of emotion for Lindsey Alexander bothered her. *What kind of person feels nothing over the death of an old friend?*

Former friend, she amended. So much for the pack of tissues she'd tossed into her shoulder bag in the event she became overcome with grief.

A sage-colored canopy had been erected graveside to protect Lindsey's mega-clients from the brutal sun. The funeral director escorted some two dozen guests to folding chairs in the shade. The lesser glitterati were left to jockey for whatever prime spots remained, standing room only.

"Look, there's Ivan."

Claudia followed Kelly's pointing finger and saw a middle-aged man of small stature in the front row, twisting in his seat to scan the crowd. Ivan Novak, Lindsey's close friend and business manager, was wedged between a handsome couple that Claudia recognized from television campaign ads. State Senator Bryce Heidt and his wife, Mariel.

Spotting them, Ivan waved at Claudia. He stood up and began to make his way to the back of the crowd, stopping to shake hands with a few of the guests who reached out to him. As he grew nearer, the puffy pink flesh around his eyes told the story. He had shed his share of tears for Lindsey; probably Claudia and Kelly's share, too.

"Hey, you two, thanks for coming," Ivan was subdued. "I know it wasn't easy for either of you. I appreciate it."

Kelly reached out to give him an impulsive hug. "Ivan, you look like you haven't slept in days. Are you okay?"

Ivan was almost at eye-height with Kelly, though she was slight and fine-boned and he was thickset, though not overweight. As he spoke, his stocky body seemed taut with the effort of controlling his emotions. "No, Kelly dear, okay is something I am definitely *not*."

He mopped his damp face with a snowy handkerchief and laid a pudgy hand on Claudia's arm. "I have to talk to you privately," he said, effectively shutting Kelly out. "You *are* coming to the reception, aren't you?"

Claudia hesitated. Joining the jet set for cocktails and hors d'oeuvres was the last thing she had in mind for the rest of the afternoon. She had only recently become acquainted with Ivan through her professional connection to Lindsey, and was certain he had invited her and Kelly because Lindsey had given him the impression that they were still dear old chums. The truth was, Claudia had tolerated her former friend over the past few months, only because it had been a financial necessity.

"Well, actually I wasn't . . ."

Ivan's big black moustache drooped with disappointment. "But you *have* to come! We can't talk here . . . the service is about to start. It won't take long, I promise." His grasp on her arm tightened. "Don't disappoint me, Claudia. For Lindsey's sake."

She's dead, but the drama continues.

Claudia watched him hurry back to his seat as the funeral director stepped up to the lectern and asked for their attention. "I wonder what's going on with Ivan," she murmured.

Kelly shrugged. "Go to the reception and find out. I'll be there, and . . . hey, there's Zebediah. That seersucker jacket is sooo Zeb."

Claudia had to smile at their friend's choice of funeral wear. The summery blue and white stripes made him easy to spot. "I guess being Ivan's ex-therapist rates him a seat in the shade."

"Yeah, well, I have a feeling Ivan's gonna need a whole lot *more* therapy before all this crap is over."

"Poor Ivan. He really cared about her."

Kelly's face soured. "He's the *only* one."

Claudia shot her an irritated glance. Considering their shared history, she didn't blame Kelly for the way she felt about Lindsey. Still, she felt compelled to register a protest. "How about putting a sock in it, Kel? There's a better time and place for that discussion."

Kelly stared straight ahead, her chin jutting defiantly. "I don't give a shit about the time or place."

A woman standing in the row ahead turned a shocked glare on them. Kelly returned the glare, but lowered her voice a notch. "The only reason I came here is to make sure the bitch really *is* dead."

Claudia caught the faint whiff of alcohol on Kelly's breath and it came as no surprise. Since their early teens Kelly had dealt with stress by drinking, Claudia by working more hours. Soon, someone would need to find a way to cram twenty-six hours into a day.

"We can talk about it later," she said a little more firmly, but Kelly wasn't ready to let go.

"It's a good thing the casket's closed. I can see her rising up and sinking her fangs into someone's jugular, can't you? I'll *never* forgive her for the things she did to me. She ruined my wedding night, not to mention all the other times she fucked me over. Fucked *you* over, too, in case you've forgotten."

Claudia certainly had not forgotten any of the cruel tricks Lindsey had played in the name of fun, nor the easy shifting of blame for her own misdeeds. She and Kelly had debated several times over the past week whether or not to attend the funeral. There had been as many reasons to stay away as there were to come. In the end, it was probably curiosity more than anything else that had brought them here.

As she sought an appropriate response to Kelly's tirade, the funeral director stepped to the podium and the hum of conversation abruptly died. He introduced Bishop Patrick Flannery, who looked pale and soft in white vestments as he opened his gilt-edged missal and peered over the assembled crowd.

He'll be lucky if he doesn't end up with a nasty sunburn,

Claudia thought, noticing that his bald pate was already an interesting strawberry shade.

"We are gathered here today on this sad occasion to bid a final farewell to Lindsey Alexander, a woman much revered . . ."

"Good thing he didn't say 'much *loved*,' " Kelly stage-whispered.

"Shut *up*." Claudia gave her friend a sharp poke with an elbow.

". . . often seen on the evening news, with the clients to whom she devoted her life, Lindsey came to Hollywood with nothing but raw energy and a unique gift for recognizing talent in others, on which she built an empire . . ."

The bishop's reedy tenor was no competition for the eggbeater clatter of Channel Seven's news chopper circling overhead, and Claudia could barely make out the words. The sun beat against her neck like an angry drummer and her right temple began to throb. She needed water. Or better yet, a vodka tonic.

Is this funeral ever going to end? Or is this really hell, and we're all sharing it with Lindsey?

She gave up trying to listen. The way she saw it, Lindsey had been a self-serving ball-buster. But brutal truths like that didn't belong in a eulogy. Her thoughts gravitated inevitably to the final act of betrayal that had severed their friendship. Events that had burned deep into her memory and still had the power to mortify.

But that was more than ten years ago, and now, Lindsey was dead.

Chapter 2

Lindsey Alexander had lived at one of the most desirable addresses along the Wilshire Corridor. Thanks to its elegant line of high-rise condos and apartments, this stretch of the Boulevard had become known as the "Golden Mile."

Claudia checked the invitation. Fifteenth floor penthouse. She and Lindsey hadn't been on visiting terms for a long time, and their last face-to-face had been at the publicist's Century City office.

Leaving her elderly Jaguar with a valet, she crossed the lobby of the high-rise, heels clicking an irritable staccato on the marble floor. Receptions were for weddings, not funerals. Besides, whatever it was labeled, the scene of Lindsey's untimely transition from this world to the next seemed like an inappropriate location for this event, whatever you called it. But then, *inappropriate* had always been Lindsey's middle name.

The maroon-uniformed concierge at the ultramodern black and chrome lobby desk looked up with a professional smile and asked how he could help her. Claudia told him her destination and he requested to see a picture ID.

She flashed him her driver's license with its nearly decade-old photo. She'd just hit thirty when it was taken. Intelligent emerald eyes gazed frankly back at the camera, framed by attractively winged brows. A slightly pouty mouth. The auburn hair had been perm-frizzed back then, looking as if she'd been plugged into the nearest electrical socket. Now she wore it shoulder-length, straight and glossy.

Giving the license a cursory glance, the concierge thanked her and passed her a pen and clipboard with sign-in sheet attached. Before adding her name, Claudia ran a practiced eye over the signatures already covering the page. Force of habit for a handwriting expert.

The names read like opening night at the Dorothy Chandler Pavilion, but the who's who interested her less than what the signatures told her about the personalities behind them—the tall capital letters and strong rhythms of the powerful; the showy styles of the rich and famous who wanted everyone to know it.

As she stepped out of the elevator at the fifteenth floor, Claudia's ears were assaulted by the din of music and loud conversation from the penthouse. Entering the open doors, she found herself in a circular foyer illuminated by a thousand crystals sparkling in a chandelier that would have done the Governor's Mansion proud.

The attack on her senses was softened by the glorious bank of floral tributes lining the walls. She stopped to sniff at the rose sprays and mum crosses, the carnation hearts and arrangements of lilies in vases. They might as well have been silk, all scent having been bred out of the hothouse blossoms. Like Lindsey, they looked good on the outside, but were lacking that ineffable quality, soul.

A half-dozen steps led to a sunken living room about thirty feet wide. Claudia stood on the top step, feeling as if she'd stumbled into a blizzard. Stunning white-on-white art deco furnishings reminiscent of the movies of the thirties; an Italian leather banquette along one wall; conversational groupings that made the space about as personal as a hotel lobby. The decor made a startling contrast with the guests' dark funeral apparel—as simultaneously stark and beautiful as an Ansel Adams photograph.

Lindsey gazed down on them all from a life-sized oil portrait in the place of honor above the fireplace. She wore a low-cut, satiny Harlow gown and stood beside the pearl Steinway grand where one of her famed guests now sat, plunking tunelessly. The artist's brush had captured a wistful expression in her eyes, far from the hard-boiled stare she'd cultivated over the years, and used to intimidate anyone who was bold enough, or stupid enough, to cross her.

What was on her mind to produce that look?

Claudia turned away from the portrait, scanning the room for Ivan. He didn't seem to be among the rich and famous.

Warm breath touched her neck, startling her. "Darling," a voice said close to her ear. "I've been waiting for you."

Old friend, one-time lover, a bear of a man. These days he had more hair on his chin than his head, but daily workouts on Venice Beach had kept his body tanned and muscular.

Claudia stepped into the arms of Zebediah Gold with a smile. "Well, look what the cat dragged in."

Zebediah released her with a hard squeeze. "I didn't see you at the cemetery. Were you there?"

"Kelly and I were sweating it out with the other peons. Unlike you, I might add."

"Front-row seat, sweetie, where else?"

"Who'd you sleep with for that privilege?" The gleam in her eye took the edge off her words.

He looked amused and squeezed her again. "I see you're in a bitchy mood."

"Put it down to heatstroke."

"Poor baby. Where's the elfin Ms. Brennan?"

"Probably seducing one of the pallbearers. She had her eye on them." Claudia shifted her gaze to the plain vanilla furnishings, the dearth of ornamentation in the place. "I can't imagine Lindsey living here. It doesn't suit her personality."

Zebediah studied her with clinical interest. He'd given up a lucrative Beverly Hills psychology practice a couple of years back for semi-retirement as a consultant, and her comment clearly intrigued him. "Our Lindsey was a woman of many faces," he said enigmatically. "Come on sweetie, let's free ourselves from this iniquitous din."

He draped an arm across her shoulders and shepherded her through the guests, following a wall plastered with photographs of Lindsey posing with clients clutching various statuettes at prestigious awards ceremonies. They passed through a formal dining room, maneuvered around caterers scurrying from the kitchen bearing trays of wine and hors d'oeuvres, until he brought her to glass doors that led to a sun deck high above Wilshire Boulevard.

Claudia drifted to the railing and looked over the side. The West Side sprawled fifteen stories below—a panorama of old and new LA, shoulder-to-shoulder like old pals: dwellings and commercial properties, the UCLA campus, the Armand Hammer Gallery. In the distance, a bloody sun lolled just above a Pacific Ocean that glowed sapphire in the late afternoon haze. Muted traffic noise floated up but it seemed as though they were in another world.

She turned back to Zebediah, who sat on the edge of a chaise lounge. "It's all so unreal. I keep expecting her to pop out of a cake and yell *'Surprise.'*"

He leaned back, his lips thinning into what Claudia called his Clint Eastwood smile. *Wry.* "You think she'd enjoy the shock value?"

"You're the shrink, you tell me. Personally, I think it gave her a sense of power to shock people. She had to stay up nights, dreaming up some of the stunts she pulled."

He tipped his head to one side, considering. "Mmm, she had a dark imagination all right."

"Dark?" Claudia echoed. "That's a tame word for it. She did some really nasty shit. Kelly's *still* talking about what happened at her first wedding. She brought it up at the funeral."

"Her wedding? That would have been before I knew her. Do tell."

Claudia made an a*re-you-really*-sure-*you-want-to-know* face. "Okay, you asked for it. It was one of those defining moments. The last time they spoke to each other for ages. Nearly twenty years ago." She leaned back against the balcony railing and looked him in the eye, wanting to gauge his reaction to the story she was about to tell.

"Kelly and Greg . . . he was groom number one . . . got married in Las Vegas. About a dozen of us went with them and afterwards everyone got pretty hammered. We finally all went up to our rooms. Next morning, Kelly woke up and found herself in bed, nude, with *Lindsey.*"

Another couple wandered out onto the deck and Claudia lowered her voice. "Greg was in the other bed with some *guy* friend of Lindsey's. Neither he nor Kelly had a *clue* as to what happened."

Zebediah's jaw dropped. "Good god, woman, she slipped them a mickey?"

Claudia nodded. "Some kind of date-rape drug. She thought it was brilliant; couldn't understand why nobody else was amused."

She refrained from describing how Lindsey had laughed herself silly at Kelly's reaction; how she had tormented poor Kelly into a state of hysteria because the young bride couldn't remember anything that had happened the night before.

"The wedding night from hell," Zebediah muttered. "Jesus Christ!"

"Kelly would've killed her if Greg hadn't . . ." Claudia broke off as Kelly's bitter words at the funeral came back.

Unaware, Zebediah laughed. "You know, maybe you're right. Maybe this whole suicide thing *is* just one of her bad jokes. She's probably in the Witness Protection Program, living the high life in Brazil."

Knowing Lindsey, it didn't seem such a far-fetched conclusion. "Maybe that's why they had a closed casket," Claudia said thoughtfully.

"No, love, it was the twelve hours in a hot tub. That wouldn't leave the human dermis in any condition for viewing. We have the coroner's word on that."

The thought made Claudia shudder. She nodded, reluctantly relinquishing the Witness Protection theory.

According to the media, Ivan Novak had guessed that something was wrong when Lindsey failed to show up at a press conference for one of her high profile clients. She hadn't risen to the top of her profession by missing important events. When Ivan went to the penthouse looking for her, he'd found her dead in her bathroom Jacuzzi.

It was the coroner's opinion that she had been in the

water overnight; enough drugs and booze in her system
to seriously impair someone twice her weight. A note had
been found near the body—a note whose contents were
not reported in the press, but which led the investigating
detective to conclude that Lindsey Alexander's death had
been by her own hand.

*Maybe the world is better off without someone who made
a career of hurting others.*

The news that arrogant, self-important Lindsey had killed
herself had shaken Claudia. She hated to admit it, but she
had also experienced a twinge of relief, along with all the
other mixed feelings that had been part of her relationship
with Lindsey.

Claudia moved to perch on the chaise next to Zebediah and turned her face toward a welcome breeze. He had
known Lindsey almost as long as she had, and certainly
more recently.

"Do you believe she really killed herself?" she asked.

He made a show of shrugging out of the thumb-your-nose-
at-convention blue and white jacket Kelly had commented
on and folded it over his arm. "That's an odd question.
What makes you ask?"

She related what she'd overheard at the cemetery.

"You're saying those women think someone killed
her."

"Well, there *are* plenty of people who hated her."

"You said yourself you didn't overhear the whole conversation," he countered, looking away. "You probably took
it out of context."

"Come on, Zeb, I know what I heard. So, what do *you*
think?"

Zebediah stuck his hand in the pocket of his jacket and
took out a coral carved pipe. He'd given up smoking long
ago, but he liked to hold the stem in his mouth while he
contemplated the universe. It satisfied his oral needs he said,
half-joking. He caressed the empty bowl before returning it
to his pocket. "I don't have any reason to doubt it."

He hadn't answered her question, but she decided to let
it go with a slight change of topic. "I was surprised they got

a bishop to officiate at the funeral. I doubt Lindsey had seen the inside of a church since she was baptized."

"Isn't it amazing how a hefty donation can change minds?"

"Change minds?"

"The powers-that-be were *dead* set against burying a suicide in consecrated ground, if you'll excuse the pun."

"*Bad* pun. And you know this? How?"

"The ubiquitous grapevine, of course. Flannery was in the news a while back, defending a priest. The priest had been arrested for keeping the altar boys on their knees too long."

"I knew I'd seen him before! What a pompous, holier-than-thou asshole. Ivan really scraped the bottom of the barrel if he had to resort to someone like that."

Zebediah grinned. "Don't hold back, darling. Tell me, how do you really feel?"

Claudia stood up and stretched. "So, I have an opinion, sue me. What will happen to the agency? Lindsey had no heirs, she never married."

Zebediah pushed himself up from the chaise and dusted off his trousers. "My guess is, Ivan will run it until the estate is settled. After that . . ." He shrugged.

"I hope she made a will. Suicide is such a selfish way out." Claudia glanced past Zebediah to the mob of guests, animated but silent behind the barrier of dual pane doors. Still no sign of Ivan.

". . . some high-priced talent in that stable," Zebediah was saying as she returned her attention to him. "I'm sure the lawyers will get fat trying to figure out what to do with all those contracts." He shook his head, like a dog drying off after a swim. "Come on. This conversation is getting maudlin. Let's go back inside and get shitfaced."

Back in the great room, a musical combo played dangerously close to an up-tempo beat, the mood conspicuously lighter. The funeral reception had turned into a shindig of major proportions—graveyard tears were recycled into cocktail-party chatter: *Let's do lunch; have your people* _call my people; kiss-kiss, yada yada, byeee._ Lindsey would have approved.

Zebediah claimed space at one end of the long sofa and Claudia settled next to him on the arm. They chatted about the child custody case she was consulting on until Kelly sauntered over, munching on a cracker smeared with pink paste.

"What took you so long?" asked Claudia. "A little afternoon delight with a pallbearer?"

Kelly grinned, unrepentantly lascivious. "Uh huh. One of those gorgeous Chippies stopped me for speeding on the way out of the cemetery. M'mm. Motorcycles are sooo phallic. Take me for a ride!"

Claudia rolled her eyes. "Did you get a ticket?"

"Of course not. I promised to fuck his brains out if he'd let me off. Works every time."

Kelly directed her posterior onto Zebediah's lap and put her arms around his neck. "My turn. You've monopolized this stud long enough."

Zebediah leered back at her and pretended to nuzzle her neck.

"Okay, that's it." Claudia rose to her feet. "I'm going to find Ivan and see what he wants."

The air in the penthouse was heavy with a potpourri of big-ticket perfumes and the slight hint of perspiration from dozens of bodies packed as closely as the Roxy on a Saturday night. Bel Air stick-figure women. Men who spent as much time at the beauty spa as their wives.

Claudia made her way through the Beautiful People, looking for Ivan. She wasn't prepared for the shock of a size twelve brogue landing on her foot.

Her vision blurred with pain and the floor seemed to tilt beneath her. Recovering her balance, she whirled and found herself face-to-face with a man roughly the size of an industrial refrigerator.

She took in the wide face, sensual lips, a graying hairline that receded well past low tide. He wore a conservative charcoal-grey suit and white shirt with a black silk tie, but

looked as though he might be more comfortable in Tommy
Bahamas.

"Oh god, I'm so sorry!" Refrigerator grabbed her elbow
to steady her. As if that would put out the fire in her toes.

Claudia yanked out of his grasp and extended both hands
to hold him off. "I'm fine. Don't worry about it."

Before she could stop him, he was on his knees, making
a clumsy attempt to remove her strappy sandal. "Do you
think any bones are broken?"

"No! *Stop* it!" Battling the impulse to spit a few choice
words at him, Claudia put her hands on his shoulders and
pushed at him. She might as well have tried to push a
car.

"Martin, *what* are you doing?"

The voice had a slight southern twang. It belonged to
a woman with a forty-something face and parchment-thin
skin stretched tight over a carefully sculpted chin. Her Vera
Wang dress whispered *money*.

The man hauled himself to his feet. "I just mashed this
poor lady's toes," he confessed, looking abashed. "Tell her
I'm harmless, honey." He grabbed Claudia's hand, envel-
oping it in his beefy one and pumping it. "Name's Martin
Grainger and this is my wife, Lillian. In case you hadn't
figured it out, I'm the neighborhood klutz."

I *had* figured it out.

Even in her snakeskin pumps, Lillian Grainger's coiffed
platinum head barely reached her husband's lapel. She extended a manicured hand weighed down by a twelve-carat
headlight, looking at Claudia as though she were an experi-
ment in a petri dish. "And you are?"

"Leaving," said Claudia. "Goodbye."

"One moment, if you please." Lillian Grainger's drawl
sharpened. Her body language said, *Obey me. Everyone
does*. "I'd like to have your name in case you need medical
attention, thanks to my husband's clumsiness."

Claudia gave her a cool smile. "Don't worry, I'm not
going to sue."

"No, wait." Lillian's tone had warmed by several degrees.
She actually reached out and touched Claudia's arm. "Didn't

I see you on the news last week? I never forget a face. Don't tell me . . . Poppy. No . . . Camellia?"

Channel 2 News had done a series highlighting women with unusual careers. A three-minute profile of Claudia titled *Handwriting on the Wall* had run several times.

Resigning herself to the encounter with a silent sigh, she said, "Claudia Rose."

Lillian snapped her fingers. "*Rose!* I knew it was a flower. This is incredible." She grabbed Claudia's hand with both of hers and squeezed as if they were old friends. "When we saw that piece, I told Marty we should call you, didn't I, Marty? This is serendipity."

Martin Grainger gave an affirmative nod and snagged a server who was passing by with a tray of glasses. "Wine, Ms. Rose? No? You sure?" He handed one to his wife and downed half his glass. "It's true. Ever since Lil saw that news show, she's been talking about getting you to do some handwriting analysis for us. Tell us who we oughta hire."

"Were you a friend of Lindsey's?" Lillian broke in.

Claudia hesitated. "I knew her a long time ago. We were friends in school. How about you?"

"Business acquaintances." Lillian snapped open her Gucci handbag, took out a gold card case and offered an embossed business card.

Grainger & Grainger, World Class Events. A prestigious Century City address in the same building as Lindsey's office.

"We've been catering parties for Lindsey's clients for years," Martin said expansively. "In fact, we're handling *this . . .*" He broke off as his wife interrupted him with a glare, her cheeks splotched a dull red with embarrassment.

"It's so lucky, meeting you like this, Claudia. As it happens, I do have an applicant I'd like you to take a look at. I want to know what his handwriting says about him. What do you need?"

Doing business at her dead client's funeral reception—tacky.

Claudia managed a faint smile. "Why don't we get together and talk about it next week? Right now, I need to find Ivan."

"Yes, let's. Call my office and set it up with my assistant, Yolande Palomino." Lillian paused, suddenly thoughtful. "We're giving a Halloween party on our yacht. Why don't you come? I'd love to introduce you around."

Claudia read between the lines and didn't like the subtext: come to our party and entertain the guests by analyzing their handwriting. She'd been there too many times to mistake the message. "That's kind of you, but I'm not much one for parties."

"Don't be silly, we know some very influential people. Senator Heidt will be there for one. Have you met him yet?"

"No, but I saw him at the cemetery."

"Well, dear, he's somebody you should know. I'll make sure we send you an invitation."

Claudia found Ivan Novak standing alone in a corner of the formal dining room, his face a blank. She took his hands and gave them a brief squeeze, wondering if he'd been smoking something potent. "So, tell me, Ivan, what did you want to talk to me about?"

He stared at her as if he wasn't quite sure who she was, then his eyes focused and he sniffed loudly. Reaching into his pocket, he took out a silk handkerchief and dabbed at his nose. "It's a confidential matter, Claudia," he said. "Let me take you upstairs to Lindsey's office so we can have some privacy."

He led her to the spiral staircase that led to the second floor. They'd only made it up the first dozen stairs before a commanding voice called Ivan's name.

Senator Bryce Heidt, waving up at them.

Hand-tailored black silk and the slight dusting of silver at the temples that labeled men as distinguished, women as old. Tanned, and looking as fit as if he'd just stepped off the slopes, he reached up to smooth back the thick dark wave of hair on his forehead.

Claudia remembered seeing Heidt's signature on the sign-in log. Attention-grabbing capital letters, an elaborate swirl under his name. More style than substance, she'd thought at the time, and was glad she hadn't voted for him.

Swearing under his breath, Ivan trotted back downstairs and accepted the Senator's hug.

Heidt clapped him on the back before releasing him. "I meant to mention earlier, Mariel and I want you to come to church with us tomorrow. The minister told me he's written a special addendum to his sermon, a eulogy to Lindsey. We've reserved a place for you in our family pew."

Ivan looked less than thrilled, but he quickly pasted on the Hollywood version of sincerity. "That's so thoughtful, Senator. I'd be delighted."

"Lindsey meant a lot to us all," Bryce Heidt said, the lines around his eyes tightening with the gravity of the occasion. "I know she'd want you to be there."

Ivan let that go and beckoned to Claudia, who was still waiting for him on the stairs, wishing for some heavy-duty painkillers.

"Have you two met?" Ivan asked. "Senator Bryce Heidt, Claudia Rose. Claudia, Senator Heidt."

Bryce Heidt flashed her a high-intensity smile that made his eyes crease at the corners, and took her hand in a firm grip. "Delighted to meet you, Ms. Rose." He was undeniably handsome, with the benevolent look you'd want in someone who represents your interests. Claudia searched her memory. He'd managed to keep his Senate seat for a second term, so he must be doing something right.

Except that looks aren't everything and handwriting always tells the truth.

"Did you see Claudia on the news last week, Senator?" Ivan prattled on. "She's a world-famous handwriting expert."

Heidt shook her hand with warm, sweaty fingers, appraising her. "Is that right? Do you work for the police, Ms. Rose?"

She smiled and took back her hand, battling an impulse to wipe it on her dress. "I'm an independent handwriting analyst, so I work for whomever needs my services. Even the police."

Heidt favored her with another thousand-watt smile. "So, a crook forges someone's signature and you figure it out, is that it?"

Claudia nodded. "Forgery identification is part of it, but a significant portion of my work involves behavioral profiling."

Those magnificent brows shot up. "*Profiling?* From *handwriting?* You can't be serious. You're saying you can tell how someone *behaves* from their handwriting?"

Claudia was used to dealing with skepticism. At least he hadn't held out his palm for her to read. It wouldn't have been the first time someone had asked her to tell their fortune.

"Handwriting is like body language or tone of voice," she explained. "It reveals a lot of important information about the writer." She'd repeated the words so many times before, they came as automatically as a taped message. "Most people don't realize that handwriting analysis is based on scientific research. It gives clues about how the writer functions. Potentials, weaknesses."

"Well, that's really something," he said when she'd finished her spiel. "Maybe I'll get you to analyze my opponent's handwriting in the next election. You could be our secret weapon."

Right. When pigs fly.

She glanced around, surprised to find herself alone. "Would you excuse me, Senator? Ivan's been waiting to speak to me. I need to find him again."

He frowned. "Don't go yet. I'd like you to meet my wife. You can look at her handwriting and tell me what she's been hiding from me all these years."

The unpleasant drumming in Claudia's head was now clobbering her right eye from inside her skull. *Migraine.* She didn't have the patience to think up a polite answer.

"Sorry, Senator, I don't do quickies."

"Oh, come on, be a . . ." Heidt broke off, his eyes veering off to her right, filling with panic. His lips worked, but no sound came out.

Turning to see what had caused his reaction, Claudia stepped back hastily as the beaded-haired woman from the cemetery swept past her as if she were not there, and eased up to Senator Heidt.

The woman slipped her arm through his, pressing her body against him. Her mouth brushed his ear intimately. "*Hello* there, Mr. Senator."

Heidt recoiled as violently as if she had held a match to his bare feet. "Excuse me," he said a shade too loud. "I'm afraid I er . . ."

The woman's smile revealed a set of film-star-perfect teeth. "Your victory *party,* Senator. You remember, don'chu? I was with Lin'sey."

For an instant, though the chatter went on unabated around them, the three of them occupied a private zone of frozen silence. Heidt darted a quick glance around as if gauging the need for damage control, but no one seemed to be looking their way. The moment passed and the consummate politician recovered his poise. He gave the woman an apologetic smile. "I'm sorry, miss, you must be mistaken."

Undeterred, the woman winked, long and slow. Seductive. "No, no, *no,* Senator. Let me remind you, I am *Destiny.*"

He shook his head, his lips stretched into a bad excuse for a smile. "I'm sorry, it doesn't ring any bells."

She gave a throaty laugh. "Oh, but I thought it *would* ring *your* bell."

"Destiny darling, how *are* you?" Ivan had returned. "Let me get you a drink." He took the woman's arm in a firm grasp and hustled her away, glancing back over his shoulder. "Claudia, don't go anywhere, I'll be right back."

Claudia stared after them. Was the woman drunk? A spurned lover? She had appeared neither spurned nor drunk. She'd looked downright pleased with herself.

Ivan and Claudia ascended the swirl of white Carrara marble stairs, party noises chasing them to the second floor.

"Lindsey never expected to live a long life, poor darling," Ivan remarked as he led her along a hallway lined with framed photographs: Lindsey, at a restaurant, laughing with

Johnny Depp. Lindsey, snuggling up to Tom Cruise. Lindsey having drinks with Donald Trump. None of them had turned out for her burial. "She made plans for her funeral a long time ago. She hated looking at long faces. A party was more her style."

"You've certainly given her that," Claudia said, blanching at the odor of stale cigarettes as Ivan opened the door to an elegant home office.

Ivan crossed to the six-foot desk that dominated the spacious room and offered Claudia a guest chair. He removed his coat and hung it on the back of the throne-like executive chair before seating himself behind the desk. "Thank god," he said, rolling up his shirtsleeves and fanning himself with his hands. "I've been dying to do that all afternoon."

He shook a smoke from the pack of Marlboros that lay on the glass-topped desk and lit up with a silver lighter. Leaning back against the inset moiré silk he sucked in a generous drag and puffed it out on a long sigh, watching the blue smoke curl toward the ceiling. It wasn't until he had finished enjoying the nicotine rush that he broke the silence.

"Lindsey may have planned her funeral, but one thing she *never* planned was to kill herself."

Carefully setting the cigarette on an ashtray filled with half-smoked butts, he stared at Claudia, as if daring her to dispute him. She waited in silence as he opened the top drawer of the desk and removed an envelope, tossed it across the desk.

She opened the envelope and withdrew a single sheet of paper, folded in half. Six words had been block-printed on Alexander Agency letterhead in black ink.

IT WAS FUN WHILE IT LASTED.

"This is the suicide note?"

"That's what the cops called it."

Claudia's brain flipped to automatic as she studied the note: Nothing remarkable in the style. Not enough handwriting to suggest depression or suicidal ideation; none of the tremor that would be expected in a case of illness or drugs or forgery. No signs that the writing might have been coerced. Nothing unusual at all. A lengthier sample would have offered further insight. "You don't believe Lindsey wrote this?"

"Hell no."

"What makes you so sure?"

"She never printed. *Ever*. She *never* wrote in black ink, and she wouldn't have used company letterhead."

Ivan's words struck a chord. Lindsey's odd quirk had always irritated Claudia. Twenty years earlier, when Lindsey had lived on a large Bel Air estate, she'd bragged to anyone who would listen that she had money to burn. Yet, when she sent personal letters, they invariably came written in her trademark green ink on the backs of junk mail or bills, sent in reused envelopes; a mailing label slapped over the original address.

Extreme recycling.

Ivan lit another smoke from the first, which was only half-consumed, and pointed at the paper Claudia held. "I'm not satisfied with the way the police handled this situation. They came up with some dumbshit theory that she wrote it, changed her mind and then went ahead and killed herself anyway. It's ridiculous. I'm not buying it, not for a second."

Unwilling to accept what he was suggesting, Claudia shrugged. "Okay then, it was an accident. Too much booze and . . ."

Ivan slammed his fist on the glass top hard enough to make the silver lighter jump. "No! Lindsey was *murdered*."

She'd known it was coming, yet the bald words still shook her. She massaged her throbbing temple, not wanting to hear what she knew was coming next. "I suppose you've told the police what you think?"

Ivan slumped back against the chair, his face crumpling. "They weren't interested in my opinion."

"Wouldn't they have to do a thorough investigation for someone as high profile as Lindsey?"

"If she'd been one of our clients they would. But the

only time Lindsey was in the limelight was when she stood next to them. Reflected glory, isn't that what they call it?" Rancor curled Ivan's lip. "That damn detective never took it seriously. He claimed he had it examined by their experts and that they said she wrote it, but I'm telling you, *she didn't!*"

They had come to the crux of the meeting. Claudia tensed as Ivan rested his hands on the desktop and leaned forward.

"I need you to prove she didn't write the goddamned note. The life insurance companies are jerking me around. They don't want to pay on a suicide." Opening the drawer again, he took out a Waterman fountain pen and a leather bound checkbook. "Will a retainer of three thousand be enough to get you started?" He folded open the checkbook and began to write, the platinum nib scratching against the paper.

Claudia's hands shot out, palms forward. "Hold on a minute, Ivan."

"Four thousand? Five? Tell me what you need."

"It's not the money. I need time to think."

Ivan sprang to his feet. "There *is* no time! Look, everyone knows you're the best in the business. But you were also once her friend. Don't you want to know the truth about her death?"

Sitting in front of Lindsey's desk with Ivan's eyes boring into her, Claudia silently reviewed the catalog of inexcusable acts Lindsey had accumulated and weighed them against the earlier years when they had still been friends. There could only be one answer.

Chapter 3

Claudia kicked off her sandals and trudged up to her second-floor office, more than ready for some down time after the loud crowd at Lindsey's. Her bruised toes throbbed, keeping time with her headache. She sank into her desk chair with a sigh of relief and a tall glass of iced tea, and downed a handful of Ibuprofen.

Before she'd taken her leave from Lindsey's apartment, Ivan Novak had urged her to agree with his belief that Lindsey had not written the alleged suicide note. She'd had to lay down the law with him. Her opinion was not for sale.

In as clear terms as she could manage, Claudia had explained that before she would be able to give an opinion on the authorship of the note, a thorough examination of many handwriting samples would be required. Because the handwriting on the alleged suicide note was block printed, she would need to see a selection of block printed samples of Lindsey's true, known handwriting for comparison.

Once she was in possession of those comparison samples, Claudia would measure the size and proportion of the letters, the angle of slant, the amount of space between letters and words. Her stereo microscope would reveal some important pieces of the puzzle. A special piece of equipment called a Handwriting Comparator would add more.

Only after the handwriting had yielded all its secrets would Claudia know whether or not the samples had sufficient similar characteristics to qualify as a match.

If she were unable to make an identification—if she reached the conclusion that Ivan was correct and the note was written by someone other than Lindsey—Ivan would take her report to the police and attempt to persuade them to reopen the investigation.

Kelly was right, Lindsey had made more than her share of enemies. But was that simply the price of a trip up the Hollywood ladder? Or had someone hated her enough to kill her and arrange her death to look like suicide?

Claudia considered the other option. What if the samples *were* authored by the same hand? If she determined that the suicide note was indeed genuine, Ivan would have to accept that, for whatever reason, Lindsey had found her life too unbearable to live.

She focused her gaze on the hand-printed note, now encased in a protective plastic sleeve, mulling over the reasons why people kill themselves.

Money worries, being jilted by a lover, fear of damaging information being exposed, terminal illness. Hopelessness that life will ever improve.

Lindsey had been one of the top PR agents in the country and usually appeared in the company of some gorgeous male. Judging from the luxury of her penthouse apartment, money appeared to have flowed freely, but was it possible that things were not as rosy as they appeared to be? Could she have made unwise investments or otherwise be struggling for money? Or had she been jilted by a lover? In Claudia's memory, Lindsey had never allowed herself to care enough about a man to be annihilated by a breakup.

Yet another possibility came to mind. What if Lindsey had authored the note under duress? Had someone forced her to write her own death sentence and then carried it out?

Claudia kicked herself for agreeing to get involved with *anything* to do with Lindsey Alexander. What the hell had she been thinking?

She took Ivan's retainer check from her purse and studied the little string of zeroes following the number he had insisted on. The plain truth was, work had been slow for the past couple of months and she couldn't afford to turn down such a healthy retainer. The same reason she had accepted a few recent handwriting analysis assignments from Lindsey herself.

Claudia scowled at the mail lying in an untidy heap on her desk, daring her to attack it. She considered giving Kelly a call and asking her about what she'd said at the cemetery, but enough time had been spent on matters concerning Lindsey for one day. She rummaged in the pen cup for the letter opener.

Twenty minutes later, she turned to the computer, where a string of spam and unsolicited porn e-mails filled the screen, a stubborn leftover from the last guy she had dated oh-so-briefly. After deleting a half-dozen e-mails with subject lines like, *"Here I cum," "Barnyard Beauties,"* and *"I'm lying here waiting for you,"* she clicked open a message from her brother.

Pete was in his second year as a widower, still making the adjustment to single-parenting a teenage daughter. His e-mail pleaded for her help with Monica. As if Claudia knew anything about raising kids. She'd given up trying to get pregnant after the third miscarriage, unable to face another bitter blow.

After answering Pete as best she could, she worked on whittling down the e-mails from the handwriting analysis Listserv of which she was a member. She kept hard at it until after nine, when her neck and shoulders began to protest that she had been too long in the chair.

Pushing away from the desk, she headed downstairs, stopping in the kitchen long enough to splash a shot of vodka into a glass, followed by a generous helping of cranberry juice. She took the drink with her and crossed the dark living room, stepping through the open door to the deck that jutted out over the front of the house, facing the ocean.

The night called to her. She went back inside and ran upstairs, changed into sweats, and jammed bare feet into grubby sneakers without bothering to untie the laces. Locking the door behind her and pocketing the key, she hurried down the steps.

Wisps of fog curled around her in the darkness. She lifted her face to the cool dampness of marine air on her skin.

"Walk, Flare?" she called softly, crossing her neighbor's front lawn. A loud bark came from the other side of the wooden fence separating the houses. Even in the relatively safe beach community of Playa del Reina, walking alone at night was an itty proposition. Claudia was as grateful for the company of her neighbor's massive German Shepherd as the dog was eager to go.

She rang the doorbell and heard it play the opening bars of *Strangers in the Night*. Seconds later, her neighbor, Marcia Collins, looked through the peephole, then opened the door. She stood tall and slim in cutoff blue jeans and a man's Oxford shirt, a cigarette in her hand. "Hey, Claudia, wanna buy a dog?"

"I'll just keep on borrowing yours if you don't mind. I'd never be able to give one of my own enough attention."

Marcia stood aside to let her in. "You look a little shop-worn, neighbor. What's up?"

"Went to a funeral. You'd have had fun. Movie stars up the yin-yang."

"You're kidding. The funeral on the news tonight? Russell Crowe was there—did you see him?"

"Only from a distance."

Marcia moaned. "He is *so* hot."

Claudia followed her into the kitchen. "I just caught a quick glimpse. He rushed off right after the service. So, how's work?"

Marcia waitressed at Cowboys, the bar and grill down the hill at the beach end of the short string of shops and restaurants comprising Playa del Reina's tiny main drag. She scowled. "One of the waitresses took a hike, so yours truly got stuck with the extra hours till they hire someone else. I totally hate having no time to myself. Lucky for Flare you're here. She wouldn't get diddly squat of a walk out of me tonight."

Claudia grinned. "Good, 'cause I need the beach. Desperately."

"Honey," Marcia admonished, wagging a finger at Claudia, "what you need is a man."

"Thanks for the advice, but I've bagged my limit for this year."

"Oh come on, you're too young to give up on men."

"I haven't given up, I'm just taking a time-out."

Marcia unwound the dog's heavy leash from around the doorknob and attached it to a harness. She opened the back door and the big Shepherd bounded in, paws clicking loudly on the tiled floor as she slid to a stop at Claudia's feet and began nosing her.

Marcia snapped the harness around the excited animal's forequarters. "Dammit, Flare, don't do that!" She looked up. "So, this woman who died; she killed herself, right? Flare, sit! Why d'you think she did it?"

Why did Lindsey do any of the crazy things she'd done?

Maybe one of those crazy things got her murdered.

Claudia shook her head with a sigh. "Kiddo, I haven't a clue."

As they started back across the kitchen, Marcia stopped to pick up a greeting card lying on the table and thrust it at Claudia. "What do you think? It's this new guy I've been seeing."

Claudia knew she was talking about his handwriting. She looked at the message scrawled inside: *"You're the greatest. This is going to work! Love Justin."*

"One thing's for sure: It won't be easy to get him to commit."

"That's okay; I'm not looking for anything permanent right now."

"So, go for it. But see how he disconnects the last letter of this word, *'going'*? He rushes into new relationships, but come time to put his money where his mouth is, he's gone. He's also emotionally needy. He doesn't put a comma after writing the word, *'love.'* It says *'Love Justin.'* He's begging for your love."

Marcia looked confused. "But you just said he wouldn't commit."

"People don't always want what they need. At least he isn't a psychopath, like the last one."

"You sure had *him* pegged right. Fantastic in the sack, but honey, could he turn ugly fast."

"Handwriting never lies."

"You probably oughta listen to your own advice, my friend."

Claudia tightened the leash around her wrist as Flare began tugging her toward the door.

"You know how it is. The shoemaker's kids go barefoot."

The dog padded a few feet ahead, leading Claudia down the steep hill, keeping the leash taut but never taking advantage. They zigzagged left, then right at the next two streets, passing Tyler's Coffee House. She could hear the noisy late evening crowd laughing over beer and burgers at The Shack across the street. Marinelli's Italian restaurant was on the opposite corner, its red, white, and green lights twinkling garishly on the roof like a perpetual Christmas.

Pulling Flare to heel, Claudia crossed the highway and stepped onto the path to the darkened beach. Sensing impending freedom, the dog dragged her across the sand to the water's edge. She unhooked the leash and let Flare run while she followed.

Alone again.

She couldn't help thinking of the string of disastrous relationships she'd had over the six years following her divorce. None had survived her all-encompassing compulsion to work, including her five-year marriage to Alan Rose, which had crumbled under the weight of his relentless need for her total devotion. Therapy had taught her that she'd turned work into a compensation for the lost pregnancies, until overwork became a way of life.

Alone is emotionally safer than a bad relationship: no one to complain that I work too much. That's good. But no one to love, no one to love me. Not good.

She'd failed to pay attention to the growing distance between them until Alan consoled himself with another woman. He deserved someone to give him the love he needed, and Claudia hadn't been the one.

Maybe being alone was okay. She had her house, her career, her freedom.

Better than what Lindsey has.

Chapter 4

Groaning, Claudia reached out to silence the persistent buzzing of the alarm clock. The small amount of alcohol she'd consumed the night before couldn't account for the grogginess she felt as she crawled out of bed and dragged herself to the bathroom.

In an effort to improve her attitude, she set the shower jets to a hard pulse and let the steaming water beat a tattoo against her head and shoulders, lathering up with soap that didn't deliver on its promise to make her feel like a spring morning.

After drying off, Claudia swiped her towel over the foggy mirror. Her reflection stared back at her. When had the web of tiny lines first begun to appear around her eyes? she wondered with a little shock. The hot breath of her fortieth birthday seared her neck, and her mother's voice, carping about her lack of a permanent relationship, echoed in her ears.

Telling the voice to shut up, she wiped off the rest of the steam and went to get a handwriting sample that had arrived in yesterday's mail. An employment applicant from one of her steady clients who owned a Beverly Hills furniture store.

Propping the sample on the vanity where she could see it, Claudia aimed the hair dryer at her hair and let the handwriting work at the edges of her consciousness. Like most of her clients, Rick Taylor wanted the results yesterday and would have faxed the handwriting if she'd let him. But the faxing and scanning process could affect important nuances, such as pen pressure and line quality, so her clients learned to send original handwriting samples whenever possible.

Nearly every centimeter of the sheet of paper was covered with large, round letters and excessively wide g and y loops. To Claudia's trained eye, the grouping of characteristics bespoke a strong need for approval, plus low objectivity. The writer could be expected to engage in attention-getting behavior and would probably be flirtatious. The extra-short upper loops suggested that the young woman who had written it would have difficulty accepting responsibility for any mistakes. If Rick hired her, he would need to provide close supervision and plenty of pats on the back to keep her happy.

Two cups of coffee and a toasted bagel later Claudia had keyed her report into the computer and e-mailed the resulting file to Rick. Time to get dressed for her meeting with Ivan.

Ivan greeted her at the door to Lindsey's penthouse in baggy jeans and a red flannel shirt that had seen better days. He waved a sheaf of papers in one hand and a half-smoked cigarette in the other.

"I've gathered some samples of Lindsey's handwriting," he announced, jamming the cigarette between his lips and fanning out a jumble of bills, flyers, and other scraps— standard Lindsey writing materials. "You can see for your- self her writing is nothing like the writing on that phony suicide note. Green pen, always written in cursive. See how she makes this capital W, and here, the way she does her L. They're completely different."

Claudia took the papers and sifted through them, glanc- ing at each one before handing them back. "I'm sorry, Ivan. These are not going to work for me. As I told you yesterday, comparing cursive to printed writing is apples and oranges. The note was printed, so it's important for me to compare it to her genuine *printed* writing. These are all written in cursive."

Ivan's eyes narrowed with annoyance. "The police didn't ask for that."

"And you weren't satisfied with the police's opinion. That's why you retained me."

"But she never printed," he insisted, waving the papers at her. "Never! That's why I know she didn't write the suicide note."

"Forms are usually printed," Claudia noted, doing her best to hang onto her patience. "How about a credit application?"

"We have secretaries to fill out forms. Lindsey never did them herself."

Claudia took a deep breath, preparing to do battle. "Ivan, if you want a proper forensic examination and opinion, you're going to have to come up with some printed samples; otherwise, I can't help you."

"I'm trying to get this place closed up," Ivan snapped, a frown drawing his heavy black eyebrows together. "And I've got to keep the office running. I don't have time to go searching for some piece of paper that doesn't exist."

Mentally waving good-bye to the money she would have earned from the case, Claudia told herself that it wasn't worth the hassle. If the client started out creating problems, things usually ended up going from bad to worse. Her professional integrity was at stake. "If you want someone who'll just say whatever you pay them to, there are plenty of so called experts who'd love to cooperate. I'll return your retainer check and you can call one of them."

Ivan tossed the papers onto a side table. "Okay, okay, you don't have to get on your high horse." He started for the spiral staircase, beckoning Claudia to follow. "You can look for what you need in the files and box them up as you go through them."

On the day of Lindsey's funeral reception, her office had looked as if someone worked there. Now, less than two days later, the computer equipment had been removed, tables and bookshelves were bare. The glass top of the desk stood against the wall, leaving the black lacquer base an obelisk in the middle of the room.

Claudia was surprised at the speed with which the stack of moving boxes by the door had been filled and sealed. "Somebody must have worked like a dog over the weekend," she observed.

Ivan touched a button on the wall unit and a door slid open, revealing a walk-in closet more spacious than Claudia's bedroom. "Lindsey leased the place, which is one reason I'm in a hurry to get everything settled." He didn't elaborate further.

A row of filing cabinets stood against the far wall, a heap of collapsed storage boxes stacked on top. "You can start here," Ivan said. "Just pack the files into these boxes as you finish going through them. Maybe you'll find what you're looking for."

Claudia looked back at him, not trusting herself to speak. She was accustomed to clients having difficulty coming up with proper materials for her examination, but no one had ever offered to pay her hourly rate to search through a half-dozen file cabinets for comparison samples. At this rate, the generous retainer Ivan had paid would soon be eaten up on grunt work.

He went to the door. "I'll be downstairs on the phone. We were in negotiations for one of our biggest clients when all this went down. I haven't been to the office in days." He paused, his hand resting on the jamb. "If you need me, use the intercom on the desk. The codes for all the rooms are marked. Oh, and help yourself to coffee or cold drinks. There's a fridge in the minibar."

With Ivan gone, quiet descended. Claudia stared at the empty bookcases and bare walls. Nothing that reflected Lindsey's personality or taste remained in the room, yet her presence hovered eerily. Was she watching from some netherworld reserved for suicides and murder victims?

After gulping down the pills and booze, had Lindsey taken one last look around at all she had accumulated, the bits and pieces that had made up her life, realizing that she would never see them again? How might she have felt,

knowing that her nervous system would soon begin to shut
down; that she would cease breathing; that she would no
longer exist in the physical world?

Had she roamed the apartment, saying goodbye to her
luxurious possessions before climbing into the Jacuzzi and
sliding under the water; before consciousness gradually
faded?

Chiding herself for being melodramatic, Claudia gave the
first file drawer a sharp tug. Inside, green file folders pressed
up against each other, untidy edges of paper protruding from
the sides. Why had Lindsey, a woman of means, chosen to
live with this kind of clutter? Why hadn't she purchased more
file cabinets; hired someone to organize her papers?

Claudia answered her own question: for the same reason Lindsey always wrote on trash; she only spent money
if there was some kind of payback for her. Her disdain for
most people was evident in her refusal to use good letterhead stock unless the letter was destined for someone she
deemed important.

She assembled a file box and carried an armful of files to
a credenza. Years-old magazine articles spilled out; pages of
jokes off the Internet; files filled with correspondence; even
gourmet recipes that would never find their way into Lindsey's kitchen. Any handwriting that surfaced was Lindsey's
standard—scribbled notes in cursive, but nothing printed.

Could Ivan's assertion that Lindsey had never printed
be true? The chances were next to nil. People adopt alter-
nate writing styles for various types of communication. All
Claudia had to do was hunt through enough of this stuff
until a suitable sample turned up.

She worked her way through the drawer, reflecting on
what she considered Ivan's odd attitude. His evident lack
of willingness to cooperate in providing the materials she
needed for the job was nothing short of bizarre. Was he
simply being petty and vindictive because she'd rejected
the samples he had offered for her examination?

Two hours into the search, an insistent growling from
Claudia's stomach added to the growing list of reasons why

she should abandon what appeared more and more to be a useless task. Logically, she knew that everyone had to use printed writing at some time or another. But if Lindsey had printed *anything,* the evidence must be elsewhere.

Tension from leaning over the file drawers had bunched the muscles in her shoulders. She took a moment to straighten and clasp her hands over her head, making herself a promise as she stretched her neck to release the stress: if she had no luck in the next half-hour, she would walk.

She sealed the box she was working on. The next batch of files would be the last for the day. She was nearing the final few files when she came upon a plain white envelope, unaddressed, no postmark.

A block printed note was inside, written on a single sheet of lined notebook paper.

The pen had dug deep furrows into the paper, spawning an evil braille on the back. Heavy, slashing strokes, crowded words, letters jumping up menacingly from the paper.

YOUR GONA BE ONE <u>SORY</u> BICH!!!!!!

Definitely not Lindsey's handwriting. The undeveloped letter forms indicated someone functionally illiterate—grade school education at best.

Psychopathology was nothing new to Claudia. She had worked for years in the courts and with psychologists, analyzing the handwritings of mental patients and convicted criminals. The handwriting on this page fit neatly into the latter category. She pressed the intercom and called Ivan.

"This has absolutely nothing to do with Lindsey's death," Ivan said calmly, taking the paper from her.

Claudia stared at him in surprise. "How can you be so sure? Don't you think the police would be interested in this?"

"This note came from a security guard we fired for sexual harassment about a year ago. He was none too bright. This was just an attempt to scare us."

"This guy could do more than scare you, Ivan. His handwriting show's he's a real sicko."

"Oh, is that the technical term?"

"It's not funny. He could do some serious damage. Is he in jail, I hope?"

"No, he isn't." Ivan's tone turned decidedly frosty. "We handled the situation internally. We never heard from him again."

Claudia got the message: *Don't tell me my business.*

She had never thought of herself as psychic, but she was picking up an undertone that mystified her. Why was Ivan unwilling even to acknowledge the possibility that the writer of this threatening message might be involved in Lindsey's death?

"I could compare *this* handwriting with the suicide note." Claudia pressed him. "If you really believe Lindsey was murdered, this person could be a suspect. It's block printed, too."

With a dismissive wave of his hand, Ivan tore the paper into six jagged pieces, ignoring Claudia's gasp, and tossed it into the trash bin under the desk.

"It's not him."

"Why are you so sure?"

Brushing aside the question, Ivan took a deep drag on his cigarette and tapped it on the ashtray, sending up a shower of ash and sparks. "I think your time might be better spent talking to Earl Nelson. It's possible he might have something you can use."

"Who's Earl Nelson?"

"Lindsey's brother."

Claudia frowned, puzzled. "Lindsey had no family, she was an orphan. There certainly wasn't any family at the funeral."

Ivan blew a thick cloud of smoke from the corner of his mouth. "I can assure you, whether she acknowledged him openly or not, her brother is alive and living in West Hollywood. He wasn't at the funeral because her will barred him from attending." He scribbled on a yellow sticky note. "Here's his phone number. I don't know whether he'll see you or not, but give him a call and ask whether he has any of her handwriting—tell him what you need. He'll want something in return, so call me if he's got anything. Meantime, I'll have someone from the office pack up the rest of the files and messenger them over to your place so you can finish looking through them."

Claudia accepted the paper, noting that he had printed Earl Nelson's address. She dialed the number on her cell phone, making a mental note to check Ivan's handwriting against the alleged suicide note.

Chapter 5

Earl Nelson lived in a run-down condominium conversion in one of the less affluent neighborhoods of West Hollywood. Less than ten miles east of the penthouse his sister had called home, it could have been in another galaxy. In the 1960s, the place had been an apartment building for moderate-income tenants, but some twenty years later, mercenary owners concluded money was to be made by turning the flats into condos. Unfortunately for the buyers, new paint and carpets failed to mask the fetid smells of cooking, old kitty litter, and mildew that permeated the maze of hallways. And the passage of time had only made it worse.

As Claudia entered the dimly lit lobby a youth in black leather slouched past, his hair molded into a crown of magenta spikes. He walked in front of her as if she weren't there, and punched the elevator call button. When the car groaned to a stop and the door clanged open onto a tiny, graffiti-defaced compartment, she changed her mind about stepping inside with Spiky Boy and decided to take her chances on the stairs.

Nelson's apartment was located on the third floor at the far end of a succession of labyrinthine corridors with poor lighting and frayed carpeting. Television sounds penetrated the wall as Claudia knocked at the door. She wondered whether Earl Nelson would resemble Lindsey. He'd been anything but friendly when she'd spoken to him over the phone, but at least he had agreed to see her and even grudgingly acknowledged that he might have what she was looking for.

The door swung open and an odor stronger than anything she had smelled on her way to the third floor assaulted Claudia's nostrils with a knockout punch. The stench of old garbage and marijuana mingling with body odor made her want to pinch her nostrils shut. Even LA smog was preferable to breathing Earl Nelson's personal brand of air pollution.

Nelson bore about as much resemblance to Lindsey as he did to Brad Pitt, which was zero. He peered at her through mean eyes framed in Buddy Holly glasses, a permanent scowl etched on the sallow face. Middle-aged, maybe ten years older than his sister had been. A long ponytail hung over a soiled green golf shirt, which bore an incongruous Izod logo. The round shoulders were peppered with dandruff. A tattooed snake slithered up his left arm, its red eyes glittering with evil.

"Earl Nelson?" Claudia offered him her business card. "I'm Claudia Rose. We spoke earlier about Lindsey."

"Yeah?" He took the card and jammed it into his trouser pocket without looking at it. Flicked a glance over Claudia's body, his gaze lingering on her breasts until she crossed her arms. Turning on his heel, he went back inside. "Whaddya waitin' for?"

The postage stamp apartment was lit only by the television and what little sun leaked in around the edges of the mangy curtains. Nelson plopped into an ancient recliner that bore the clear imprint of his ass and picked up a bottle of beer from the coffee table. He didn't offer Claudia a seat, for which she was thankful, as there was no surface in the room where she would willingly sit.

She watched, fascinated, as he emptied the bottle and aimed it at an overflowing box of trash in a corner of the room. It missed, and fell clattering against its brethren already on the floor.

"Fuckin' thing," Nelson groused. "I was *that* close." He fixed Claudia with an expectant stare and pointed the remote at the TV, muting the sound on Jerry Springer. "So, she finally remembers she had a brother?"

"Excuse me?"

"Did the fucking bitch change her mind?"

No wonder Lindsey didn't want to claim this pathetic excuse for a human being as a relative.

"I'm sorry," Claudia said politely. "I don't know what you're talking about."

"Did she leave me some bank?" Nelson spoke slowly, stretching out the words as though she were a very slow learner.

Claudia gave him her iciest stare. "Perhaps I wasn't clear when I called. I'm not a lawyer, I have nothing to do with handling Lindsey's estate."

"But I thought . . ."

"I'm a handwriting expert. I'm here because the executor of her estate retained me to authenticate the handwriting on the note found with your sister's body."

"Exe-cu-tor!" He spat the word back at her, his lip curling into an ugly sneer. "Exe-cu-tor! You mean her fucking *secretary*! The selfish bitch leaves it all to her fucking secretary, and the fucking secretary sends a handwriting-fucking-expert to get something from her only brother? That's bullshit."

"Mr. Nelson, I told you on the phone, I'm looking for samples of Lindsey's printed writing that I can use for comparison to the suicide note. That's *it*. I don't know anything about her will or her estate."

Consumed with some primitive rage, Earl Nelson wasn't listening. "Too fucking good for her family! Keep her only brother out of her goddamned funeral? Who the hell'd she think she was, the fucking Queen a' Sheba? We were *partners*."

Claudia interrupted the flow of invective. "Excuse me, but do you have anything written in Lindsey's hand printing or not?"

Nelson broke off, staring at her blankly, apparently so caught up in his rant that he'd forgotten her presence. All at once, he grinned, showing nicotine-stained teeth. "How about some *live* action?" he said. "I got plenty of *movies* I could show ya."

"What are you talking about? I'm looking for handwriting samples, not movies."

"Hey, Lindsey and me, we had a nice little system going. Now *I'm* calling the shots. I could . . ."

"Mr. Nelson, you told me on the phone that you might have something I can use . . . block printed handwriting. That's the only reason I'm here, so show it to me *now,* or I'm gone."

A coffee table separated them, littered with racing forms, a smoke-stained bong, and assorted garbage. Nelson hawked up a wad of phlegm and spat it on a frozen-dinner tray, sending a cockroach the size of a small mouse scurrying, antennae quivering, across the desiccated remains of a long-past meal.

Claudia recoiled in disgust. She hiked her briefcase strap over her shoulder and started toward the door. Ivan Novak wasn't paying her enough to deal with this kind of vermin, human *or* six-legged.

"Hey, wait," Nelson yelled, rushing after her. "What's in it for me?"

Claudia stopped, her hand resting on the doorknob. "What is it you want?"

An avaricious gleam brightened the dull eyes. "Ivan needs what I got or you wouldn't be here. Oughta be worth somethin'."

"What do you want?" Claudia repeated, losing patience. "You want to *sell* me your sister's handwriting? I'll call Mr. Novak and see what he says."

Nelson scratched his head, releasing a shower of white flakes. "That money's mine, not his." He shuffled over to the bedroom. "He wants anything from me, he'll cough up some ducats." The bedroom door snapped shut behind him.

While she waited for him, Claudia got out her cell phone and dialed Ivan's number, keeping an eye on the cockroach, which was now examining another kind of roach lying by the bong.

Why didn't Ivan warn me about this loathsome creature?

Earl Nelson returned five minutes later with a manila envelope clutched to his undernourished chest. "What about the bank?"

"If you've got something I can use, Mr. Novak will send you a check for a thousand dollars."

The mean eyes narrowed to slits. "A thousand? Fuck that; little sister had *millions.* I want at least five big ones. That's my price."

"The offer is a thousand, take it or leave it." Claudia started to open the front door. "Personally, I think he's an ass to give you a *dime.*"

"Wait up!" Nelson sounded panicky. He reached around her, pushed the door shut and leaned against it. "Not so fast. How do I know he'll pay up if I let you just take the shit?"

This time, Claudia didn't bother to hide her contempt. "I guess you don't. Hand it over now or you get nothing; I'm not coming back here."

She could see the wheels spinning as he weighed the options. With a muttered, "Aw, fuck it," he thrust the envelope at her.

Claudia opened it and tipped out a stack of eight by ten glossies.

Not your usual Kodak moments.

The photographs starred a very young Lindsey Alexander. She appeared to be about nine, tethered to a wrought iron bed by handcuffs, wearing lingerie never intended for a child. The waifish little girl stared at the camera with a faraway expression.

"What the hell is this?" Claudia thumbed through photo after explicit photo with a rising sense of shock and outrage.

Bondage and sexual acts, many featuring a man who looked about thirty. Curly brown hair, clean-shaven chiseled features, aquiline nose. In the final image, the child now several years older—Lolita with smeared lipstick—lay on the bed beside him.

Why would someone with those knockout looks need to prey on a child?

Of course, Claudia knew the answer: feelings of inadequacy with adult women.

A tide of revulsion swelled in her and she had to fight an impulse to grind the self-satisfied smirk off Earl Nelson's face with the heel of her boot. "You filthy pervert. Why are you showing me these?"

Nelson giggled obscenely at her discomfort, delighted to have rattled her. "Little sister said they were worth money and she was right. Too fuckin' bad it's too late for *her,* ain't it?"

Claudia thrust the stack of photos in his face. "If you don't have any samples of her handwriting, it's too fucking late for *you,* moron. I'll give these to the cops."

"Hey, chill, bitch. Look on the back."

Claudia flipped the photos and saw that immature printing covered the back side of a few:

> *UNCLE PRESTON AND ME, HAVING FUN*
> *PRESTON AND HIS SPECIAL GIRL*
> *HE LOVES ME*
> *I LOVE PRESTON I HATE PRESTON*

The back of the last picture was covered with the name *PRESTON* printed over and over in green ink with adolescent colored-in hearts scattered around. Claudia's heart sank. She could immediately tell that the childish handwriting wouldn't be suitable for her examination and analysis. The twenty-five or thirty years that had elapsed was too great a time range. Lindsey's handwriting had altered significantly in that period.

She crammed the photographs back into the envelope. "Who's the piece of shit that did this to her?"

Nelson yanked open the front door with a sneer. "That ain't included in the price. You want more information, it's gonna cost. Now get the fuck out."

Chapter 6

Still shaking with anger at the way Nelson had exploited his young sister's innocence, and feeling as contaminated as if she'd been exposed to Ebola, Claudia tossed her purse into the passenger seat and climbed behind the wheel of the Jaguar. When she fumbled the keys in the ignition and dropped them on the floor, she made herself stop and take a calming breath.

Closing her eyes, she inhaled deeply, and visualized a strong vacuum sucking a thick layer of muck out of her lungs; squeezing every vestige of Nelson's vile presence out of her body as she exhaled. She repeated the process until she felt calm again, then punched in a speed dial number on her cell phone. If anyone knew the truth about Lindsey, it would be Zebediah.

"Are you available?" she asked without preamble when he answered. "I've got something I have to show you."

"Darling, for you, I'm *always* available, you know that. What's wrong?"

"Wrong? What makes you think anything's wrong? I'm having a *lovely* day."

Zebediah's voice dropped to a sensual murmur. "Bring that luscious body over here and I promise to make it all better, whatever it is."

In spite of herself, she laughed. "Ahhh, you're all talk." Once, she would have taken him seriously, but that was long ago, before their brief, blistering affair had mellowed into an easygoing friendship.

"Just give me a chance, my sweet," he said, knowing she wouldn't. "Put your panties over your heart and forget the past."

Forget the past. Forget that he was a man who loved women; who jokingly called himself a lesbian in a man's body. A man who would never confine himself to just one lover.

He couldn't see her, but Claudia rolled her eyes anyway. "Put it away, Zeb, I need to see you, now!"

Zebediah chuckled. "Ooh, I love it when you talk like that." They had their banter down pat.

"Have you had lunch?"

"No, sweetie, what d'you have in mind?"

"How about that funky little veggie place you're so fond of on Venice Beach?"

"You're buying?"

"You got it. I want to pick that devious brain of yours and I'm willing to pay for the privilege. I can be there in . . ." She checked her watch. "Forty minutes."

Despite her playful flirtation with Zebediah, Claudia couldn't have been more serious about her need to discuss with him what she had discovered about Lindsey. Child abuse was a miserable fact of life that she had dealt with more than once over the course of her career. Children treated like animals. Neglected. Beaten. Starved. Children forced to steal. Children prostituted for money. Little girls passed around to their fathers' friends. Little boys whose own mothers injected their veins with heroin-filled needles. She had worked those cases with psychologists, analyzed the handwritings of the abusers and their victims. Or, when the victims were too young to write, she analyzed their drawings.

More than once, Zebediah had cautioned her against becoming too involved. He'd suggested that she was projecting because of the miscarriages, but she'd never learned to insulate her emotions the way she did in adult relationships. The name and story of every abused child whose handwriting had crossed her desk remained indelibly stamped on her heart.

*   *   *

Aside from an elderly couple in the corner sharing a late
lunch, the Veghead on the Venice Boardwalk was deserted.
The new school year was in swing and the summer out-of-
towners had returned to work. Only the die-hard body build-
ers lingered on the sand, along with a few of their groupies.

Although the sun wouldn't emerge until the marine layer
burned off late in the afternoon, Claudia and Zebediah took
a table shaded by a big blue-and-yellow-striped umbrella
on the front patio of the café. As they sat waiting for their
meal, a tall, loose-jointed black woman in a yellow string
bikini went gliding past on roller blades. She waved at Zebediah, who waved back.

He handed back the stack of photos, looking troubled,
but not surprised as Claudia had expected. "Poor Lindsey.
She never stood a chance against all that money and power
and evil."

She tapped the top photograph. "The evil is obvious, but
money and power? You knew about this guy?"

"Yes, I knew."

"Well, come on, *give*. Don't make me go back to that
shitheel of a brother and pay for the information."

"Not so fast," Zebediah said, with a look that made her
squirm. "I still have a license to protect, and there's client-
patient confidentiality to consider."

"She's dead, and I'm retained by her estate to look into
her death, so that should let me in on the privilege."

He gave his beard a little tug and chewed on his lower
lip, considering. "That's stretching it, but it's basically true.
And seeing as I trust you completely . . ." He frowned a
warning over his glasses.

Claudia zipped her thumb and forefinger across her closed
lips. "I won't repeat it."

"Well, it *is* considered a gray area, legally, so okay, I'll
tell you what I know. Lindsey was already sexually active
by the time her brother handed her over to Preston Sommerfield when she was eight. She claimed that Earl had been
molesting her as far back as she could remember. His pals
had their fun with her, too."

The thought of being touched by Earl Nelson was enough to make Claudia's flesh crawl. "Who is this Preston Sommerfield?" she asked.

"It's a pretty sordid story," Zebediah said, leaning dangerously far back in the plastic chair. It wasn't built to support his weight and for a moment, Claudia worried that it might tip over and land him on the ground.

"Lindsey's father deserted the family when she was five. As you know, that's an especially vulnerable time for a little girl to lose her daddy. Even a sonofabitch like this fellow apparently was. Her mother took a job as a live-in house-keeper at the Sommerfield estate in Bel Air. According to Lindsey, her mother resented having to support her, and let her know it every chance she got."

"That big house in Brentwood where she lived wasn't her family home? They were just servants there?"

Zebediah nodded. "The Sommerfields employed Earl as a chauffeur. From what I understand, Preston had inherited the estate. He was a failed *artiste;* blew through the money pretty rapidly and abused every substance known to man. *Mrs.* S . . . Preston's wife, not his mother . . . was a high-powered real estate exec. She made her own money, and for reasons of her own, kept him supplied with his drug of choice, but otherwise pretty much treated him like dogshit. According to Lindsey, the wife showed how she despised him by sleeping with anyone and everyone, the more inappropriate the better . . . the pool man, the gardener."

Her raised eyebrows produced a nod. "Yes, darling, the chauffeur, too. Back then, Nelson *had* to be more appealing than what you've described. Sommerfield was inadequate and entirely incapable of an adult relationship. So he paid for sex with the housekeeper's child. And thanks to the early incest with her brother, Lindsey already had a warped view of sex, which she never outgrew. She was, shall we say, ripe for the picking."

"Didn't Mrs. Sommerfield ever hear of divorce?"

"As you know, people have all kinds of reasons for staying in a miserable situation."

The waitress arrived with a macrobiotic dish of beans and

rice for Zebediah. Claudia had opted for Chinese chicken salad. Eating raw greens made her feel virtuous, and less guilty about ordering dessert.

Zebediah plucked three pink packets of sweetener from the container on the table and sprinkled the crystals into his tea. "Lindsey was pathologically attached to Sommerfield," he said thoughtfully, stirring his drink. "But she also despised him for what he did to her."

"Do you think she could have been blackmailing Sommerfield with these photos?"

"I suppose it's possible What makes you ask?"

"When we were in school, she always had a steady stream of cash, and believe me, she flaunted it. Had her own Gold Card. She was always showing off shopping bags from Rodeo Drive. She'd show up with stuff the rest of us only *talked* about buying. French silk scarves, Italian leather sandals. Always the very item she'd heard someone else say they wanted."

"Darling, you know she had to be on top in everything."

"I guess you'd know more about that than I would."

Zebediah shook his head in pretend despair. "You are truly wicked."

"She had this gorgeous white Mercedes convertible," Claudia continued, as memories continued to trickle back. "She'd deliberately park it in the red zone. Naturally, she'd get cited, but would she pay the tickets? Of course not. She'd stick 'em in the glove box for a couple of months, and when she finally got around to it, she'd write out one big check for all the fines."

Zebediah adjusted his chair upright, stuck his long legs underneath it, and attacked his food with the anticipation of a starving man. "If she was blackmailing Sommerfield, I'd guess she must have made him pay in spades over the years."

"What about her mother? Why didn't she do something about the abuse?" Even as she asked the question, Claudia guessed the answer.

"She claims her mother knew all about it, but she didn't want to lose all the perks, so she kept her mouth shut. She was only too happy to look the other way."

*Looked the other way while her child was used as a
sex slave. Lindsey must have been crushed by the emotional abandonment, along with everything else she had
to suffer.*

It was not uncommon for victims of long-term abuse
to eventually identify with their abuser. Like Patti Hearst
and the Symbionese Liberation Army, back in the seventies. Psychologists had dubbed it the Stockholm Syndrome,
after a botched bank robbery in Sweden, where the hostages
had eventually refused rescue. One of them even became
engaged to her captor.

"So, what happened to this guy?" asked Claudia.

"I don't know, but as I said, Lindsey was pathologically
attached to him. She talked to me about it, but she didn't
want him prosecuted for the prior child abuse. She was an
adult, which meant I didn't have the same legal obligation
to report it, as I would if she'd been a minor." Zebediah
looked thoughtful. "If she *was* blackmailing him she probably made more money than she would have been awarded
in a lawsuit. He must be delighted that she's dead."

"Do you think Preston Sommerfield could have killed
her?" Claudia breathed, then immediately wondered how
she could obtain a sample of the pedophile's handwriting
to compare to the suicide note. What were the chances that
he used a block printed style?

"If Earl Nelson thought Sommerfield was involved in
Lindsey's death, he'd cash in on it, big time. I doubt he'd
worry about a paltry thousand bucks from Ivan."

"But if he and Lindsey were blackmailing Sommerfield,
Nelson must have the negatives or he wouldn't have given
up the photos. Lindsey may have hated her brother, but he
said something about them being partners." Claudia tore
off a hunk of bread and dipped it in the blue cheese dressing
she'd requested on the side. "If Nelson was blackmailing
Sommerfield, why is he living in such a dump?"

Zebediah waved at the bikinied skater again as she rolled
past them, going the other direction. "My guess is, any money
he gets goes straight up his nose or into his veins."

"Good point. Okay, first things first. I haven't examined the suicide note yet. I've been waiting, hoping to find some good block printing samples for comparison. Ivan is sending Lindsey's files over, so I'll need to finish going through them and decide whether she actually wrote the note or not. The handwriting on those photos Nelson gave me was done too long ago to be useful, except for one thing. It's block printed, which tells me that block printing *is* a style of writing within Lindsey's personal range of variation." Claudia sighed. "I need to find out whether a police expert actually examined the handwriting on the note, as they told Ivan."

"Do you know any of the detectives at the PD in her district?" Zebediah asked.

"No, that would be Wilshire or Beverly Hills. I'll call my contact at Pacific Division and see if she can find out for me which detective was assigned to Lindsey's case."

"Do that, sweetie. Who knows? He might be just what you need."

Dialing the number for the Pacific Division police station an hour later, Claudia couldn't get the images of the young Lindsey and her abuser out of her head. What she had learned about Earl Nelson and Preston Sommerfield turned her stomach and had put Lindsey in a totally different light. Her appalling childhood experiences explained so much of her behavior.

"Records," a formal voice said. "Jackson speaking."

"Hey, Dana, what's up?"

The voice relaxed as Dana Jackson recognized her caller. "Don't *even* ask. It's been crazy around here, all the gangs shooting each other and anyone else who gets in the way."

Pacific Division was responsible for a twenty-four-square-mile territory covering Venice Beach, Oakwood, Mar Vista, Playa del Reina, where Claudia lived, and Westchester, an area attractive to tourists, and rife with gangs and drug dealing.

"Keeps you in a job," said Claudia.

"Yeah, thank you so much, Ms. Citizen," Dana said sarcastically. "Hey, I'm glad you called. Much as I hate to admit it, I'm dating another cop. I've got some of his handwriting to show you."

"Send it over," Claudia said with sudden envy. Lately, it seemed as if all her friends had new loves in their lives. They all wanted her to analyze their handwriting samples, while *she* hadn't dated anyone steadily in more than a year. In fact, over the last few months she had dated very little. Her personal life seemed to be headed nowhere. She could practically feel her allure slipping away.

"I need a favor, too," Claudia said. "I have to find the investigator on a case I'm working. He's either from Wilshire or Beverly Hills. His name's . . . hold on." She read the note she had scratched to herself during her last update with Ivan Novak, where she had filled him in on her meeting with Nelson, and her lunchtime conversation with Zebediah.

"It's Vanderbosh. Detective Eugene Vanderbosh."

"Vanderbosh?" Dana repeated. "Sorry, girl, he's in the hospital. Last I heard, he's not expected to make it."

"No shit? What happened? Shot in the line of duty?"

"Nah, heart attack. Too many donuts."

"Your compassion is touching, Dana."

"Aw, he's a fat fuck. No one around here's sheddin' a whole lot of tears."

"My client didn't think much of him, either," said Claudia, idly doodling boxes around the edges of the electric bill that lay on her desk. "Listen, this is a suicide case. The heirs want me to look at the handwriting on the note. Can you find out if someone examined it on your side?"

Dana gave a contemptuous snort. "Knowing Vanderbosh, he probably just made something up. That's the kind of hardworking sumbitch he is. Was." Claudia heard her fingernails clicking on her keyboard. "Someone has to be filling in for him on his cases. Let me find out who it is and get back to you."

"Can you get me the autopsy report, too?"

"Why do you need that?"

"For the tox screens. I need to know exactly what drugs were in her system. If she actually wrote the note, the drugs would have an effect on her handwriting."

"I get it. Okay, I'll see what I can do. I can probably get you a cleansed copy of the Incident Report, too."

"Cleansed?"

"The witnesses' names are redacted. That's blacked out to you."

"What's the point of that?"

"Hey, if someone got pissed off about something they read in our report and went after a witness, we'd be in deep shit. Gotta protect our asses from lawsuits, you know?"

"Yeah, I bet. Okay, thanks, Dana, I owe you."

"That's right, you do. I'll fax you my guy's writing when I send the reports. Just tell me the bad stuff. I already know the rest."

Claudia was rinsing out the plastic tray from her frozen lasagna when the phone rang and Kelly's number popped up on caller ID. She hadn't heard from her friend since the funeral reception on Saturday.

"Where have you been?" asked Claudia. "I've been calling you."

The boozy voice that answered was an instant red flag. "You gotta help me, Claudia."

"What's wrong?"

"You have to tell me what to do. I'm scared. I don't know what to do. *Help* me!"

"Take it easy, Kel, just tell me what happened."

"I don't . . . I can't . . . just forget it, I'm hanging up now."

Claudia sighed inwardly. Kelly after a few cocktails could do drama better than Meryl Streep. "Don't hang up, Kel; just tell me what's wrong; everything's going to be okay."

Famous last words.

Kelly began weeping convulsively, big, heaving sobs. "I . . . oh my God. Claudia . . . I think I killed Lindsey."

Chapter 7

Claudia stared at the phone as if it had suddenly taken on a life of its own. "What the *hell* are you talking about? She committed suicide, remember?"

"You don't know what happened. I'm so . . . so scared."

Something in Kelly's voice warned Claudia not to blow this off as her usual run-of-the-mill theatrics. "Just tell me what happened," she repeated gently, feeling like a therapist. "Start at the beginning."

Through the phone, she could hear glass clinking on glass. Kelly, pouring another martini. Extra dry, two olives.

Claudia paced the room, pausing at the open door that led out to the deck. Autumn in California was fire season, and smoke from a blaze twenty miles up the coast in Malibu had painted a stunning sunset of feathery pink and gold fingers on the evening sky.

Kelly began to speak in a shaky voice. "It started last month. Remember that guy I was seeing, Sean?"

It would take a scorecard to keep up with Kelly's dates. Tearing her gaze away from the scenery, Claudia made herself concentrate, replaying conversations they'd had over the past few weeks. Kelly liked them young, she was fond of saying, so she could train them. Was Sean the one who resembled Orlando Bloom, or Jason Patric? "Sean's the actor, right? He plays a doctor on *Tender is the Night*?"

"Well, yeah," Kelly said, as if Claudia should have known. "I had to dump him."

"And, this is connected to Lindsey's death how, exactly?"

"Wait, I'm getting there. The week before Lindsey . . . died, Sean and I went to Busby's for drinks. We're at the bar and lo and behold, *she* shows up."

Claudia knew the club. Popular with the upwardly mobile Westside singles crowd, Busby's boasted go-go girls, pool tables, and abundant couches on which to snuggle, if that was what you were looking for.

"So, what happened?"

"I might as well have been invisible. She was on him like a bitch in heat; kept leering at his crotch."

For a millisecond, Claudia had the urge to ask what was so special about Sean's crotch, but she thought better of it and let Kelly continue her story.

"She never would have looked at him twice if he hadn't been with me. Why was she like that, Claud? She could have ten guys crawling all over her, but if she saw *me* with someone, she'd go after him instead." The bitterness in Kelly's voice brought back their conversation at the gravesite. Hatred had sprouted like a prickly shrub and was bursting into full, thorny bloom.

"Sounds like insecurity to me," Claudia offered, thinking of Preston Sommerfield, and Earl Nelson's repulsive photo gallery. But Kelly knew nothing of that.

"Insecurity my ass. I got her into the ladies' room. Told her to keep her goddamn hands off this one. I said, 'I've had enough of you fucking up my life.' "

Kelly's anger dissolved into sobs. "Like always, she thought it was a big joke. Then she called him *the next day* and asked him out, Claud. And he *told* me about it. He was actually flattered! She told him she'd introduce him to Spielberg. Like that was ever gonna happen."

"Creep," Claudia agreed automatically, wishing Kelly had more discriminating taste in men.

Look who's talking. Like you've done any better.

"That bitch had more balls than a two-pecker billy goat. Can you believe she'd go after him like that?"

"We're talking about Lindsey, here."

"God, I hated her."

"I get that, honey, but what makes you think you *killed* her?"

"This isn't easy, Claud. Gimme a minute." Kelly paused, catching her breath. Claudia could hear her gulping her cocktail, then she started talking, faster and faster until the words ran together. "I couldn't get it out of my head, what she'd done with Sean; *all* the things she did. I thought about my wedding; about what she did to you. By Friday night I was going crazy. I thought . . . I thought, maybe if I saw her face-to-face, I could make her understand that . . . hell, I don't know. I just went over to her apartment and started banging on the door. She wouldn't open it; probably saw me through the peephole.

"I could hear music inside. I started yelling and kicking the door. Shit, I know I was acting like a baby, but I *couldn't* let her get away with screwing me over that way again. Sean was the last straw. I wanted to kick her skinny ass."

Under other circumstances, the idea of petite Kelly going ten rounds with the much taller Lindsey like a couple of mismatched boxers would have made Claudia laugh, but Lindsey's death had changed so many things. She leaned her head back against the cushions and closed her eyes. "Did she open the door?"

"No, but she was there." With the stability of a yo-yo, Kelly's mood shifted back to anger. "She called the cops on me! Must have taken them all of three minutes to get there. I guess you have to live in a penthouse to get that kind of service. They busted out of the elevator, pointing their guns at me and yelling! God knows what she told them. It was a nightmare. I thought they were going to shoot me."

"Holy shit, what time was that?"

"What time?"

"Yes, about what time were you pounding on her door?"

"Around eight, I guess. Why?"

"The police report would show what time they arrived and that they saw her alive then. Were you arrested?" Kelly would surely have told her if she'd gone to jail, even if it had been just long enough to post bail. But Kelly had kept surprisingly quiet about the entire episode.

Claudia flopped full-length on the couch and put her hand over her eyes, as if that would blot out the scene that her friend had described. "Please tell me that this is the *whole* story. That you just turned around and left. You did, right?"

"Well I *had* to leave. She kept laughing that stupid donkey laugh of hers. She said she wasn't going to press charges . . . for what? I didn't do anything! They escorted me downstairs and told me to go home. It was all so humiliating."

Kelly *sounded* humiliated, but Claudia wondered uncharitably if she hadn't enjoyed the drama, just a tiny bit. "I have a sinking feeling there's something else," she said.

Silence, then the sounds of a glass being refilled.

"Kelly?"

"Yeah, there's more. I went back later. I . . ."

"You went *back?*"

"I know, I know, it was a stupid thing to do. It was a couple hours later."

A couple of hours. That had given Kelly enough time to knock back a few more martinis.

Media reports had put Lindsey's death sometime between midnight Friday and dawn Saturday. The condition of the body had made it difficult for the coroner to be more exact.

"I drove around for a while and just got madder." Kelly gave a humorless laugh. "I went back and the police cars were gone. I was expecting the guy at the desk to stop me, but he was eating; hardly even noticed I was there. I went up and knocked on her door again. Not like before, just a regular knock. She opened up right away, like she was expecting someone. She was wearing this black satin *come-fuck-me* bustier and garter belt."

Claudia could visualize the scene: Lindsey flinging open the door, anticipating a late-night visitor, certainly not expecting to find Kelly on her doorstep again.

"What'd she do?"

"She was shocked to see me. I pushed past her and went inside. She asked what the hell I thought I was doing."

"And?"

Long pause. "I said I was through with her messing up my life. I said . . . I said, if she didn't stay away from me . . . I said I'd *kill* her." Kelly's voice cracked. "She just laughed at me again. Why did she always do that, Claudia? Why'd she always have to laugh at people that way?"

That godawful mocking, nails-on-a-blackboard laugh.

Claudia rolled off the sofa and took the phone out to the deck. It was too dark to see the ocean, but she could hear the shushing of the waves, feel the mist on her cheeks. "What happened after that?"

"I don't remember."

"What do you mean, you don't remember?"

"I . . . I blacked out."

Kelly had begun drinking in middle school, where she'd discovered that alcohol could deaden the pain of dealing with a drug-addicted mother who was often out of touch with reality for days at a time. As the eldest child, the responsibility of parenting four younger siblings had fallen on Kelly's young shoulders. Neighbors of theirs for years, Claudia's parents had tried to help fill in the gaps so that Child Welfare wouldn't split up the children in foster care, and Kelly had become an unofficially adopted member of Claudia's family.

"Do you remember leaving the apartment?"

"That's the worst part. When she started laughing at me I lost it. I just lost it. I don't *know* what happened afterward. I woke up in my car a long time later, feeling like shit on toast. I drove home and threw up." The tears began to flow in a torrent and it was all Claudia could do to make out the words. "Then it was all over the news that she was dead and I . . . I . . . I . . ."

Kelly's blackout had been smack in the middle of the coroner's estimate of when Lindsey had died. Claudia's heart sank a few degrees lower.

"They said she drowned. I think I might have pushed her into the Jacuzzi and held her head under the water,

Claud. I was angry enough to do it, *and* buzzed enough. I just don't remember!"

Claudia's hand went to her neck and she began massaging the knots of tension that had formed. "Let's think this through. You said you thought she was expecting someone, right?"

"Yeah, she was all made up, lipstick, everything."

"Well, in the event she *didn't* kill herself, what makes you so sure that this other person didn't show up and kill her after you left?"

"Jeez, I hadn't thought of that." Kelly's voice brightened as she latched onto this explanation like a life preserver. "That *must* be what happened. She didn't act like someone who was about to kill herself."

"Don't repeat that," Claudia cautioned. "It could easily work against you." If the police got wind of Kelly's story, they would be on her like a pack of starving mongrels. Yet, what if a killer was on the loose? "The cops need to know someone else might have been there, Kel. You'll have to tell them."

Kelly's voice grew shrill with panic. "Forget it! Not after Lindsey called nine-one-one. They can't know I went back."

"There wasn't a restraining order against you and the coroner ruled her death a suicide. Unless there's evidence that someone else was there, that's how it will stand."

If another visitor had arrived after Kelly, that person's name might be in the log, although the concierge had let Kelly pass without signing in. Claudia made herself a note to suggest Ivan Novak have the log checked.

"Claudia, did you hear me?" Kelly was asking in a plaintive voice. "What if I *did* kill her?"

"I'm going to have to examine the suicide note tomorrow. If Lindsey wrote it, you won't have to say anything. But if it's not her handwriting, you'll *have* to tell the police that you saw her again and that she was alive at ten o'clock."

"I'm not talking to the cops, Claudia." All of a sudden Kelly sounded stone cold sober. "And neither are you."

*   *   *

By the time she'd cleaned up the kitchen and dumped the bag of trash into the plastic bin in the alley behind her house, Claudia had resolved to get to the bottom of Lindsey's death.

It was not her job to reopen the investigation. Her obligation ended with authenticating the suicide note. But after Kelly's little bombshell, she knew she would have to do everything within her ability to uncover the truth.

What if she uncovered evidence that incriminated Kelly? Could she remain objective? Maybe she should resign from the case before it was too late. Torn by second thoughts, Claudia went upstairs to the office and got out the suicide note.

IT WAS FUN WHILE IT LASTED.

Block printing. She reflected on some of the general interpretations that she could make about printed handwriting and personality. People who block print only occasionally are usually making a point, being emphatic. *Habitual* printers generally tended to have intimacy issues. By breaking the links between their letters, they were symbolically breaking their connections to other people. Also, those who chose the *block* style of printing were often egocentric, seeing themselves as the center of the universe.

Those characteristics fit Lindsey.

From what Claudia knew of Lindsey's handwriting from years ago, the style of writing had been distinctly different from the printed words on the paper—cursive, with large lower loops. Yet, she knew that when life takes traumatic twists and turns, handwriting changes.

IT WAS FUN WHILE IT LASTED.

She could see Lindsey uttering those pragmatic words before downing the lethal cocktail and stepping into her hot tub. But again Claudia asked herself, why would Lindsey choose to end her life at this particular point in time?

Or did Kelly's story hold the answer after all?

Questions plagued her long into the evening, until doubt became a living thing, choking her with uncertainty. Was it possible that her closest friend might be responsible for a monstrous crime like murder? *Ridiculous.* Yet, the window of opportunity yawned just wide enough to make the ridiculous possible.

Only nine-thirty, but Claudia's eyes burned with fatigue. She undressed and threw on her favorite ratty T-shirt and stretch pants, fed an Eric Clapton CD to the stereo and went into the kitchen, where she poured a vodka and cranberry. Grabbing the heavy afghan that was draped across the back of the couch, she went out to the deck, dodging the large potted asparagus fern that she had purchased a week earlier. She had yet to find the right home for it on the deck, and needed to move it before she tripped over the long fronds and broke her neck. *Tomorrow.*

Clapton's voice followed her outside as she hummed along to "Layla," wrapping herself in the afghan and settling into the cozy basket chair suspended from the rafters.

She was excessively proud of that chair. Drilling the hole for the big hook and hanging it without any help had been a small symbol of her independence after Alan had moved out, destroying the imperfect life they had built together. Overcome by hurt and remorse, she had been unable to work for weeks afterward. Ironic, since it was her work that had driven them apart.

Claudia cuddled the afghan around her, a poor substitute for a lover's arms. This was her favorite part of the day: a moment to savor, when she could relax, unwind, and recharge her batteries. No questions to answer, no clients' demands or friends' problems to deal with.

Yawning, she set her half-empty glass on the redwood deck, certain of only one thing—if there had been foul play, the killer must be brought to justice, *whoever* he or she might be. No matter how hateful Lindsey's behavior had been; however many nasty tricks she had played, she had been molded by horrible childhood abuse. She didn't deserve to die.

*   *   *

Startled from a disturbing dream, Claudia was out of the chair and halfway into the house before she became aware that it was a ringing telephone that had awakened her.

Chapter 8

Her heart was galloping like a racehorse in the home-stretch, as Claudia stumbled into the kitchen and squinted at the phone's caller ID: *Private Caller.* The LED clock on the microwave told her she'd been asleep for about twenty minutes.

Waiting for her respiration to slow, she listened to her own recorded voice on the answering machine: *". . . and please leave your name and number after the beep."*

"Claudia, if you're there, pick up. Claudia?" She recognized the voice and its insistent tone even before the caller said, "It's Ivan Novak, please pick up the phone. It's urgent."

She grabbed the handset, too jarred by the sudden wake-up not to let her irritation show. "*Yes*, Ivan?"

"I've found something I need you to take a look at."

Still fuzzy from her dream state, Claudia turned on the faucet, and splashed cold water on her face. "What? I was asleep."

"Asleep?" Ivan repeated. "Good God, Claudia, it's not even ten o'clock."

"I apologize for being tired after running around all day, working on your case."

Her sarcasm was lost on Ivan. "I've got to see you, this is important."

"What's this about?"

"I'll tell you when you get here. I'm about to leave for Chicago on the red eye, so you need to come right away."

"You want me to come back to Lindsey's place tonight?"
She felt foolish, echoing him, but this call was far from the
standard client request.

"I've found a letter from Doctor Gold written to Lindsey
that you need to see," Ivan said.

"From Zebediah? About what? You can fax it to me."

"No, that's not all. I need you to hold some other things
for me until I get back from Chicago and figure out what
to do with them. Tapes and, well, this material is just too
sensitive to leave lying around here."

"What material? What tapes? Ivan, what the hell are
you talking about?"

"I can't discuss it over the phone. It's not secure." He
lowered his voice almost to a whisper. "Someone could be
listening in."

His words sent a little chill up her spine. "Ivan, are these
tapes evidence in Lindsey's death? If so, you should take
them to the police."

"No! Look, I've found something that could put a new
light on Lindsey's death. Claudia, I know Doctor Gold is a
close friend of yours. When you see this letter I think you'll
agree it's in his best interests for you to . . ."

His words slammed her in the face and brought her fully
awake. "You can't possibly think Zebediah . . ."

"Come now, *please*. We'll talk when you get here."

Claudia didn't immediately answer. Even though he occasionally confided in her, she was well aware that Zebediah
Gold was a man with secrets of his own. But what Ivan was
implying . . .

"Believe me," Ivan continued, "I'd rather put all this
crap into a safety deposit box, but I have to be at LAX by
eleven. You can drop me at the airport on your way home.
It will give us a chance to discuss everything."

Claudia tensed with frustration. "*Ivan . . .*"

"I'll wait for you in front of the building. You can drive
by and I'll just jump into your car. It's a white Jag, right?"

Zebediah had always been there for Claudia when she
needed to talk about a difficult case, or make her laugh with
a bawdy joke when she needed a break; someone to discuss

things that she didn't want to share with Kelly. She owed it to him to see what it was that Ivan had.

Or thought he had.

And what about the tapes he had mentioned?

Tapes of what?

Claudia pushed the Jag as much as she dared through surface streets, speculating on what the letter might contain. There was no denying Zebediah was a man of powerful appetites, impulsive when he wanted something. Her mind raced through the possibilities. What were the chances he had violated the ethics of his profession and the law and had an affair with Lindsey while she was his patient? Zebediah had long ago confided in Claudia that Lindsey had tried to seduce him. He said he had immediately referred her to another therapist, but she'd never kept the appointment.

Had he been telling the truth when he said he'd rejected her advances? What if Lindsey had threatened to expose him; blackmailed him as she may have blackmailed Preston Sommerfield?

She remembered Ivan's words: *"This could put a new light on Lindsey's death."*

The morning's tête-à-tête with Earl Nelson came back like a news flash. Was his claim that Ivan was Lindsey's only heir a reason for Ivan to throw suspicion onto someone else? If Nelson was correct, Ivan was the one who stood to gain from Lindsey's death. If Ivan had something to hide, maybe accusing Zebediah could be to his advantage.

But if Ivan himself were in some way involved in Lindsey's death, why would he need to divert suspicion when it had already been ruled a suicide?

The insurance money.

He'd said the insurance companies wouldn't pay out for a suicide.

Maybe he needs a patsy.

His reluctance to help her come up with the materials she had requested for the handwriting comparison continued to perplex her.

"Please don't let Zebediah be involved," she prayed aloud,

although she had long ago left religion behind and couldn't
say for sure to whom she was praying.

Arriving at the Wilshire Boulevard high-rise, Claudia
found the sidewalk deserted. She parked the Jag behind a
florist's van with a bouquet of red roses stenciled on the
side, and cut the engine, irked that Ivan was not where he
had promised to be. At this time of night, LAX would be a
thirty-minute drive and she would need to break speed limits
to get him through security on time to make his flight.

She dialed Lindsey's number and got a busy signal. Ivan's
mobile number went right to voice mail.

Goddammit.

Claudia flipped the phone shut and leaned over the seat
back, straining to see through the glass doors fronting the
lobby. She got out, slammed the car door, and ran up the
half-dozen steps, doing a slow burn. Jesus, this case was
bringing out the worst in her. Was it only that morning she
had been here, poking through Lindsey's files? It felt like
a month ago.

No valet or doorman was in evidence, but she could see
a security guard behind the reception desk where the concierge normally stood. Fat and fiftyish, he had a Big Mac
in one hand and was fully occupied with stuffing a fistful
of fries into his mouth with the other.

The front doors were locked and she held up her ID, prepared to make a fuss if he gave her a hard time. But the guard
just waved his sandwich at her and buzzed her in. When she
hurried over to the desk, he gave her a friendly greeting and
didn't bother checking her ID or make her sign in.

"They just had a flower delivery up there," he said when
she told him her destination.

The delivery might explain Ivan's delay, but it didn't explain why the telephone was busy when he was supposed
to be meeting her outside.

The luminous green eyes that stared back at her from
the mirrored elevator walls were strained and fatigued. For
a brief moment, Claudia nurtured the bizarre notion of
getting a tattoo on her forehead to remind her every time

she saw her reflection: *Personal acquaintances make the worst clients.*

The door to the penthouse stood ajar. Claudia pushed it open and walked into the foyer. A folded Louis Vuitton overnight bag and black attaché stood against the wall. Atop the attaché was a white business envelope with her name written in handwriting she recognized as Ivan's. Before stuffing it into her purse she automatically assessed the large, right-slanted, loopy script: *Overemotional, highly reactive, quick to jump to conclusions.* That was the Ivan she had come to know.

"Ivan," she called. "Let's go!"

No response. She raised her voice a few notches. "Ivan! Come on, it's late."

She was struck, suddenly, by the overwhelming stillness of the place. It felt almost as though the apartment were holding its breath.

Where is *Ivan?*

Still on the phone? Probably in Lindsey's office where he couldn't hear her.

Passing a large arrangement of fresh funeral lilies on a table in the foyer, Claudia paused to check out the gift card. The logo on the envelope matched the florist's truck behind which she had parked the Jag. The delivery person must have taken a service elevator, or she would have run into him on the way up.

In the living room, a single dim lamp in a distant corner cast more shadows than light. Just enough light to reveal a half-dozen or so large moving boxes. Claudia crossed to the spiral staircase and began to ascend, calling Ivan's name again.

A few steps before she reached the second floor landing, she was halted by the sound of a yell, a muffled thud, a crash. The sounds came from below, deep in the apartment.

Ivan!

Adrenaline surged through muscles paralyzed by fear and sent Claudia racing the rest of the way up to the landing, her mind filled with one thought: *get help.*

Fumbling in her purse in the dark corridor, she came to the awful realization that she'd left her cell phone in the car.

Lindsey's office had a phone. She felt her way along the wall until she reached the door that she believed was the office where she had spent the morning. Locked.

Shit!

With as much caution as her shaking legs would allow, Claudia started back down the stairs. The sound of running feet below halted her once again, raising the fine hairs on her arms.

Someone was following the path she had taken through the living room, not bothering to cover the sound of heavy feet thumping across the foyer's terrazzo floor.

Claudia stood still, straining for any sound. The silence was complete, except for the pulsing of her own heart in her ears.

Dropping to her knees, she crawled to the banister and looked down. A man stood near the bottom of the staircase, his back to her, listening. Oily black hair, dark, long-sleeved shirt and trousers. Average height.

Claudia held her breath.

Please don't come upstairs!

A weapon—she needed a weapon—although God knew if she'd have the guts to use one. Even spiders got a second chance in her house.

His sudden movement took her by surprise. She'd lost sight of him. Had he gone out the door, or back the way he'd come?

Claudia counted to one hundred. Hearing nothing, she tiptoed back down to the first floor and into the living room. What had happened to Ivan?

Apprehension twanged along nerves as taut as piano wire as she scanned the room. Her eyes lit on a cut-crystal ashtray on an end table. She picked it up, hefting it in her right hand. Heavy enough to do some serious damage if it connected with a vulnerable spot.

Treading silently on spotless white carpeting, she took the direction Ivan's cry had seemed to come from, making her way past the sofa where she and Zebediah had sat chatting with Kelly after the funeral, past the doors to the deck where they had savored the view.

In the dining room, Claudia took in the empty breakfront, the blank spaces on the walls where artwork had hung. The moving boxes that had been torn open, their contents scattered, as if someone had been searching for something. A chair lying on its side.

A door neatly concealed in the wallpaper pattern stood open. She paused there, listening to the silence.

What the hell am I doing?

Behind the door was a utility corridor. Clutching the ashtray like a pitcher winding up for the throw, Claudia took a deep breath and forced herself to keep moving forward.

Hoping her sneakers would mask her footfalls on the unglazed floor, she eased into the shadows and crept along the wall, toward the rectangle of light at the end of the passage.

Chapter 9

A spray of blood arced across the wall, splattering glass-fronted kitchen cabinets with crimson, like the work of some macabre graffiti artist. From the floor, the telephone handset emitted an insistent "off-the-hook" beep-beep-beep. A bloody handprint smeared the stainless steel refrigerator door.

Claudia's horrified gaze registered the carnage, bile surging into her throat.

Don't get sick. Keep your mind blank. Don't get sick. Don't think. The mantra pulsed in her head as she swallowed hard to keep from heaving.

A seven-foot island dominated the center of the kitchen, blocking her view. She edged along it and turned the corner. The ashtray slipped from her hand and the puny weapon crashed on unforgiving terra cotta tile. "Holy Christ."

Ivan lay on his side, his head bathed in a scarlet halo. His knees were drawn up in fetal position, one arm defensively covering his face.

Can anyone lose that much blood and still be alive?

Fighting nausea, Claudia did her best to avoid the gore, and crouched on her heels beside him. Gently, she removed Ivan's arm away from his face and pressed her fingers to his throat. Almost dizzy with relief when a pulse quivered under her touch.

"Ivan," she murmured. "It's Claudia. Can you hear me?"

Ivan's eyelids fluttered. His mouth moved, emitting a

few meaningless sounds. Abruptly, he turned his face away
from her, exposing blood-matted hair and flesh the texture
of tenderized meat.

Claudia had a sudden, sharp recollection from a high-
school first-aid class: head injuries were the bloodiest of
all, and often deadly. But it didn't take a trained nurse to
recognize that Ivan needed expert help. Fast.

"Ivan, I'm going to call nine-one-one." Straightening,
she shakily silenced the still-beeping phone, not at all sure
that Ivan was able to comprehend her words.

"A man's been attacked," Claudia told the dispatcher,
hearing her voice rising in panic. "He's unconscious, he's
lost a lot of blood."

"Calm down, ma'am."

"His head's bleeding. There was a man . . ."

"Ma'am?" The dispatcher's voice was stern. "I need you
to be calm. Now, are you safe? Where's the assailant?"

*How in God's name am I supposed to be calm while
I'm standing in a sea of blood, watching a man's life trickle
away?*

"I'm not sure, but I think he's gone."

"Okay, ma'am, they're on their way. Now, I want you
to look for some clean towels so we can try and stop the
bleeding."

Claudia took the phone with her and began to search
drawers and cabinets. She found a stack of clean dishtowels
and carefully wadded them under Ivan's head, Kelly's tale
of showing up here on the night of Lindsey's death, and
Ivan's innuendo about Zebediah, hammering away at her
as she worked. Neither of them was capable of this kind of
violence; she would stake her own life on it.

The electric hum of the utility clock seemed as loud as
a thousand-kilowatt generator, ticking the minutes away in
slow motion. The refrigerator motor cycled on and off as
always, as though a vicious crime had not been committed
right in front of it. Ordinary kitchen sounds; things you
never usually notice.

Shouldn't something be different?

The 911 dispatcher was still talking, but Claudia wasn't

listening. Mutely, she laid the phone on the counter and leaned against the doorjamb. The tears came then, hot, and in a rush. She bent over, hands on knees, rocking a little as emotion poured out in ragged sobs.

For a minute or two, she let herself go. Finally, exhausted, she tore off a paper towel, wiped her nose on it, and told herself she should turn on more lights for the paramedics.

She went around the apartment flipping switches, turning knobs, until all the downstairs rooms glowed as bright as daylight. But all the light in the world couldn't blot out the scene in the kitchen.

Returning to Ivan's side, Claudia felt like a rubbernecker on the highway, slowing to gawk at a horrible crash, denying what her eyes were telling her. She stroked his arm, murmured reassuring words, though she was worried about the thin trickle of blood that seeped from his ear.

Suddenly, his body spasmed, arms and legs jerking. He twisted away from her, exposing a small object lying on the floor beneath him. It looked like a miniature cigarette lighter with a plastic cap covering one end, which Claudia knew would plug into the USB port of a computer.

A flash drive—a miniature but powerful storage device for electronic media. She stared at it, her mind buzzing, yet strangely anesthetized.

A loud shout came from the living room, announcing the arrival of police.

Claudia called out her location. A moment later rapid footsteps came along the utility corridor. She stared down at the flash drive in her hand, hesitating for an instant, then dropped it into her purse.

Chapter 10

The lead detective strolled in at close to one in the morning with the casual air of a man who feels no sense of urgency and no great concern for his witness's shaken sensibilities. In fact, Claudia decided, with his open-necked shirt and Haggar sport coat, and the toothpick dangling from his lip, he looked as if he didn't give a rat's ass about much of anything.

Around six-two, fortyish. Broad-shouldered, untidy thick brown hair shot through with silver. A patrician nose and devilish eyebrows, the left one curved in a permanent question. An interesting face that gave away nothing.

He passed through the living room on his way to view the kitchen crime scene, nodding in Claudia's direction, but not stopping to speak to her.

Before his arrival, one of the female patrol officers on the scene had taken Claudia down to the high-rise lobby to wait with the shaken guard at the front desk until the penthouse had been cleared. After they had made certain that no one was hiding in any of the rooms, she was escorted back upstairs to Lindsey's apartment. Meantime, paramedics had arrived and loaded Ivan onto a gurney, talking to a doctor by cell phone as they performed emergency aid.

Claudia had offered to accompany Ivan to Cedars-Sinai Medical Center, but the cops asked her to stick around and give them a statement, confining her to a sofa in the living room to await the arrival of the detective assigned to handle the investigation.

As she waited for the detective to finish his inspection and return to her, she heard the patrolmen repeating the litany of events she had related. A bark of laughter erupting as someone cracked a joke offended her. Nothing about this evening was even remotely amusing. The realization that gallows humor was the cops' safety valve was cold comfort. The image of Ivan lying senseless in his own blood remained etched on the insides of her eyelids.

Maybe I can learn to sleep with my eyes open.

"Ms. Rose?"

She jerked awake, wondering for an instant where she was. A drop of drool had dried at the corner of her mouth. Blinking, she swiped at it with the back of her hand, embarrassed to be caught dozing, though the hour was late and she was exhausted.

The detective was leaning over her. "My name is Joel Jovanic. I'm in charge of the investigation. I need to ask you some questions." His voice wasn't unkind. It wasn't cold. It wasn't really anything. Claudia couldn't even identify a regional accent. She pulled herself from her sleepy sprawl into a more dignified position and took the hand he offered. "Is Ivan going to be okay?"

"He's still unconscious. The next forty-eight hours seems to be the critical period." Jovanic seated himself beside her on the sofa so they were almost knee-to-knee. "I'd like you to tell me everything you can remember."

"I already told the other officers," Claudia said, still feeling disoriented from the shock of the violence she had witnessed. "Can't you get my statement from them? I don't want to talk about it anymore tonight."

His expression was serious, but she couldn't help noticing the smile lines crinkling the corners of his eyes, contradicting the serious set of his mouth.

"If you don't mind, ma'am, I'd like to hear it directly from you." Jovanic took a small spiral notebook and black rollerball from his pocket, holding the pen in his left hand, ready to take notes. "What did you see when you first arrived?"

Through the cloud of fatigue, Claudia noted that small detail. A lefty. She raked her hair away from her face. "Does it matter if I mind?"

"A serious crime has been committed here, ma'am, and we need your help. The sooner we get the information, the sooner we'll find out who's responsible for the assault on your friend."

Feeling like a jerk, she pulled herself together. "I got here a few minutes after ten. The front door was open, it was pretty dark, I . . ."

"It was dark?" Jovanic cut in. "Who turned on all the lights?"

"I did. When I first arrived, only that light over there was on. I didn't want to sit here alone in the dark until your people showed up."

Jovanic gave a noncommittal grunt. "Yes, ma'am. Did you see anyone?"

"Not at first. I was trying to figure out where Ivan was. Then I heard him cry out and there was a loud noise, which I assume was him falling after having his head beaten in. I hid up on the second floor landing. Then I heard someone running, but when I looked down, I could only see from behind."

"What makes you so sure Mr. Novak was beaten?"

"I don't . . . I don't know," she said slowly, wishing she could go home, curl up in her bed and escape into sleep. "I didn't hear a gunshot. All that blood . . . I just assumed . . ."

If she could see the detective's handwriting, she would know how to handle him. She tried to sneak a peek, but he held his pad at an angle, out of her line of sight. *Probably a block printer.* Most cops were trained that way. Block printers tended to be unemotional, harder to get close to. Harder to read.

"You're sure you didn't see anyone else?" Jovanic repeated.

"No."

One dark brow arched. "No, you're not sure, or no, you didn't see anyone?"

Claudia rubbed her eyes, realizing too late that she had smeared what was left of her mascara onto her cheek. "No, I didn't see anyone."

"What's your relationship with Mr. Novak?"

"He's a client."

Jovanic cocked his head to the side and studied her through intelligent grey eyes flecked with brown. "What business?"

"I'm a handwriting expert."

More scribbling in the notebook. "What were you doing here tonight?"

"Ivan called and asked me for a ride to LAX."

"He was going out of town?"

"That's why *I* usually go to the airport." Claudia regretted the sarcasm as soon as it left her lips. Jovanic gave her the raised brow again. "He was booked on a redeye to Chicago," she amended lamely.

"What does Mr. Novak do?"

"He's in public relations."

Jovanic looked attentive, waiting for her to elaborate, but Claudia held her tongue. She had learned interview technique from years of giving expert testimony in court. A good witness answered only the question asked, nothing more.

He who speaks first loses.

"Do you know of anyone who might want to harm him?" Jovanic asked at last.

"No. He only retained me yesterday morning."

"Yet, tonight he asks you for a late-night ride to the airport? I didn't know handwriting experts provided taxi service."

"He wasn't a total stranger. I'd met him before, through the woman he worked for."

"So, how long *have* you known him?"

"A few months, and only very slightly."

"Then why didn't he call a cab or the Super Shuttle?"

"He wanted to give me something. Since I would already be here to pick it up, he thought it made sense for me to drop him at the airport. LAX is near my house."

"Did you get it?"

"Get what?"

"What he had for you. Did you get it?"

"Oh, uh, yeah."

"I thought you didn't get a chance to talk to him."

"I *didn't*. He left an envelope in the foyer for me. Maybe you noticed the suit bag? That's where I found it."

Would she be forced to hand over the letter if Jovanic pursued the matter? She probably should have opened it before he arrived, but everything had happened so fast. *Shit.*

The detective unwrapped a new toothpick and held it like a cigarette. A reformed smoker, she would bet on it. He asked her to tell him once again what had happened, starting with Ivan's phone call.

Claudia's relief that he didn't ask her for Zebediah's letter was immediate and intense. This time around she remembered about the matching logos on the florist's van and the flowers in the foyer.

"Is there any more you can tell me, ma'am?"

The "ma'am" annoyed her, made her feel ninety-nine instead of thirty-nine. She wondered if he did it deliberately.

"No."

But he continued asking questions and making notes, with an occasional grunted, "Uh huh" as she answered. Then, almost as an afterthought, he asked, "What was it he wanted you to pick up?"

"What? Uh, that's confidential."

"Must have been pretty important to bring you out here so late on a Monday night."

"It was related to the case I'm working on for him. As far as I know, it has nothing to do with what happened here tonight."

"What kind of case is it you're working on, Ms. Rose?"

"As I told you, I'm a handwriting examiner. He asked me to examine some handwriting."

Jovanic made no response to that and a long silence ensued, during which she concluded that he wasn't going to say anything further.

Point conceded. Score one for Detective Jovanic.

"Ivan worked for a woman named Lindsey Alexander, who recently committed suicide," Claudia explained. "*Apparently* committed suicide, but Ivan didn't believe it." She watched him closely as she described Ivan's suspicions about Lindsey's death and saw the flicker of disbelief in his eyes.

"I'm familiar with the case," he said. "There was nothing to suggest it was anything other than suicide." He sucked thoughtfully on the toothpick, looking at her straight on with eyes sharp enough to penetrate the smallest white lie. She would hate to be a suspect if he were doing the interrogating. Being a witness was uncomfortable enough. "What makes you so sure your case isn't related to the attack on Mr. Novak?"

"What makes you think it is?" she countered. There she went again, letting the words rush out without thinking. She needed some sleep. Real sleep; not the nightmare-inducing catnaps she'd been allowed this night.

"It's my job to investigate," said Detective Jovanic. "And I'm investigating. Doesn't it seem a little strange to you? It just *happens* that he calls you to come over, then, *voila*, he's attacked?"

"What's that supposed to mean? *I* attacked him?"

His face was expressionless as he replied, "We're just beginning the investigation. I'm not ruling anything out at this point."

"Oh, for crying out loud, now I'm a *suspect*?" Outraged, Claudia glared at him. "I'm the one who called nine-one-one, remember? What motive would I have for attacking Ivan?"

Jovanic shrugged. "If you have a motive, I'll find out. Meanwhile, do you really believe that two acts of violence in the same place inside of two weeks is a coincidence?"

"You're the ones who are so sure Lindsey committed suicide. That's a very different kind of violence than this! Come on, detective, it's nearly two in the morning; I'm wiped; I can't think straight. Or is that why you've kept me here? So I won't know what I'm saying?" Suddenly, Claudia's anger deflated like a popped balloon. "Can't we finish this some other time? Please?"

Jovanic pointed to his own cheek. "You've got blood on your face."

Her hand flew to her cheek, felt the dried spot on her skin. "Why didn't you tell me before?"

"How'd the blood get on you?"

She rolled her eyes. "Have you *seen* the amount of blood in there, Columbo?"

"You know, Ms. Rose, you might want to consider changing your attitude. At the very least, you're a witness at a serious crime, and I expect you to explain yourself, not smart off."

Claudia stared at him.

"Wait here," he said. "And don't touch that blood." He got up and strode out of the room, returning a moment later with a young woman who awkwardly approached the sofa with him.

"This is Daleesha," Jovanic said. "She's a crime scene technician and she's going to swab the blood on your face."

"So you can make sure it's Ivan's blood?"

"I see you've been watching Forensic Files," Jovanic said, and Claudia wasn't sure whether he was being sarcastic, or it was an attempt at humor. "We're also going to need a blood sample from you, to rule you out. You can come down to the lab to do that."

The technician showed Claudia a cotton swab. "It'll just take a sec," she said, reaching forward to swipe it across Claudia's cheek. "Okay, got it. Thanks." She dropped the swab in a paper bag, sealed it and wrote something on the seal, then nodded to Jovanic and left.

Detective Jovanic sat down beside Claudia and took a clean linen handkerchief from his pocket, offering it to her. She took it with reluctance and scrubbed at her face, stunned at being considered a suspect, even though she understood that he was following standard procedure.

"Thanks," she said begrudgingly. "I'll have it cleaned."

"Not necessary," Jovanic said, then returned to his earlier question. "Can you think of *anyone* who might want to harm Mr. Novak?"

She thought of the threatening note she'd found in Lindsey's files. Ivan had rejected her suggestion that it might be connected to Lindsey's death, but it seemed too much of a coincidence to ignore. "There was a letter that I discussed with Ivan this morning," she began. "He said it was from a former employee who had been fired for sexual harassment. I told him that the guy was dangerous. He disagreed and tore the letter up."

"Dangerous? How did you reach that conclusion?"

"From his handwriting. I'm a graphologist as well as a document examiner. There were a lot of red flags in the writing."

Jovanic's neutral expression puckered into scorn. "*Graphology?* Come on, Ms. Rose, you don't expect me to believe that BS, do you?"

Claudia was used to dealing with skepticism and should have been prepared for his response, but her customary aplomb deserted her. She sprang up from the sofa, her hands balled into tight fists. "I really don't give a shit whether you believe it or not."

Before she knew what was happening, he was on his feet, scowling down at her. Claudia's pulse raced with a mixture of emotions, but she'd be damned if she would let him know he intimidated her. Like a cat puffing out its fur to scare off the enemy, she straightened her spine and tried to make her height work for her.

They glared at each other, the atmosphere thick with antagonism, neither willing to give way until Jovanic gave a short laugh. He backed up a step and took a business card from his jacket, scribbled something on the back. "Here, you can analyze this."

Claudia snatched the card and thrust it into the pocket of her Levis without looking. "I don't need to see your handwriting to know you're being rude."

Unexpectedly, he smiled. A nice smile that softened the lines around his mouth. What the hell was he doing? Playing good cop/bad cop, all by himself?

"Call me when you've had some sleep," he said. "You'll need to sign your statement once I've got it typed up."

Chapter II

The morning light and the shimmer of dawn on cold, blue water had sold her on the place. Sunrise cascading through the glass wall that fronted her office. Even when the marine layer obstructed the sun, the light was there to give her a lift. But today, when morning arrived—far too early after a night far too short—the light battered the backs of her eyes.

She would have slept on but for the intrusion of the ringing telephone. When pulling the pillow over her head failed to shut out the third call, she gave up and turned off the ringer. After that, sleep was impossible and she headed downstairs.

On her way to make coffee, Claudia's eyes drifted to the couch, where she had tossed her purse upon arriving home from Lindsey's apartment only a few hours earlier. Ivan's envelope was inside, still sealed. She had been loath to open it before, and she was loath now, afraid that his suspicions about Zebediah would have some basis in fact.

She crossed to the kitchen, moving away from the purse with quick strides. But professional curiosity and personal friendship jerked her to a halt. Feeling like a marionette on a string, she did an about-face.

As she picked up the envelope she spotted the flash drive lying beneath it, forgotten in the chaos of the arrival of the police and the EMS crew. Detective Jovanic's stern countenance popped into her head as she carried both items to her desk. Would she be in trouble if he found out about that?

Yeah, she would be in trouble. Big trouble.

With a sigh, she set aside the drive and slit open the envelope, removing the single sheet of paper. Claudia swore under her breath, immediately recognizing the jerky, malformed strokes. There was no denying that Zebediah had written the letter.

He had always been self-conscious about writing in Claudia's presence, blaming his strange handwriting on a learning disorder. More than once, he had complained that letting her see his unique scrawl made him feel naked. And yet, he had felt compelled to write a letter to Lindsey.

Lindsey:
Get out of my life! Mexico was a huge mistake. I should never have let you talk me into it. Don't you understand? I want nothing more to do with you. Stop calling me, stop writing to me, stop following me around. Just stay the hell away. Don't force me to do something drastic. I don't want to hurt you.

His distinctive *"ZG"* was scrawled across the bottom of the page.

Reading his words, Claudia's heart sank. It was easy to see why Ivan had interpreted the letter as damning.

She read the letter over a second time and a third, debating what to do with it. California law expressly forbade counselor/patient liaisons for a period of two years after discontinuing therapy. How much time had passed before Zebediah had succumbed to Lindsey's manipulations?

She pressed his speed-dial number on the phone. What would she say to him? *Say, Zeb, did you kill Lindsey? Did you attack Ivan?*

Would he tell her the truth? Would she know the difference?

She chickened out and hung up before the call connected.

Staring through the office window she watched the surf, lazily drifting in and out on the other side of the highway. Beach-goers studded the sand, ants from her perspective a half-mile away. They had no idea she was watching them, just as Zebediah was unaware that, with his letter to Lindsey, she might be holding his fate in her hands.

She could burn it and no one would be the wiser. Even if Ivan fully recovered from his injuries, chances were, he might not even remember the letter. Claudia replaced it in the envelope, memories of Zebediah's many kindnesses blurring the lines of ethics. Besides, she had introduced the two of them when Lindsey had turned to her for a good therapist referral. That made her partly responsible.

You have to turn the letter over to Detective Jovanic.

She did her best to shout down the little voice in her head, drown it out. But this letter was no minor stretching of the facts. Claudia had sworn too many oaths to tell the truth over the course of her career to abandon those ethics now.

But could she betray her old friend that way? His Buddhist principles precluded harming any living creature. Violence was against everything Zebediah stood for.

Maybe she didn't have to take action immediately. Going to the small safe that the last owner had cut into the wall, she slid aside the Egyptian Eye of Horus papyrus and dialed the combination. The letter would stay with her computer backup disks for now.

She slammed the door on it both literally and figuratively and poured herself a cup of strong coffee, the image of Detective Jovanic flitting through her head again. After their final heated exchange in the apartment, he'd said very little as he escorted her to her car in the pre-dawn.

Positioning her mug at a safe distance from the computer keyboard, Claudia finally turned her attention to the flash drive she'd picked up in the penthouse kitchen. She uncapped the plastic case and plugged the metal tip into an empty USB port on her computer. A few clicks of the mouse accessed the drive.

Only one file name appeared: *LACONABK.xls*. Its three-letter extension designated it as a spreadsheet. Double-clicking the file name launched the appropriate program, but a small warning box popped up: *LACONABK.xls is password protected.*

In other words, Claudia, butt out.

She wondered what Ivan might have chosen for a password. Or Lindsey, as it was more than likely her file. The "LA" could be her initials. Lindsey had been computer literate—her home office had been equipped with state-of-the-art computer hardware on Saturday when Claudia had first seen it.

Chewing on her lip, Claudia typed, "LindseyAlexander" and pressed Enter.

The password you supplied is not correct.

That would have been too easy. *Okay, how about her birth date?*

The password you supplied is not correct.

She tried experimenting with variations on Lindsey's and Ivan's names and what vital statistics she knew. The result was consistent: *The password you supplied is not correct.*

She cursed at the screen and gulped more coffee, then tried a few more combinations of letters and words. No dice.

The password could be any of a million words or combinations of letters and numbers. Continuing to guess from now until a week from Tuesday would probably not produce the right one. How had she gotten herself into this predicament? She wished she had left the flash drive at the penthouse.

Launching her Web browser, Claudia popped open instant messenger. Her brother, Pete, was a computer geek and always online.

His screen name, BlackCars, popped up right away and Claudia keyed in an instant message:

> *GraphoPro:* Hey, you!
> *BlackCars:* What's up, Sis?
> *GraphoPro:* How do you break a password on a spread sheet?
> *BlackCars:* You going into the hacking business?
> *GraphoPro:* LOL. I need to open a file. Any ideas?
> *BlackCars:* What file?
> *GraphoPro:* You don't want to know.

BlackCars: Okey dokey, call the software company
    and ask for a back door.
GraphoPro: Huh?
BlackCars: They might break the password with a
    back door. You'd have to be the registered owner,
    of course.
GraphoPro: I knew I could count on you! How's my
    favorite niece?
BlackCars: She's great.
GraphoPro: Tell her to call me, ok? Thx for the help.

Obtaining the number for tech support from the software
company's Web site was easy. The argument Claudia waged
with herself about what she was doing was another matter.
If the contents of the flash drive had nothing to do with her
friend, she promised herself, she would immediately turn
it over to the police. If there was something that further
incriminated Zebediah, that was a murky pond she hoped
she wouldn't be required to wade into.

The tech support phone number accessed a recorded
message advising her to log onto their Web site for free support. Fifty bucks would get her to a live person. The Web
site wasn't going to tell her how to hack into a file.

The image of Ivan's blood pooled on the kitchen floor
still haunted her. And there was a possibility that the flash
drive might reveal something important about Lindsey's
death. The way Claudia saw it, she had no choice.

Before dialing, she rehearsed what she would say, so that
when the tech came on the line and asked for her name,
"Lindsey Alexander" slipped out with ease. But a stress rash
warmed her throat and she found herself fumbling over the
tale she had fabricated. Maybe her father was right when he
kidded her about being too honest for her own good.

"Uh, I have this file," she blurted. "I uh, I need to get
into this uh, this file. It's really important. A disgruntled
ex-employee password-protected it out of spite before he
left. Can you help me get into it?"

The tech spoke with a Pakistani accent so thick it took her
a minute to understand that he didn't care *why* she wanted

the password. She probably could have just told the truth. It wouldn't have mattered to him, and she could have saved herself the kick in the butt from her conscience.

"Can you not e-mail me the file?" he asked. "I shall see if I can find a back door. If indeed I can, I will e-mail back the password to you."

Just like that. *Pete's a freaking genius!*

In a matter of seconds, the tech told her that the file had arrived in his mailbox. Decoding the password would take longer and he promised to immediately begin work on it.

While she waited for the results, Claudia telephoned Cedars-Sinai Medical Center and asked for ICU.

The duty nurse was less than cooperative when she asked for information about Ivan's condition. "Are you a relative?" the nurse inquired.

"No, I'm a . . . a friend."

"I'm sorry, this is a police matter. We can't give out information except to family members."

"I understand, but I'm the person who made the nine-one-one call last night when he was attacked. My name is Claudia Rose. Couldn't you . . ."

"I'm sorry, Ms. Rose, you'll have to check with the police."

"Can you at least tell me if he's conscious?"

"Like I said, Ms. Rose, if you're not a family member, I can't answer any questions. Oh, just a minute." Her voice became muffled while she covered the mouthpiece and spoke to someone in the background.

Jovanic's voice came on the line.

"He's still unconscious," he said without preliminaries. "The doctor says there's brain swelling. They don't know yet when, or if, he'll come out of it."

Claudia's throat constricted in dismay. "He might not make it?"

"That's a possibility."

"Have you been there all night?" As she said the words, she bit her tongue. The fact that he sounded worn out was none of her business.

"Yeah," he said. There was a long pause while she tried

to think of something to say. Jovanic broke the silence.
"Can you meet me around five tonight? I'd like to talk to
you some more about what happened last night."

A glance at her calendar showed nothing that couldn't
be easily cleared. Besides, the opportunity to make a better
impression appealed to her.

The tech support guy cracked the password and e-mailed
it to her inbox.
FQU6969
Typical Lindsey, to give it a sexual twist.

The spreadsheet opened instantly. Claudia's eyes widened as she read the data that filled the rows and columns
on her screen.

When the fax rang ten minutes later, she was still trying to
work out how to hand over the spreadsheet to Jovanic without getting herself arrested. And there was no question—it
had to be turned over immediately.

For a moment, she toyed with the idea of sending it to him
anonymously, then ridiculed herself for being a coward. She
would give it to him when they met that afternoon.

Pages began dropping into the fax tray. God bless Dana,
she'd come through with the autopsy report. Gathering up
the handful of sheets, Claudia began to read.

*Decedent: Alexander, Lindsey Elaine. Identifica-
tion: Height 70 inches; weight 128 pounds; diffuse
skin slippage; unembalmed; long blond hair; rigor
present; blue eyes, free of conjunctival hemorrhages;
mouth, own teeth.*

Skipping the external examination, she went straight to
the summary:

*A 38-year-old white female was found in a hot tub
at her residence. The woman was pronounced dead at
the scene. The decedent is received in a white sheet.
General Description: Rigor Mortis is generalized
and full. Lividity is developed on the anterior sur-*

*faces of the trunk and face. The corneas are markedly
opaque and the body is cool to the touch. The body is
well-developed and well-nourished. There is diffuse
skin slippage with only a rare intact skin blister. The
skin slippage is most pronounced in the same dis-
tribution as the pattern of lividity. Upper and lower
extremities are normally developed and free from
apparent antemortem injuries.*

She'd read enough Patricia Cornwell to know what lividity meant—the pooling of blood where the body made contact with a surface. The dry description of Lindsey's body,
inside and out, continued. There was something obscene
about the reduction of vibrant, high-spirited Lindsey, who
had laughed and cried and raged for thirty-eight years, to
a bald recitation of her stomach contents and the weight of
her internal organs. So unavoidably, sadly cold.

At last, the cause of death: *Drowning.*

The coroner had deduced that once the significant
amount of alcohol and barbiturates present in Lindsey's
system had taken effect, she'd simply slipped under the
water and drowned. The alleged suicide note made that
conclusion seem plausible.

Claudia still needed to review the police report and any
handwriting examination that might have been conducted
on the alleged suicide note. According to the comments
Dana had written on the transmittal, it wouldn't be available for a few more days.

Leaving the autopsy report on her desk, Claudia went
downstairs. She sliced an English muffin and dropped the
halves into the toaster, then turned on the small portable
television on the kitchen counter. With a fresh mug of coffee and the toasted muffin, she slid into the breakfast nook
and flipped to one of the morning news shows. Within five
minutes, the lead story was screaming at her: *Violent assault in Beverly Hills.*

The story of the attack on Ivan featured a photo of Claudia herself in a corner insert, with an account of her connection to Lindsey Alexander. She recognized the photo from

an interview she had given when a man named John Mark Karr had been questioned in the murder of child beauty queen, Jon Benet Ramsey. She had been asked to compare Karr's handwriting to the ransom note left by the child's killer. Someone in the newsroom must have connected her name from the 911 dispatch and pulled the file photo.

Home invasion attacks were not uncommon in LA, but this was a tale to make a reporter salivate: The suicide of a hot Hollywood publicist, an attack on her associate, and the intervention of a well-known forensic handwriting analyst. The news anchors speculated among themselves about the reasons for the attack, and whether it was connected to Lindsey's death.

If it bleeds, it leads.

All the makings of a miniseries. Deals were probably already in the works.

"You have ten new messages," the digital voice intoned when Claudia switched the telephone ringer back on and pressed the blinking message indicator.

Reporters from the two major LA newspapers and a couple of television stations wanted personal interviews. Three calls from Kelly, demanding to know what was going on. One from her brother, Pete, another from Zebediah. Apparently, they all watched the early morning news. Thank goodness her parents lived in Arizona.

The last voicemail was from Lillian Grainger's assistant, Yolande Palomino, asking when Claudia could meet with her boss about the handwriting sample she wanted analyzed. She did a quick search of her memory. Lillian Grainger was the woman whose clumsy husband had practically crushed her toes at Lindsey's penthouse.

Kelly answered the phone halfway through the first ring. "Claudia!"

"Jeez, Kel, are you sitting on top of the phone?"

"My God, honey, what's going on?"

"I only wish I knew."

"Tell me everything, and don't leave anything out!"

When Claudia had finished, Kelly was practically in tears.

"Oh, poor Ivan, it's so awful. I know he can be a pain in the ass, but why would anyone *do* that to him?"

"I don't know, Kel, but I've got a hunch it's tied to Lindsey's death."

When Detective Jovanic had suggested a connection between the two events she'd denied it out of fear for Zebediah.

Kelly's voice rose with excitement. "Do you think this clears me? I mean, I sure as hell didn't attack *Ivan*. I was doing the nasty all night with this *amazing* firefighter."

"*Doing the nasty*? Kelly, where do you get this stuff?"

The call-waiting beep sounded. Claudia put her friend on hold.

"I saw the news," said Dana Jackson. "Girlfriend, what have you got yourself into now?"

"Don't ask."

"Can't let you outta my sight for a second."

"Hey, it wasn't my fault. I was just in the wrong place at the wrong time."

"Wouldn't be the first time. Hey, listen, I found out who's taking over Vanderbosh's cases. His name's Joel Jovanic." She made it sound like "Joevanick."

Claudia's heart gave a funny little bump. "It's pronounced Yo*van*itch."

"Oh. You know him?"

"We've met."

Chapter 12

Jovanic had suggested they meet at five at Cowboys, Playa del Reina's neighborhood bar and restaurant. But the twenty-year-old Jaguar stubbornly refused to start, as it did on a semi-regular basis.

Temperamental British electrical system, grumbled Claudia, slamming the door shut on her house. Cowboys was walking distance, if you didn't mind the mile-long downhill trek. She wouldn't have minded the walk, but Marcia Collins, who was on her way to work the dinner shift, offered a ride. Like Kelly, she had seen the news and wanted to hear first-hand about the previous night's misadventures.

Dressed in a maroon *Cowboys* T-shirt, tight blue jeans, and running shoes, her hair pulled back in a ponytail, and no makeup, Marcia could easily have passed for a teenager at a distance. *She drives like one, too,* Claudia thought, folding herself into her neighbor's VeeDub and taking a firm grip on the roll bar.

Playa del Reina's main drag was a half-mile of aging storefronts, restaurants, and seventies apartment buildings undergoing facelifts. An incognito beach town, no longer quaint, it was frequented mostly by locals and the few LA residents who happened upon it in search of unspoiled stretches of sand and surf. Tourists looking for street vendors selling Blu Blocker sunglasses and T-shirts with inane slogans had to venture farther north, to the Venice Boardwalk or the Santa Monica Pier.

Situated near the beach end of the strip, Cowboys had

a red tile roof and yellowed stucco walls, surrounded by a redwood deck. It squatted across the street from a strip mall that included a pint-sized post office, boutique, candy and gift shop, barber, fortune teller, dentist, and a nightclub that had been closed for at least a year. Out front on the sidewalk a chunk of rock hung from a chain beneath a sign:

> *If the rock is dry, it's sunny.*
> *If the rock is wet, it's raining.*
> *If the rock is white, it's snowing.*
> *If the rock is swaying, it's an earthquake.*

At four forty-five, only a handful of vehicles dotted the parking lot. A couple of SUVs, a Harley, a black Jeep. Crossing the wooden deck, Claudia wondered whether one of them belonged to Detective Jovanic.

She followed her neighbor into the dimly lit restaurant through French doors that opened onto the bar, where a couple of customers slouched over their beers, and the television blared up-to-the-minute coverage of the latest high-speed police pursuit. No one was paying attention; high-speed chases were so commonplace in LA they scarcely produced a blink.

Not seeing Jovanic, Claudia circled the bar to an arched doorway that opened onto the dining room. Shelves of paperback books lined the back wall, and a faded hand-lettered cardboard sign tacked to the frame invited patrons to take a book home and replace it on their next visit. The smoky aroma of hickory wafted through the open doors from the barbecue pit on the patio, an olfactory announcement of the evening's fare.

Across the room, the detective sat alone at a table for two covered with a red-checkered tablecloth, reading a dog-eared Ludlum he'd probably borrowed from one of the shelves. His hair was still damp from a shower, and he wore the same sport coat from the night before, but with a clean, open-necked white shirt and grey flannel trousers. A dark tie hung from his pocket, a toothpick from his lip.

As if he had her on radar, Jovanic glanced up as Claudia appeared in the doorway and inclined his head. He wasn't obvious about it, but she couldn't help being conscious of his eyes on her as she crossed the bare wooden floor. She'd dressed in snug jeans, a black T-shirt, tucked in, and sandals. Her hair swung loose, hanging just below her shoulders.

Jovanic removed the toothpick as she approached, stood and drew out a chair for her.

What do you know—a gentleman.

The clean scent of Zest soap clung to him.

"Car trouble," Claudia said in greeting. "So, I guess you found the place all right?"

"I've been here before. I live a couple miles away."

He didn't say exactly where and she squashed her curiosity like a bug. "Anything new on Ivan?"

Jovanic shook his head. "The hospital has instructions to page me if he regains consciousness. How about you? Now you've had a chance to rest up, have you thought of anything more?"

The plastic flash drive throbbed accusingly in her purse like Poe's *Telltale Heart.*

He must feel its presence, Claudia thought, her mouth going dry. So far, she had failed to come up with a satisfactory explanation for having it in her possession.

Before she could respond to his question, Marcia appeared to take their drink order. She gave Jovanic an approving glance and winked at Claudia over his head. Pretending not to see, Claudia introduced them and her neighbor lingered, chatting, until another couple wandered in looking for a table.

"I think your neighbor's more interested in our conversation than serving drinks," Jovanic said when she left.

Claudia gave him a slow smile. "Are you detecting again?"

"Just can't seem to help myself."

"I have an idea," she said, wanting to stretch the light mood and delay her confession a little longer. "How about showing me your handwriting? Maybe I can change your opinion about graphology."

"I gave you a signature on my card last night, wasn't that good enough?"

"If I handed you a close-up photo of my nose, how much would it tell you about my face?"

His grin softened his features and made him look younger. "Okay, I get the point."

"Your signature is just your public image." Claudia leaned an elbow on the table and cupped her chin in her hand, vamping a little. "I rarely make an offer like this, detective. You should take advantage of it. What are you afraid I'll see? Come on, the real you can't be all *that* bad."

He cocked a brow, eyeing her without comment, then reached over to the empty table next to theirs and filched a cocktail napkin. He took out his pen. "What should I write?"

"What you write isn't important. How about, *I know that this is a true sample of my handwriting.*"

His pen flew across the square of paper, printing the first few words block style, the rest in cursive. "My handwriting changes," he said, handing her the napkin. "Depends on whether I'm writing for work or something personal."

"That's what they all say."

The restaurant was crowding up with diners arriving for the early-bird special: bacon-wrapped tri-tip, and ice cream for dessert if you ordered before six. Marcia arrived with coffee for Jovanic, iced tea for Claudia, then hurried off.

Claudia appraised the handwriting on the napkin. She held it at arm's length, taking into account the less-than-ideal writing materials and uneven surface of the table-cloth. "You're a fast thinker, good intuition, flexibility. All very important qualities for your work." Turning the napkin over, she touched the back, where she could feel the pen pressure on the other side. Heavy, but not overly so. Full lower loops in the cursive writing: *healthy sex drive.* "Strong physical drives, good stamina . . ." She noted that he formed his personal pronoun I with a loop at the top, but at the bottom there was a small tic. "Some unresolved issues with your father."

His smile flash-froze and the poker face was back. "He's dead."

"And you're angry about it."

Jovanic searched his pockets for a new toothpick and jammed it between his teeth. "My father became a homicide victim when I was thirteen. Yeah, I'm angry about that."

Getting too personal was an occupational hazard that Claudia had never learned to curb. She crushed a desire to reach out and touch his hand. "I'm so sorry."

"Hey, it helped me choose a career."

He spoke lightly, but she could feel the world of pain behind his words. "I didn't mean to sound blasé," she said. "You have every right to be angry."

"He was mugged." He recited the facts in a flat tone that didn't invite sympathy. "He was only carrying three bucks and change, so they beat him to death with a baseball bat. That was thirty years ago."

Something told her that Jovanic was not the type to give out this kind of personal information easily. She wondered why he was offering it now.

"I'm sorry," she said again, uselessly. An awkward silence stretched and she stared at his handwriting on the napkin. Confession time. How would he take it?

His handwriting—not the words themselves, but the patterns and rhythms of the ink trail—informed her of the best approach. The writing was stripped down, simplified, with no extra loops or strokes. That told her that if she tried to make excuses for what she had done, he would lose patience and stop listening. She would need to keep her explanation direct, no frills.

Her heart started to thump a tango as she screwed up her courage. "A few minutes ago you asked if I knew of anything that might help your case."

His eyes instantly pinned her like a butterfly on some collector's wall. She wanted to look away, but found she couldn't. Would he Mirandize her on the spot once he heard how she'd come by the flash drive? It would be embarrassing to be hauled out of the bar in handcuffs.

Jovanic waited.

"I have something to give you." Reaching into her purse, Claudia took out the plastic flash drive, wrapped in the printout from the Pakistani tech support guy.

"What's this?" he asked as she handed it across the table.

"It's a flash drive, for the computer."

"Let's pretend I'm not computer savvy. What's a flash drive?"

"It holds files like an old floppy disk, but has lots more storage space."

"And this flash drive is connected to the assault on Mr. Novak?"

Claudia nodded. "Apparently. There's just one file on it. It's a spreadsheet with a lot of names, financial information, and . . . uh . . . other things."

"What *other* things?"

"Sexual things."

Jovanic's body went still, the keen grey eyes alone betraying his interest.

"Why don't you tell me about it."

Claudia sipped her tea, noticing that the glass trembled slightly in her hand. She wiped the condensation with her napkin and cleared her throat. "Remember Lindsey Alexander, the publicist Ivan worked for? According to the file on this drive, she was into more than just repping big-name celebrities. She was providing, uh, services to a whole other clientele."

"How do you mean?"

"The services?"

"Yeah, the services." He held her in his gaze and apparently was going to show her no mercy.

Okay then.

"Bondage," she said, meeting his eyes. "S&M, golden showers, group sex, animals. That kind of thing."

"I see." Jovanic rubbed his hand over his face and gave a long sigh, as if he were very weary. "So, would you care to tell me how it is that you just happen to remember that you had this interesting spreadsheet on a . . . what did you call it?"

"Flash drive. But I didn't . . ."

"Yes, this flash drive, which apparently belongs to a dead woman?"

"Okay, I have a confession to make," Claudia said, wishing she could slide under the table and crawl away. "Uh, I found it at Lindsey's penthouse."

"Lindsey's penthouse? You *found* it at Lindsey's penthouse?"

She nodded and he sat back in his chair, crossed his arms, and fixed her with a grim look. Moments passed in silence while he stared her down.

Conversation buzzed all around them, the scent of hickory-smoked meat drenching the air, but for once, Claudia had no appetite.

Jovanic said, "When, Ms. Rose? Exactly when did you *find* this flash drive?"

She cleared her throat again, moistened her lips. No sense pretending, she was a lousy liar. "Last night."

"Last night. Okay, next question. Exactly *where* did you find it? You'll need to come back to the apartment and show me."

"That would be difficult."

His left brow shot up. "And why's that?"

"Ivan was lying on top of it."

Jovanic looked at her for several seconds with a chilling expression. When he spoke, his voice held a barely controlled explosion. "You removed evidence from a crime scene? Do you know what the penalty is for tampering with evidence?"

Claudia was afraid to speak. Just what had she expected? That she could charm him into letting it go that she had broken the law? *That would have been nice.*

She lifted her shoulders slightly.

"It's called obstruction of justice and it carries a fine of up to one hundred thousand dollars and a prison sentence of up to forty years."

Oh, shit.

"Are you going to arrest me?"

He seemed to be debating with himself. Or maybe he was just playing her. "Why'd you take it?"

"I didn't know what it was. I mean, I knew it was a flash drive, but I thought there might be something on it that would be damaging to a friend of mine." That didn't sound right and she knew it the moment the words were out. "Well, I mean, obviously, I wouldn't have kept it. I'm giving it to you now, aren't I? Oh, hell, I really didn't think about it, I just took it."

He gave her a skeptical look that said he wasn't sure whether or not to believe her. "How do I know you haven't messed with it, changed something?"

"I wouldn't do that!" Claudia declared with more righteous indignation than she probably had a right to. "Anyway, there's more."

"This wasn't enough?" Jovanic examined his toothpick. He'd chewed it flat. "Okay, what else?"

"The names in the spreadsheet."

"What about them?"

"They're, shall we say, recognizable? High profile people."

"How high profile?"

"*Very.*"

She leaned forward on the table and lowered her voice to a confidential near-whisper. "One of them was at Lindsey's apartment after the funeral last Saturday . . . *Senator* Bryce Heidt. I thought at the time that he was a sanctimonious SOB. That evangelist who's always in the papers, movie stars." She named a few notables, counting them off on her fingers. "And there's this plastic surgeon who runs an infomercial on late-night TV . . . um, Bostwick? Does that sound right?"

Jovanic's look was speculative. What he saw every day in his job probably eliminated the surprise factor. "Anything else you might have missed?"

Claudia wasn't sure whether the irony in his tone was a good sign or a bad one. "These people have some pretty interesting proclivities."

Wisps of a long-ago conversation floated back. "*Interesting,*" Lindsey had once said, "*is a word people use when what they really mean is perfectly awful.*"

"What makes you think these people are clients and it's not just her Christmas list?"

"It's got an accounts receivables worksheet and accounts paid. These people are playing expensive games."

Jovanic turned the flash drive around in his hand, as if staring at it would tell him everything he wanted to know. "So now you believe Ms. Alexander was killed because of this?"

"Well, isn't it a bit strange that Ivan's beaten half to death when he's obviously about to give me *this file*? I thought he was just being paranoid when he said someone might be listening in on the phone."

"You know what they say . . . just because you're paranoid, it doesn't mean they're not out to get you."

Claudia wrinkled her nose at him, relieved that he was joking with her.

"Why do you think the assailant didn't attack *you* and keep looking for this little piece of evidence, if that's what he was really after?" Jovanic asked, slipping the flash drive into his pocket. "If Mr. Novak had it on him, he didn't have far to look."

"Hell, I don't know. I'm just glad he didn't."

"What was Novak's relationship to Ms. Alexander?"

"Ivan was like a silent partner, I think. He pretty much ran the business. Lindsey's brother . . . who's a real dirtbag, by the way . . . told me that Ivan was Lindsey's heir."

"I see. I don't suppose you printed a copy of this *damning* spreadsheet for me?"

Claudia slowly released a breath. Maybe he wasn't going to haul her sorry butt off to jail after all. "No, but I could print one for you if you'd like."

Detective Jovanic folded the paper with the password and put it into his jacket pocket. "Okay. I'll give you a ride home."

She took it as an unspoken truce. Later, she wondered if she were being naive.

Chapter 13

"Tell me more about Lindsey," Jovanic said, settling into the puffy cushions of the office couch.

The short ride to Claudia's house had been cordial enough, but now his body language was keeping secrets. If he had an opinion about the spreadsheet printout she'd just handed him, he wasn't sharing it.

Claudia swivelled her chair around to face him. Seated at her desk, she was ten feet away and she needed the distance. "Back in school, we used to say that if sex were an Olympic event, Lindsey would be a gold medalist. She liked to brag about being into kink."

Lindsey.

Twenty years since she had first invaded their lives like a colorful jungle bird, showing off its plumage.

Tall and bony as a high-fashion model, she had entered the lecture hall that first day, and turned it into her personal catwalk. She wore a brief halter top and a gauzy skirt that danced well above her knees. Dishwater-blonde hair cascaded in a tangled mane over her bare shoulders. Posing against a backdrop of bright sunlight, it was apparent that in an era where bra-burning was in vogue, her panties had gone up in smoke, too. Marilyn Monroe on a sidewalk grate was a prude next to Lindsey Alexander.

Down the aisle she had sauntered, stopping to drop a casual remark to a student here and there—always male, of course—her high-pitched laughter reverberating in the silence. The psych professor had halted mid-sentence and

stared, annoyed by Lindsey's disorderly entrance, but clearly
intrigued.

"Who does this chick think she is?" Kelly whispered.
Lindsey was certainly no great beauty, and her loud laugh
turned more heads than her looks.

"She must have made a lot of enemies," Jovanic cut in,
snapping Claudia back to reality.

"Eventually she did, but at first we were all fascinated
by her. She had a real talent for turning everything into a
party. We had a lot of fun. For a while, anyway."

"So, what happened?"

Time collapsed as more long-buried memories, blurred
around the edges, spun like a rewound video and focused on
a gathering at a hotel in San Francisco. Feeling the need to
detach herself from those long-ago events, Claudia sought
for the right words to describe them.

"After we'd both gotten our psych degrees, Lindsey and
I studied graphology . . . handwriting analysis. We actually
worked together for a while. This was years ago. I guess
you could say that we both made it to a certain level of
leadership in the field. Lindsey cultivated some very high-
powered contacts in the corporate world, and that gave her
a certain . . . edge.

"So, here's the thing. She and I were asked to set up a
symposium. The top professionals from all over the world
were being invited to discuss the future of handwriting
analysis . . . whether we needed to focus on becoming a li-
censed profession; how to get people to stop thinking of us
as fortune tellers. You know . . . take us more seriously?"

Jovanic glanced down at his notebook and Claudia de-
tected a smile. She figured he was remembering his own
negative reaction of last night, when she'd told him her
profession.

She went on with her story. "Lindsey wangled an appointment as chairman. She really wanted the title, but not
the job. She was great at starting things and then dumping
them onto someone else to finish up."

"Did that show in her handwriting?"

Claudia shot a quick glance at the detective. "Of course it

did," she assured him, refusing to take the bait. "She asked me to handle the publicity. I told her I didn't know jack about PR and frankly, by that time, I didn't want to be that closely involved with her. But she kept pressuring me. *It's eeeeasy. I'll help you!* Silly me, I let her talk me into it.

"The trouble was, I was pretty successful and she couldn't stand that. Lindsey wouldn't let anyone look as good as or better than her. So she started sabotaging everything I did. Very subtly, of course, but in the end, nothing I did had a snowball's chance."

And just like that, Claudia was flung back into the symposium audience, reliving the humiliation.

"She waited until the closing ceremonies to stick it to me. It was very clever the way she shifted the blame onto me for *everything* that had gone wrong with the symposium. And believe me, that was plenty. It made me look a complete fool."

Jovanic removed the toothpick from his mouth, giving her his full attention, which she found damned uncomfortable. "What'd you do?"

"What *could* I do? It was a catch twenty-two, and she knew it. If I'd publicly called her on her lies I would have just looked defensive. The truth came out later and she was eventually discredited. That's when she decided to switch careers. But you know how these things go . . . everyone comes to the wedding, but they don't always show up for the divorce. It took a long time to rebuild my credibility. It might not sound like much to you, but it was pretty traumatic for me."

Claudia watched his hands as he wrote in his notebook. Big hands, strong-looking, very short, neatly trimmed nails that looked as if he'd taken some time with them.

When he'd finished writing, he glanced over at her. "What about after that?"

"I completely cut her out of my life, avoided her for years. Then, after all that time, we suddenly ran into each other at a restaurant a few months ago."

Claudia and Kelly had walked into the Great Wall in Venice together, and there was Lindsey, alone in the lobby, waiting for a table. She had greeted them both with warm hugs, as if they were still the bosom buddies they used to be.

Kelly had shoved her away, angrily demanding to know what made Lindsey think she could justify the betrayals of both Claudia and herself. For a tense moment, it had looked as if Kelly would physically attack Lindsey. But Claudia didn't mention that to Jovanic. Instead, she offered a watered-down version, omitting any mention of her friend.

"Lindsey did what she did best . . . laid on the charm and suggested we hash it out over *moo goo gai pan* and good wine, her treat. But she pretty much kept the conversation on the polite amenities and by the time the fortune cookies arrived, we'd agreed to leave the past dead and buried."

"You were willing to just let bygones be bygones?" asked Jovanic, sounding skeptical.

"So many years had gone by. Holding a grudge is bad karma, don't you think?"

"After what she did to you?"

Claudia sighed. "I tried to remember the good things she'd done for me way back when. She got me my first big client. She was well-connected, even back then."

"So, did you see her after that?"

"We got together a couple of times, but just at her office. She hired me to do some handwriting analysis for her, which is how I came to know Ivan. He's the one who made the arrangements."

Up went the brow. "Excuse me for being confused, but you said she had trained as a handwriting analyst, too. Why would she hire you to do something she could do herself?"

"She told me she felt rusty. That might have been true, but my feeling was, she didn't want to bother. Sitting at a desk, figuring out personality traits, wasn't her big priority. Let's face it, analyzing handwriting is work like anything else, regardless of how *some people* want to look at it."

His lips twitched again as he scribbled in his notebook.

"Was it anyone on the list?" he asked when he had finished writing.

"What?"

He tapped the printout that rested on his knee. "The handwriting analysis you did for her, was it anyone on the sex list?"

"No. One was a new client. The other was a problem competitor she wanted to know how to handle. Strictly mundane stuff."

"So, there was no big rekindling of the friendship?"

"I may have let go of the past, detective, but I'm a wee bit smarter now." Claudia leaned her head back against her chair and closed her eyes for a moment. It wasn't easy to explain Lindsey. "You have to understand something. Lindsey was a classic narcissist. She truly believed the world revolved around her, and she was very good at manipulating people to do whatever served her needs. I'm not sure she even understood what she'd done to get everyone so upset."

"She sleep with any of *your* boyfriends?"

The question came from left field. Trying to catch her off guard? Claudia smiled a wry smile. "She had a knack for knowing how to hit where it hurt. When she pulled that trick at the symposium, she was well aware that my professional life was *my* vulnerable spot."

Jovanic consulted his notebook, flipped back a few pages. "Do you know someone by the name of Kelly Brennan?"

That was the second time he'd taken her by surprise. She felt transparent, as if he'd seen inside her head and watched the memories as they'd unraveled. "Kelly? What about her?"

"How well do you know her?"

"We've been friends since we were six years old. Our families were neighbors."

He wrote something, then said, "Were you aware that Ms. Brennan made threats against Lindsey Alexander on the night of her death?"

"She told me about it, but if you think Kelly could've killed her . . ."

"Whoa, slow down. Her name came up in the file. I'm looking at all the possibilities, that's all."

"Kelly's five-foot four and weighs ninety-eight pounds fully dressed. She could never handle someone Lindsey's size."

"Is Ms. Brennan the friend you wanted to protect when you took the flash drive?"

Claudia straightened up and gazed at him seriously. "Listen, detective, my friends aren't murderers. Don't you think you ought to be looking at the names on that list I just printed for you? If someone did kill Lindsey, it's probably one of them."

He returned her stare. "I'll be looking at all of them. *Including* your friend, Kelly." Before she could form a rejoinder his cell phone rang. He took it off his belt and thumbed it open, listened for a moment. "When? What's the status? Has he said anything? I'll be right there." He rang off and turned to Claudia. "Ivan Novak just regained consciousness."

Chapter 14

After the detective's departure, Claudia cracked a can of diet Coke and took it out to the downstairs deck. Late afternoon traffic swished along the highway below, blending with ocean sounds as she swung idly in the basket chair, wondering what Ivan might reveal to Jovanic. She felt again the warmth of the detective's hand as it closed around hers. He'd held on a little longer than necessary, with a promise to let her know what happened at the hospital.

She was still daydreaming when Kelly Brennan's red Mustang convertible turned the corner and rolled to a stop at the curb.

Claudia hauled herself out of the chair and leaned over the balcony. "You're just in time," she called as Kelly climbed out of the car.

"For what?"

"Come on up and see."

"Okay, chill the glasses, I brought some vino." Kelly went around to the back and popped the trunk. She took a bottle of wine from a grocery bag imprinted with the logo of the local liquor store, and ran up the steps, bearing it aloft like an Olympic torch.

Inside the front door she stopped short, staring at a stack of file boxes that had materialized in Claudia's living room. "What the hell's all that?"

"Ivan messengered them over yesterday. They're files from Lindsey's apartment. The idea is to find some block printed handwriting samples I can use to compare to the suicide note." Then she corrected herself. "*Supposed* suicide note. You can help me look."

"Oh yeah? What's in it for me?"

"Chinese food. What are you in the mood for? I'll call it in."

The subject of Chinese food reminded her of Lindsey and the conversation with Jovanic. She brought Kelly up to date on her meeting with him, refraining from mentioning that her name had come up. It made no sense to throw her friend into a panic, which it would do if she knew that the detective was looking at her.

She debated whether to share the news about the flash drive and its contents. Kelly might be a ditz, but as an attorney, she knew how to handle confidential information. And she certainly hadn't attacked Ivan.

She suddenly became aware that Kelly was waving a hand in front of her face. "Helloo. Where'd you go?"

Claudia made up her mind. She and Kelly had been sharing secrets for more than thirty years. "Last night, before the cops got there, I found something . . . evidence that Lindsey was running a kinky sex trade."

Kelly's jaw dropped. "No shit! How the hell did you find that out?"

"I've been taking detective lessons," Claudia said with a grin. "Don't worry about how I found out."

Kelly glanced at her sidelong and went through to the kitchen with her bottle of wine. "I have a feeling there's a story here."

"Nah, just a very interesting policeman."

"Claudia! Don't tell me you're joining the ranks again?"

Claudia shrugged it off. "Right now, he's just investigating what happened to Ivan. And speaking of Ivan, I have a feeling he wanted me to have this piece of evidence because he suspected one of Lindsey's clients of killing her."

Or Zebediah. But Claudia was keeping that bit of speculation to herself, too.

Kelly folded her hands in prayer and turned her eyes heavenward. "Hey, as long as it wasn't me."

Claudia huffed a sigh of impatience. "The other night

you seriously thought *you* might have killed her. You think *maybe* that blackout you had is a sign?"

"A sign of what?"

"That it's time to do something about your drinking?"

Kelly hung her head, a mock penitent. "You're right. I'm a dumbshit. I'll call my sponsor, first thing next week, promise."

Claudia gave up, knowing that was one promise her friend had no intention of keeping, and turned her attention to the file boxes. She tapped the box on top of the stack. "One way or another in all this mess, maybe we'll find proof of what *really* happened to Lindsey. Look for anything with block printing on it."

They shoved the coffee table out of the way, tossed couch pillows on the floor for comfortable seating, and began to dig in.

"I don't think that woman ever wrote on a clean sheet of paper," said Kelly, arching her back in a stretch an hour into the search. She scowled at the growing stack of discarded file folders: notes, letters, and business correspondence decorated in Lindsey's familiar green ink. "I think it was a big *fuck you* aimed at whoever she was writing to. Like she thought you weren't worth the nickel it might cost to use a new sheet." She tossed a credit card receipt onto the pile and dug into the file box she was emptying.

Claudia reached for a wax-coated carton on the table and spooned a heap of fried rice onto her plate. "She claimed she was saving trees," she said. "Hey, I'm as environmentally con . . ." She broke off. Kelly was waving a leather-bound book at her. "What?"

"This could be important!"

"Printed writing?"

"No," Kelly rolled onto her knees and shoved the book in Claudia's face. "This is her calendar. Look at the note on the twenty-third. That's the day she croaked: *Remind Bos—Blue Heaven—PS*."

"Bos." Claudia turned it over in her head. "One of her

sex clients was named Bostwick. I wonder if he was who she was expecting when *you* showed up."

"That has to be it!" Kelly said, getting excited. "Damn it, why didn't she write the time down?"

Claudia frowned. "I wonder what *Blue Heaven* refers to. And what's *PS?*"

"Who the hell knows? That movie, *My Blue Heaven*? You know the one, with Steve Martin and . . . who was that guy in *Honey, I Shrunk the Kids*?"

"Rick Moranis." Claudia got to her feet and carried her plate out to the kitchen, speaking over her shoulder. "Definitely not a Lindsey kind of movie. If you're through with the won tons, let's go upstairs and Google it."

With Kelly hanging over her shoulder, Claudia launched her Web browser and typed *Blue Heaven* into the Google search engine. Forty-one thousand hits came up.

"How the hell are we supposed to know what she was talking about?" Kelly grumbled as they clicked through the first twenty links. "There's everything here from a karate studio to that movie."

Claudia leaned back in her chair and pondered the question of what Lindsey might have wanted to remind Doctor Bostwick. Assuming they were right that the notation, *Bos* was referring to the plastic surgeon. And what about *PS*?

A sudden inspiration pushed her upright in her chair. "Drugs!" she exclaimed, and began rummaging through the stacks of papers that littered her desk until she came to the autopsy report that Dana Jackson had faxed.

The drug toxicology report on the last page yielded the information she was seeking, and she keyed in a new search: *Barbiturates+Blue Heaven*

"Look, here it is . . . Amytal. That's one of the drugs listed in the autopsy report." Her fingertip left a smudge on the computer monitor where she pointed. "That makes sense. See what it says here: *Amytal is called Blue Heaven.*" She scrolled down. "And look here:"

Doctors sometimes prescribe barbiturates for people who have anxiety or can't sleep. Often, people take these powerful medications "for the fun of it," or when trying to calm down the effects of other drugs, such as cocaine or amphetamines.

"Did she seem stoned when you saw her?"

"She was always stoned when she wasn't working."

Not that Kelly had been so lucid herself that night. She probably wasn't the most reliable historian. And she was too eager to grasp an easy explanation that would get her off the hook.

Claudia glanced through the autopsy report again, then back at the monitor. "Barbiturates combined with alcohol contributed to her death by drowning. See what it says here. These drugs make you sleepy and relaxed, slow down the reflexes. By the time she got into the hot tub, she wouldn't have been able to get out, even if she'd wanted to." The realization weighed on her. "Or if someone pushed her in . . . if she didn't write the note, she *was* murdered."

"As long as it wasn't me," Kelly said. She lay down on the floor and stretched out, bending her knees, then flexing them one at a time, pointing her toes.

Claudia still wasn't satisfied. "What about the note? 'It was fun while it lasted'?"

"If *she* didn't write it, it had to be one of her clients," Kelly speculated, rolling onto her stomach and continuing her calisthenics.

"Any number of people might have wanted her dead . . . other publicists, agents, CEOs, producers, directors. You said it yourself."

"Yeah, well, *I* certainly didn't write the damn note, and right now, that's all I care about."

Claudia pushed away from the desk and did a couple of stretches of her own. "I haven't got good enough exemplars to know for sure whether Lindsey wrote it or not. Everything I've found is cursive writing, which doesn't help at all. The only printing was on the backs of some photos her horrible brother gave me, and that was too long ago to be useful."

She got up and switched on some lamps, still mulling over the possibilities.

"If this Bostwick character was there after you left her apartment, they could have partied together, with him supplying the drugs. Maybe he gave her an overdose by mistake. Or, she could have been blackmailing him about the sex stuff and he killed her. He was into donkeys. Or was it Labrador retrievers? Damn, that's disgusting!"

Kelly rolled onto her knees and jumped up with the energy of a five-year-old. "Well, he *sounds* like an ass, but that's what he gets for hanging out with Lindsey. If you lie down with dogs, you can expect to get bitten."

"You're mixing metaphors," Claudia pointed out as they went back downstairs. "It's, if you lie down with dogs, you'll get up with fleas."

Kelly gave her the skinny eyes. "You're such a freaking know-it-all." She picked up Lindsey's calendar and began flipping through it again. "This is mostly notes about meetings and parties. Big red circle around Halloween. It says 'Grainger.' "

"That's the party planner she used. As it happens, I have an appointment with Lillian Grainger tomorrow."

"You know her?"

"Met her at the reception the other day."

"What reception? Oh, the thing after the funeral? You think this Lillian Grainger might know something?"

"No, she has some handwriting she wants me to look at."

"Hey, wasn't she that itty-bitty woman with the jolly green giant?"

"Yeah, the *clumsy* jolly green giant who nearly crushed my foot."

"Well, you know what they say about the size of a man's feet," Kelly said with a wicked grin. "If that's true, his schlong must be . . ." She held her hands up, two feet apart.

They giggled like schoolgirls for a couple of minutes. After the stress of the past forty-eight hours, it felt good to laugh again.

"I thought Lillian was pretty tacky," Claudia said, slipping back into adult mode. "Talking business right after the funeral."

Kelly speared bits of cold sweet-and-sour chicken from one of the containers. "You should expect Lindsey's friends to be tacky," she said, mumbling around the chicken. "Not us, of course. We were smart enough to get out."

"But we let her back in."

"Temporarily, grasshopper, just temporarily. Hey, speaking of tacky, what about that little tart in the Frederick's of Hollywood getup?"

"At the cemetery? I don't know about her, but her friend was at Lindsey's. Remember the woman with those gorgeous beads." Claudia reached for an almond cookie and took a bite. "It didn't sound like she believed the suicide theory any more than Ivan did."

"He's probably the one who put the idea in their heads." Kelly yawned and patted her lips with a paper napkin. "I don't want to deal with Lindsey's shit any more tonight. You can stay up all night and think about it if you want to, but honeybunches, I'm over it."

"No, thanks. I've had enough, too."

They shoveled Lindsey's papers back into the file boxes and cleared away the food debris.

Claudia stood on the balcony and watched Kelly wheel the Mustang into a U-turn and accelerate away. As she turned to go inside, she heard a second engine crank over and watched a dark van parked across the road pull out behind Kelly.

Only a half-dozen or so homes stood on Claudia's side of the street, with a sheer drop to the highway on the other. She knew her neighbors' vehicles by sight and the van didn't belong to any of them. Chances were, the driver had been visiting one of the neighbors, but too many strange things had been happening lately to brush it aside.

Kelly turned left at the corner. The van turned, too. Claudia ran into the house and dialed Kelly's mobile number. "I don't want to spook you, but do you see a van behind you?"

"Yeah, why?"

"I think he may be following you."

"Hey, you're really getting into this cloak and dagger stuff, aren't you?" Kelly snickered. "Tell you what, if he's still behind me when I get to the police station on Little Culver, I'll pull right over and walk in, okay, *Mom*?"

Claudia pictured the lonely stretch of wetlands between Playa del Reina and the police station. "Just watch your back."

Ten minutes later, Kelly called back. "He turned in at the Mobil station. Quit worrying, he just needed gas."

Her words did little to allay Claudia's uneasiness. It wouldn't be difficult for the van driver to catch up with Kelly. She told herself she was being paranoid. It didn't help.

"At least put the top up on your car, would you? And keep an eye on the rear-view mirror."

"Maybe I'll pull *him* over and see if he's a hottie."

Claudia made an exasperated *tch*. "That kind of attitude is what gets you in trouble."

Chapter 15

Silvery morning mist cloaked the coastline, turning the occasional cyclist into a wraith on wheels. After another night of fitful sleep, Claudia indulged in a run on the beach, which lifted her spirits the way no amount of caffeine could. Damp sand crunched on the cement path as she jogged behind Flare. The German Shepherd's tongue dangled happily from her massive jaws and she erupted into a joyful bark at the discovery of a crab burrowing in the sand.

They ran past three Mexican fishermen lounging against the railing of the concrete pier, their lures bobbing in choppy green water; past walkers taking it easy.

Claudia covered the distance down to El Porto and back in under an hour. Her lungs were burning from the exertion by the time she returned Flare to Marcia's backyard. Feeling good about the morning's workout, she arrived back in her kitchen just as the phone rang.

Detective Jovanic, at last.

"He was awake for awhile," he said. "But I didn't get much out of him. He'd just come out of surgery and was still pretty doped up, not making sense."

"So he wasn't able to tell you anything?" Claudia felt a sharp pang of disappointment. She had hoped that Ivan had been able to identify his attacker; at least given *some* clue.

Jovanic's voice was raspy with fatigue. "He kept trying to say something, but he couldn't get the words out right. It sounded like he was saying *'take'* or *'tape.'* "

"Probably tape. He had some tapes he wanted me to hold for him while he was away."

"Did he tell you why he wanted you to hold them? What was on them?"

"No, I have no idea." Claudia thought back to her last conversation with Ivan. He'd indicated that the tapes were too sensitive to leave lying around. Which suggested to her that he had expected someone to come looking for them.

"Could I see him?" she asked impulsively.

"Sure, why not. Maybe you can figure out what he's saying. When can you get here?"

She named a time and he gave her his cell phone number. "The doc says full recovery is pretty iffy. Maybe permanent brain damage."

Brain damage. Only a couple of days earlier, Ivan had been strutting around like a little bandy rooster, handing out orders in that bossy way of his. Claudia pictured him struggling to relearn the basics of life—walking, talking, eating. The image left her depressed.

"I hope I can be of some help," she said. "By the way, I checked out Lindsey's calendar last night. There was an entry on the day she died that I think might refer to someone on her spreadsheet . . . Doctor Charles Bostwick. He's the guy I mentioned on the infomercials."

Jovanic's voice perked up. "*You* have her calendar?"

"Don't worry, detective, I have it legally. After I left Ivan at the penthouse yesterday morning, he messengered me her personal papers. The calendar was in one of them."

"Well, that's a relief." His tone was dry.

"He's got an office in Beverly Hills."

"Why, you're a regular detective, Ms. Rose. I'll put the good doctor at the top of my list of people to interview. Uh . . ." He hesitated. "Maybe you'd like to go along for the ride?"

"To see Bostwick?"

"Uh huh. Maybe you can spot some of his handwriting; tell me his secrets."

"Is that kosher?"

"No, but if you don't tell, I won't."

She couldn't stop grinning as she hung up the phone.

Grainger & Grainger occupied the entire twenty-fourth floor of a concrete-and-glass tower bordering the upscale Westfield Shopping Center in Century City. Ten million square feet of office space in the miniature city, populated by hundreds of professional practices. Claudia privately dubbed it *Lawyerland*.

Directly to her left as she stepped out of the elevator, double doors opened onto a plush reception area and an extravaganza of black marble that made up the front desk. Glass walls offered a sweeping view of Westwood and Beverly Hills. *Definitely not the low-rent district.*

The receptionist, who was speaking on the phone, raised a slender manicured forefinger, signaling her to wait. Pretty, early twenties, golden tan in a Donna Karan suit, far too self-possessed for her age.

While she waited, Claudia amused herself by watching the young woman write on a pink telephone message pad. Half-inch acrylic nails required that she hold the pen between her second and third fingers in order to write. *Large, circular handwriting. Image-conscious Valley Girl: center of her own universe.* Finally, Valley Girl glanced up. "May I help you?"

Claudia pushed her business card across the ledge. "I have an appointment with Lillian Grainger."

Reading the card, the receptionist dropped her blasé attitude. "You're a handwriting expert? How cool is that!"

Claudia smiled. "Pretty cool, I guess."

"I should let you see my handwriting," the receptionist said with mounting enthusiasm, unaware that she had already revealed plenty as she took messages.

"I've already seen it. You're the type of person who lives in the moment, you don't spend a lot of time thinking about yesterday or planning ahead for tomorrow, and you love to be in the middle of whatever's going on."

The receptionist's eyes grew round. "Wow! That's so true! How did you know?"

Claudia just smiled again and seated herself on a tobacco-colored leather chair while the young woman called Lillian Grainger's office and announced her. She glanced around at walls papered with framed photographs of the Graingers hobnobbing with famous clients at functions they had organized. A banquet with an American Medical Association banner. A political victory party with a candidate whom she immediately recognized: Senator Bryce Heidt. Oscar parties figured prominently.

And so did variations on a lily theme. A framed print of Monet's Water Lilies; calla lilies woven into the carpet border; lily of the valley on the lipstick-stained mug someone had left on the coffee table. *A conceit on Lillian Grainger's name?*

As Claudia waited, a succession of fresh-faced young men and women traipsed through the foyer. *Stepford kids,* she thought, admiring the immaculately groomed employees in conservative suits or dresses. She checked her watch. Nearly ten-fifteen. She stared pointedly at the receptionist, who ignored her.

Five more minutes and I'm gone.

Four minutes and thirty seconds later, Claudia was gathering her purse and briefcase when a striking woman came along a corridor behind the reception desk and approached her.

Late thirties like herself. Older than anyone Claudia had seen in the office thus far. She was dressed in a narrow black pinstriped suit whose crisp tailoring suggested custom-made. Dark, silver-threaded hair; serious brown eyes ringed with dark shadows. Personal problems, or work-related? Something was definitely making this lady unhappy.

"Ms. Rose." The woman extended her hand with a smile that seemed strained. "I'm Yolande Palomino, Mrs. Grainger's executive assistant. We spoke on the phone."

"Nice to meet you in person."

"Thanks for waiting," Yolande Palomino replied quickly. "Would you follow me, please?" She turned back the way she'd come and walked slightly ahead of Claudia, making conversation all but impossible.

Low-walled cubicles flanked the quiet corridor. *Human fish bowls.* People spoke on the phone or worked at computer monitors positioned so that a visitor could easily view the display over the occupant's shoulder. No secret downloading of porn or lunchtime games of Doom in *this* office. More Monet water lilies floated silently across monitors not in use.

Yolande Palomino led Claudia to an office made private by polished cherrywood doors nearly tall enough to touch the high ceiling. Lillian Grainger's personal space.

A bouquet of golden tiger lilies straight from the cover of *Town and Country* graced a table outside the door. Claudia bent to sniff. "Gorgeous!"

"Mr. Grainger has them delivered fresh first thing Monday mornings." Yolande knocked on the door and waited to be invited inside. Lillian's pleasant alto called out and the assistant stepped aside for Claudia to precede her.

A baby grand stood at one end of Lillian's office and a formal seating area at the other. More breathtaking vistas of the city through floor-to-ceiling windows.

The CEO of Grainger and Grainger wore a boxy jacket and straight skirt in a fine wool that matched the burnished gold of the tiger lilies and de-emphasized her short stature. She came forward, hands outstretched in welcome.

"Claudia, thank you so much for coming." Her voice was warm molasses. "Hold my calls, Yolande. Ms. Rose and I don't want to be disturbed." Then, turning back to Claudia, "Come on over here and let's sit down."

She led the way to a chintz-covered love seat and patted the cushion beside her. A silver tea service had been set out on a tray beside a 19th century Satsuma vase on a claw-footed mahogany table. They might have been at tea in a Charleston antebellum drawing room.

"Would you like some coffee, Claudia? Tea? How about a cold drink?"

"Tea would be great, thanks." Claudia sat down, marveling at the lushness of Lillian's office. The celebrity catering business had been good to the Graingers.

"I have to apologize for keeping you waiting," Lillian said, lowering her voice to a conspiratorial murmur as she poured the tea. "Just before our appointment time, I got a very special call. It was . . ." She paused dramatically, looking at Claudia in a meaningful way. "the *President*. I couldn't very well put *him* off, could I?"

"The President?"

"Well, I don't like name droppers, but yes, I'm talking about *the* President. Of the United States. He wants me to co-chair his new commission on women's issues. He's going to ask Senator Bryce Heidt to be the co-chair. Have you met him? He's already one of our clients, so it would be a terrific fit."

Senator Heidt, according to the spreadsheet, one of Lindsey's S&M clients, on a committee for women's issues? She wondered what Lillian would say if she knew that her proposed co-chairman figured on a kinky sex list.

"That's quite an honor," she said, biting her tongue.

Lillian reached over with a warm smile and squeezed her hand. "You never know, Claudia, there could be a place on that committee for someone with your kind of talents, if the good Lord wills it. Now, please tell me, what's all this about poor Ivan Novak? They said on the news that you were there when he was attacked. I couldn't believe it! I mean, we were all in that apartment just a couple of days ago, weren't we?"

Not for the first time, Claudia shuddered when she remembered what she had seen that night. "I arrived during the attack," she said. "From what I understand, the prognosis isn't very good."

Lillian gave a troubled sigh and shook her head. "Well, we're all praying for his recovery."

Does she mean the entire company is in on the prayers? Is group prayer part of the Grainger Company morning ritual?

"I'm going to the hospital after I leave here," Claudia

said. "If he's conscious, I'll tell him you were asking about him."

"Thank you, dear. So tell me, have they caught the monster who did this to him?"

"Not yet, but I'm sure they will soon."

Lillian shook her head again, with a bemused what-is-the-world-coming-to expression.

Sensing an opening to ask the question that was on her mind, Claudia took a moment to cross one knee over the other and smooth her skirt. "I don't suppose you might have any idea why someone would want to hurt Ivan?"

The other woman's head jerked up in surprise. "Why, no! I thought it was a botched robbery."

"No." Claudia hesitated, not sure how much she should reveal. "Ivan didn't believe that Lindsey killed herself. I've been asking myself whether that might have something to do with this attack on him."

"But if he didn't believe it was suicide, what did he think?" An expression of shock and horror crossed Lillian's face and her hand flew to the gold cross that dangled at her throat. "Oh my good Lord, you aren't saying what I think you're saying?"

"That Lindsey was murdered?"

"Oh, my Lord in heaven," Lillian said in a faint voice. The cross was getting a workout. "I can't pretend I knew either of them that well. Mostly Ivan when we organized events for their clients. Of course I saw Lindsey from time to time, too, but we never developed any kind of a personal relationship."

Claudia felt the keen sting of disappointment. Her attempt at playing detective hadn't taken her very far. She'd learned nothing new from Lillian, relative to Lindsey's death. Her hopes of having some new information for Detective Jovanic faded. She'd do better sticking to the handwriting business.

"You know," Lillian said thoughtfully, "I always got this feeling from Lindsey that she had kind of a wild side to her. I invited her to church with Marty and me several times, but she always declined."

Lindsey in church? The mind reeled. Suppressing a chuckle, Claudia turned the conversation to the subject of the job applicant whose handwriting Lillian wanted her to analyze.

Chapter 16

Jovanic was waiting for her at Cedars-Sinai Medical Center in front of North Tower parking. His jacket and slacks looked slightly rumpled, as if he'd slept in them. *If he slept at all,* Claudia thought, waving as she drove past him and turned into the lot. The five o'clock shadow that darkened his jaw suggested he hadn't.

She found a vacant spot to park on the first level and hurried outside. The hot weather had finally broken, leaving behind one of those perfect California fall days where the temperature invites sleeveless, and only the merest hint of brown haze clothes the distant foothills.

Jovanic was talking on his cell phone as Claudia exited the garage. When he saw her he snapped it shut, dropped it into his pocket, and fell into step beside her.

"You look great," he said, making her glad she'd worn the grey silk suit. The mid-thigh split in the skirt was high enough to be provocative, but low enough to be professional.

Opening the lobby door, he stood aside for her to enter. "I just got some information you'll be interested in. Remember those flowers that were delivered to Lindsey's apartment the other night?"

"The lilies in the foyer?"

"Yeah. That's how the suspect got inside. Flower delivery. Hid his face behind the flowers. The guard couldn't give any kind of description."

Claudia made a rude sound. "That guard wouldn't have noticed his *grandmother* if she was green with yellow stripes.

He didn't even look at my ID, didn't make me sign in. He was too busy scarfing down a Big Mac. *Anyone* could have gone up to Lindsey's apartment."

"He'll be at the head of the unemployment line tomorrow."

"He must feel like crap, knowing Ivan was attacked because of his laziness."

Jovanic gave her a doubting look, as if he were so jaundiced by what he had seen of human nature that he couldn't believe the guard might care about the consequences of his neglect. "The flowers got the suspect into the apartment. We don't know how he controlled the victim and got him into the kitchen. Mr. Novak was assaulted with a blunt object, which the suspect took with him."

"The guy ransacked some of the moving boxes," Claudia said. "I wonder if Ivan tried stalling for time. He knew I was on my way."

"We don't know how it actually went down."

"But it wasn't an ordinary B&E, was it?"

Jovanic regarded her with mild amusement. "And just what do you consider 'ordinary' breaking and entering?"

"Well, you know . . . they bust the lock, go inside and see what's there. It's more of an opportunistic thing. In this case, there was the flower delivery pretext, no forced entry, and the guy was really brutal. It's pretty clear *this* burglar was there with a specific purpose in mind. Ivan doesn't live there, he was just packing up Lindsey's stuff. But the way he was attacked seemed personal."

"Stranger things have happened," Jovanic said, then caught her knowing look and capitulated. "Okay, let's say you're right and it *wasn't* your run-of-the-mill B and E. What was he was looking for?"

"The tapes Ivan was going to give me?"

Jovanic took the opportunity to make a slight dig. "Maybe the flash drive you snagged?"

"Well, if that was it," she cracked back at him, "you ought to be glad I went in because now you've got it instead of him. I wonder if he got the tapes. I only saw him from behind, so I don't know if he was carrying anything."

Entering the North Tower, they headed for the Neuro Intensive Care department. Friday afternoon the hallways were bustling with volunteers pushing lunch carts. Jovanic walked with long strides, a man with places to go. Claudia kept up without difficulty.

"Like I told you this morning," Jovanic said, hitting the intercom at the locked door to Neuro ICU and announcing them. "Mr. Novak had emergency surgery last night. Bone fragments had pierced the brain."

The door swung open and they entered a world of white-stockinged feet in crepe soles that whispered on the polished floor as nursing personnel scurried from one room to another. Given the level of activity, a surprising hush hung over the unit, broken only by the purr and occasional beep of machinery.

Neuro ICU was arranged in wagon-wheel fashion, with the nursing station at the hub. Eleven beds made up the spokes, separated from the nursing station by a wall of glass. Jovanic had explained that each patient had his or her own case-manager nurse, along with a team of nurse-assistants who divided their attention between the cubicles.

He flashed a smile at the duty nurse and she flashed one back. The casualness of the exchange suggested prior acquaintance, and Claudia made a guess that he must have visited other cases in the unit.

"Hi, Grace," Jovanic said, dropping some of the cop coolness and confirming Claudia's impression. "Any change in Mr. Novak?"

The nurse, who hadn't seen the kind side of fifty in a while, shook her head and fluttered her eyelashes at him with a coyness that irked Claudia.

"His vitals are stable and he came through surgery just fine. The doctors did what all they could, but he's not even close to being out of the woods yet. It's gonna take a while before we know just how much damage was done. Don't know what your suspect hit him with, but they meant business."

"Do you think we could see him for just a few minutes?"

The nurse cocked her head in a half-shake that looked

as though it might turn into a refusal. "You know he's sedated."

"Come on, Gracie, just five minutes?"

Gracie? He probably has the babes wound around his little finger with those puppy-dog eyes.

The duty nurse's starch visibly melted and her gaze invited Jovanic to beg some more. When he didn't, she smiled faintly. "Well, five minutes, just because it's you, Joel. But then he gets his dose of Valium."

She turned to Claudia with a tone that was all business. "Just don't expect too much. Most times, people with severe head injuries don't remember what happened to them. Sometimes they don't even know who they are." She eyed her watch. "It's nearly shift change and I'm going to have to tally all his hourly meds."

"Thanks, Grace," Jovanic said. "We won't take long."

He guided Claudia to Cubicle Four. A sign was taped to the dimly lit window: *"Family only, short visits expected and appreciated. No flowers."*

In the lowered light, propped up in the hospital bed, Ivan appeared bionic—part of the machines that connected him to life—seeming less than human, somehow, and smaller. Tubes and drains were taped into place, and he wore wrist restraints to prevent him from tearing out the IV lines. At the head of the bed, a grey metal box monitored changes in vital signs. A bag dripped blood, a tube fed oxygen, a breathing apparatus clicked and sighed.

Ivan's chest rose and fell with a steady rhythm. Half-closed lids revealed unfocused eyes. Like a boxer whose head had taken a pounding, the flesh around his eyes was purplish and swollen from the slow leakage of blood vessels. But Ivan had never been a boxer.

A lump of emotion clogged Claudia's throat. "Does he have any family?" she whispered. "Isn't anyone staying with him?"

Jovanic shook his head. "No one at his office knew of any relatives and we haven't found any, either."

Maybe that's what drew Ivan and Lindsey together—no one to care for but each other.

The detective moved the only chair in the room next to the bedside on Ivan's left, then stationed himself on the other side.

Claudia sat down on the chair and reached through the bed rail, careful not to disturb the IV needle as she took Ivan's limp hand in hers.

Could he feel the human contact? Maybe on some level it would make a difference.

"Ivan," she said softly, "it's Claudia. If you can hear me, please squeeze my hand."

No movement.

Was he even aware of her presence? She looked over at Jovanic with a little shake of her head. "Ivan, can you hear me? Squeeze my hand if you can."

For a moment there was no reaction, then she felt, almost imperceptibly, the movement of Ivan's fingers curling around hers. She glanced at Jovanic and nodded. He gave her a thumbs-up.

"That's good, Ivan," she encouraged. "Really good. I need to ask you some questions, but I don't want you to tire yourself. If the answer is yes, I want you to squeeze my hand once like you just did, and if the answer is no, squeeze twice. Do you understand?"

Ivan's fingers responded again, and the pressure seemed to gain a little strength.

"Good. Do you know me?"

Squeeze.

"Okay, do you know where you are?"

Squeeze.

The rhythmical whooshing of machines punctuated the silence as Claudia sought the right questions, reluctant to upset him. Jovanic came around the bed and stood behind her. He touched her shoulder, prodding her.

She shrugged him off. "We need to go slowly."

"We can't. We might not have another opportunity." Jovanic leaned forward, his jacket brushing her cheek. "Mr. Novak, do you know who attacked you?"

Ivan turned his head, moaning, a guttural, animal sound.

Instantly, the heart monitor changed rhythm, peaks and valleys squeezing together. Heart rate 140.

"Dammit, don't push him," Claudia said, feeling a flash of irritation heat her face. "I thought we agreed that I'd handle this."

"We need to get some answers."

Jovanic had his own agenda. As a cop, he saw things through a different lens than she did. His first concern was apprehending the suspect.

Ivan's hand moved in Claudia's, squeezing with an urgency that made her lean in closer. "I know you want to tell me something, Ivan, but please don't try to talk."

She glanced at the heart monitor. Still too fast.

"Call the nurse," Claudia said to Jovanic. "I'm worried about him."

He shook his head. "If anything's really wrong, they'll know it. That's what all this equipment is for. Keep going; we have to find out what he knows."

Misgiving flooded over her, but she saw again in her mind the bloody scene in Lindsey's kitchen. Jovanic was right. They had to draw out whatever information they could. But she would do it her own way.

"Give me your pen and notebook; I have an idea."

Jovanic flipped to a blank page in the little book and handed it to her along with his pen. "What's the plan?"

"Different areas of the brain govern speaking and writing skills. It's just possible that he might be able to communicate better in writing. I need you to hold the pad steady for me."

Restraints were loosely tied around Ivan's wrists. With the reflexive grasp of an infant, he grabbed the pen in his fist the moment Claudia touched it to his fingers. She covered his right hand with hers, using a light touch that would allow her to assist the writing movement and at the same time give the plump fingers some support.

As his hand moved in an unsteady, circular pattern, Ivan's first efforts were like a toddler's scribbles. But as he continued to struggle at it, the mental images of letters learned in childhood gradually began to be restored, impressing themselves on his injured brain to begin forming new neural pathways.

Soon, a teetering line appeared next to a jagged oval, then another oval with a line going through it. Then a possible letter '*e*.'

When he'd finished, Claudia looked at the marks Ivan had made, then at Jovanic. "Do you think this is an '*l*'?"

"Hard to say. You're the handwriting expert."

"Analyzing personality doesn't mean you can always read the words," she retorted. Jovanic's presence in the small room made her uncomfortable. She wished she could have been alone with Ivan and taken things at her own pace.

Ivan was tugging at the pen. He drew a shaky horizontal line above the vertical one. A new form took shape as they watched. All at once, it became clear to Claudia.

"It's not an *l*, it's a *t*. I think it says . . . is this word '*tape*,' Ivan?"

Affirmative pressure on her fingers. "You wanted to give me a tape, didn't you?"

Stronger pressure.

"Now we're getting somewhere," Jovanic said, watching their hands closely. "Where is the tape, Mr. Novak?"

Ivan tried to say something, gagged. The monitor beeped a caution.

"Dammit," Claudia snapped at Jovanic. "Don't upset him. Only ask yes or no questions."

Jovanic backed off.

She worked to get Ivan settled down, expecting the nurse to respond to the alarm. A couple of minutes passed and the alarm stopped beeping.

Claudia rolled her shoulders to release the tension and repositioned the pen in Ivan's hand. This time a clear letter *B* emerged, but the rest was chicken scratch.

Ivan jerked on her hand, attempting to speak.

"Ivan, is it a videotape you wanted to give me?"

The sounds he made were thick, alien. Words that Claudia could not understand. She glanced back at Jovanic, but his face was a blank. His shoulders lifted, and he shook his head in frustration.

Ivan struggled to sit up. The ventilator alarms went wild and Claudia felt her stomach drop as the blood pressure display on the monitor glowed 220 over 120.

The duty nurse flew into the room, a cannonball in tennis shoes. She did a brisk check of her patient, pushing Claudia and Jovanic aside as she recycled the blood pressure cuff and reset the alarms.

Having satisfied herself that the readings had dropped to a more normal range, she swept them both with a stern glare. Before she could scold them, Jovanic said, "We were just starting to get somewhere; could we have a few more minutes?"

Claudia stared at him in amazement. *The man has balls the size of grapefruits.*

Her amazement doubled when the nurse threw Jovanic a wink and said, "Just make it quick," then hurried away to answer another call.

Claudia watched her leave, her expression darkening. "If it was me prodding her like that, she'd have tossed me out on my ass in a flash."

What the hell is wrong with me? He's just a passing acquaintance. What do I care who flirts with him?

This thought was followed by a flash of brutal honesty. She was attracted to him and she'd better get over it fast. The urgency to get whatever information Ivan had was far more important than a case of the hots for the inscrutable detective.

"It pays to know the right people," Jovanic said placidly. "I helped her kid out of a jam last year."

"Well, I think we should stop." She indicated Ivan, slowly writhing in the bed. "This can't be good for him."

Jovanic stared her down. "Bowman's the nurse, not you. We need this information. Keep going."

"Do you have to be an asshole about it? He needs to rest. Let's come back tomorrow."

"Listen, *Ms. Rose,*" he said, giving her the granite stare. *Do they teach it in the Detective's Manual?* "This could be our only chance. It's the best lead we've gotten so far. The longer we wait, the less chance of catching the guy who did this to him. He's responding to you. Ask him, otherwise, I will."

Silently cursing the detective's impatience, Claudia took Ivan's hand again. His skin felt cooler, almost clammy to her touch. "Ivan, did the guy who attacked you get the tapes?"

Squeeze, squeeze—No.

She looked at Jovanic in excitement. "So, the tapes are at Lindsey's apartment?"

Squeeze, squeeze—No. Then squeeze—Yes. What the hell?

She looked down at him in confusion. His eyes were fully closed now, his breathing labored from the effort of trying to communicate.

"You're doing great, Ivan. I can't read the second word you wrote. Can you try writing it again?"

The affirmative pressure on her hand had weakened significantly. They repeated the routine with the pad and pen, but Ivan's hand grew heavy, even with Claudia's help.

A series of illegible marks crept across the paper, crooked curves pitched at odd angles. A capital *B*, maybe; what looked like an *r*, a *d*, a couple of other marks that might have been *n* and *I*, but Claudia was far from confident that she had it figured out.

"B-r-n-d" she said, puzzling it out. "Burned? Brand? Barn?"

Ivan's body twitched restlessly as he again strained to form words that were unintelligible to Claudia's ears.

"I think he's out of it," Jovanic said softly. "He doesn't know what he's doing."

"Shhh, he hears you!"

Jovanic bent over Claudia's shoulder, leaning toward the injured man. He spoke with a surprising gentleness that revealed something decent in him after his earlier insensitivity. "Mr. Novak, Ivan. What are you trying to tell us?"

Ivan's body jerked. The wrist restraints tightened against his struggles, draining the blood from his hands. The pen clattered to the floor.

Suddenly, his eyes flew open and he stared wildly at Claudia. "Bran," he cried, his arms flailing violently against the restraints. "Branbranbran."

Then, chaos.

The heart monitor exploded in a riot of peaks and valleys that widened with each beat. The screen flashed *V-tach*.

The duty nurse ran in, took one glance at Ivan, hissed "Get out," and hustled Claudia and Jovanic through the door. "Go. Hurry." She shouted down the hallway, "Code Blue, get a crash cart."

In moments, the small hospital room was overflowing with nurses, doctor, a respiratory therapist. The duty nurse expertly whipped the pillow from under Ivan's head. A technician rolled the bed flat and raised it to waist level.

The respiratory therapist connected an ambu bag, pumped it up to one hundred percent oxygen and gave Ivan a few breaths. An IV team nurse grabbed his left arm and began a new IV. Doctors and nurses shouted commands:

"Get the defibrillator charged up."

"Give him some Epinephrine ... an amp of Bicarb ..."

"Draw some gases."

"Get ready to defibrillate."

A stream of personnel squeezed into the room while others hurried out with specimens for the lab. In a matter of moments, plastic bags and bits of paper littered the floor. The duty nurse ripped away the hospital gown and squeezed gel onto Ivan's chest.

Watching the activity through the window, an icy fear chilled Claudia to her bones.

We shouldn't have pressed so hard.

The doctor barked, *"Clear!"* and applied the paddles.

Ivan's body bucked on the bed.

Again the doctor called, "Clear!" Electricity slammed through Ivan a second time.

A third.

Chapter 17

Twenty minutes into the crisis, the doctor came out into the hall, wearing the face of one who has looked death in the eye too often for it to make much of an impact anymore. He assured them it wasn't their fault; that Ivan had not succumbed because of their questions.

"We'll have to wait for the autopsy to be sure," he said, "but it was probably a subdural hematoma . . . a blood clot in the brain. We're able to revive the patient in about sixty percent of the cases, but I'm afraid this wasn't one of them." He patted Claudia's arm in a practiced way. "Don't blame yourselves; it most likely would have happened anyway."

Outside, the sun still shone brightly. Two orderlies strolling behind them were cracking jokes. An elderly woman steered her husband's wheelchair. Life went on as usual outside the hospital walls, but not for Ivan.

The day, which had started out so promisingly, had turned Kafkaesque.

"I don't care what that doctor said," Claudia said bitterly. "We shouldn't have pushed him so hard."

Jovanic's mouth was set in a hard, thin line, and she was having trouble reading his emotions. But when he spoke, he surprised her again with an unexpectedly gentle tone.

"We had to," he said. "Those couple of words you got him to write are the only clue we've got. If we can't find the tape, we're up shit creek. Assuming it actually exists."

"It won't matter much to Ivan, will it?"

"We have to get the guy who did this," Jovanic said, anger building in his voice. "We're talking about a murder charge, now."

"Yes, of course. You have to catch him."

"You got any idea what he was talking about?"

Claudia took a deep breath and blew it out slowly, shaking her head. "No. We know he wrote 'tape.'" She looked down at Jovanic's notebook still clutched in her hand, and returned it to him. "And he said 'brand,' or something that sounded like it." She sighed heavily. "I just don't know."

"So what the hell is on this tape he was so anxious for you to have?"

Claudia thought of the photos she had acquired from Earl Nelson, still in their envelope on her desk. The handwriting on them hadn't provided any clues about the authorship of Lindsey's alleged suicide note, but now she remembered that Nelson had mentioned videos.

"I bet it's sex videos. Videotaping her clients and blackmailing them is exactly the kind of thing Lindsey would do."

The cell phone was already out of Jovanic's pocket and he was punching buttons. "I'll call the property manager and make sure we can get into the penthouse. We've got to find that tape."

They reached Claudia's Jaguar. "I wonder who'll take care of burying him," she said as she unlocked the door. "I'd like to attend, if there's a service."

"I'll talk to the people at his office and let you know." Jovanic opened the door for her. "But first, I'll follow you home."

"Don't bother, I'm fine." She didn't feel fine. She felt punch-drunk, and appalled at the ruthless way Jovanic had pressured Ivan. But at the same time she knew it was more crucial than ever to discover the true cause of Lindsey's death and, now, of Ivan's, and she was determined to participate in finding the answers. "Are you still meeting with Doctor Bostwick?" she asked.

"I'm heading over there now."

"I'd still like to go, if you're willing to take me."

He stepped into her space, just a little too close. "Sure you're up for it?"

She stood her ground, staring back at him eye-to-eye. "Listen, Columbo, I'm involved up to my eyelashes in this case. I'm not about to sit around at home like some meek little mouse, waiting by the phone to hear what happens next. Ivan was my client. We weren't exactly bosom buddies, but I owe it to him to follow through. Besides, I've done a lot of police consulting, so you shouldn't get in too much trouble for letting me tag along."

He put up his hands in mock protest. "Fine, okay! How about I drive?"

"Why? You still think I'm not up to it?"

"Nope." A half-smile dimpled one cheek. "I just always wanted to drive a Jag."

No one but Claudia was allowed to drive the Jag.
Ever.

She tossed him the keys and went around to the passenger side. He opened the door for her, climbed into the driver's seat and fired up the engine, reverently caressing the burled-wood dash. The smile he gave her almost made her forget his merciless prodding of Ivan.

Charles Randolph Bostwick III, MD, owned a venerable old building of medical suites on San Vicente, a mile or so east of Cedars. Jovanic drove into the subterranean parking garage and parked the Jag on the second level next to a late-model Rolls Royce that had been polished to a high sheen. The Rolls occupied the space closest to the elevator and bore a personalized license plate: "HARDUP."

"There's a good word for that," Claudia said, curling her lip in distaste. "*Rodomontade*."

Jovanic stood aside, allowing her to precede him into the elevator. "You just swallow a dictionary?"

"It means braggadocio. I hate that kind of crap."

"What do you want to bet that's Bostwick's car?"

"No takers on that one. Is he expecting us?"

He grinned nastily. "The element of surprise works wonders. No time to invent an alibi."

"How do you know he'll see us?"

"He'll see us."

In the lobby they switched elevators and rode to the eighteenth floor, headquarters of the Bostwick Maxillofacial Surgery Group, which also occupied the floors three and four.

Walking into a vestibule decorated with understated elegance, they found a woman seated behind an antique writing desk, working at a computer. She glanced up with a smile of anticipation. "Good afternoon, may I help you?"

In her demure, white silk blouse with its Peter Pan collar, and a soft cardigan sweater, she could have stepped out of *The Donna Reed Show* of the fifties.

Probably wears pearls and high heels while she bakes chocolate chip cookies for the kids.

Jovanic flipped her his badge. "Detective Joel Jovanic, LAPD. I need a few moments with Doctor Bostwick, please."

The smile instantly vanished, replaced by a worried frown. "Oh dear," the Donna Reed clone said in a breathless voice. "Uh . . . can *I* . . . uh, help you? The doctor is with a patient . . ." She broke off mid-sentence. "There's someone already waiting to see him."

Catching the glances they cast at the empty lobby, she hurried to explain. "We have private waiting rooms. I'm sorry, but the doctor is already forty minutes behind schedule. I don't see how . . . perhaps you could . . . there's an office manager downstairs . . . down on the fourth floor."

"This won't take long," Jovanic assured her. Something about the set of his jaw must have convinced her that he wasn't going away. Or maybe it was the purposeful way he looked around, as if he might start looking for the doctor himself.

Donna Reed glanced uncertainly at Claudia, perhaps hoping for some moral support. When none was forthcoming, she pressed her lips together in disapproval and touched a button on the phone.

They heard a beep, shortly followed by an irritable voice

that boomed through the intercom. "What is it, Frances? I'm in a consult."

"I'm so sorry, Doctor, please excuse me," the woman stammered. "Um, uh, when you have a moment . . . there's, uh . . . there's someone here . . . someone who wants to speak with you."

"I told you not to bother me," the voice snapped back.

"I'm really sorry, Doctor, but I, um . . . I think it's important . . . if you could just . . ."

Was her inability to finish a sentence her natural mode, or a sign of habitual intimidation? In her imagination, Claudia gave the woman an overbearing husband who believed in wifely submission. He would have made her a doormat through years of abuse that was seconded by her employer.

Somewhere out of sight, a door slammed. A man in a snowy full-length lab coat with his name embroidered on the pocket careened around the corner and charged toward them with the force of a storm trooper.

Frosty blue eyes glared through gold-rimmed granny glasses that perched on the end of a well-shaped nose. He was past his prime, but would have still been handsome if his face hadn't been twisted in temper.

He strode right up to Jovanic and for a moment Claudia thought he was going to jab him in the chest. She didn't know Jovanic well, but something told her it was lucky for the doctor that he stopped short.

"Who are you and what do you want?" the doctor demanded.

Claudia had met men of Bostwick's ilk before. Analretentive, bad-tempered, hating life, even when life had been good to them. She could guess what his handwriting might look like: heavy pressure, extreme right slant, long lower loops and plenty of sharp strokes. A man with a personality this angry might prefer red ink for emphasis.

Jovanic flashed his badge. "Detective Joel Jovanic," he said. "LAPD. I'm sorry to disturb you, Doctor, but we need a few minutes of your time."

"I'm trying to run a medical practice here. I don't have

time for bullshit. I'm not interested in tickets to the policeman's ball."

"This is a murder investigation, Doctor," Jovanic announced, smooth as glass. The threat in his voice was nothing more than a subtle undertone. "It involves a former patient of yours, Lindsey Alexander. Perhaps we could speak in private?"

Bostwick swung sharply on his heel and returned the way he had come. "Ever hear of making an appointment? You've got five minutes." To the woman at the reception desk: "Get Myron Gershman on the phone, then get Ron up here to finish the consult."

Claudia and Jovanic followed Doctor Bostwick to a door at the end of the hall. Hewn from black walnut and polished to a high gloss, it had a brass plate with his name engraved on it.

He unlocked the door and they walked into a room that must have spanned the width of the building. Bostwick stepped onto a raised dais upon which stood a long table covered with stacks of books and papers. Standing above them. Putting psychological distance between them.

Behind him was an unobstructed view of the Hollywood sign. At the other end of the long room was a life-size jungle tableau in a glass case, where a magnificently maned lion tore at the bloody flesh of a downed zebra. A taxidermist's dream.

Bostwick caught Claudia's stare and mistook it for admiration. "Bagged him myself," he declared with pride. "African safari, 1973."

Before she could launch into her views on trophy hunters, Jovanic broke in. "About Lindsey Alexander . . ."

"I have no intention of talking to you about any of my patients," Bostwick said. "Doctor-patient confidentiality. Perhaps you've heard of it?"

"That privilege ended when she died," Jovanic said, brushing off the sarcasm. "Perhaps you've heard of *that*. We're not here to talk about your doctor-patient relationship."

Bostwick swung his cold gaze onto Claudia. "Who are you?"

"Claudia Rose . . ."

"Ms. Rose is helping with the investigation," Jovanic interrupted her with a warning look. "Why don't you tell us about your *personal* association with Lindsey, Doctor."

"There *was* no personal association. She was my patient. That's all there is to tell."

"That so? Do you have office hours on Saturday?"

"Sometimes. Why?"

"She had an appointment with you on the day she died."

"So what?" Bostwick retorted. "She killed herself, didn't she?"

"Did she?"

The doctor puffed out his chest, managing to look like the injured party. "Why are you asking *me?* I know *nothing* about her death."

The intercom sounded and the receptionist's timid voice came over the speaker. "Uh, excuse me, Doctor Bostwick, I have . . . uh, Mr. Gershman is on the line."

Bostwick threw them a smug look and pressed the speaker button. "My attorney," he announced. Then, addressing the speaker, "Myron, there are some detectives here, asking questions about a patient of mine who recently committed suicide."

The lawyer cleared his throat. "Are we on speaker?"

Bostwick affirmed that they were.

"Detective? I don't know what you're looking for, but I'm going to advise my client not to answer any questions without my being present. Perhaps you'd be kind enough to make an appointment for a time when we can all meet."

Jovanic inclined his head at the doctor and replied to the speakerphone. "Certainly, sir. We're just asking a few questions, but if you think your client needs an attorney, you're welcome to bring him to the Wilshire Division police station this afternoon and we can conduct the interview there."

"Now wait a goddamn minute," Bostwick interjected. "I'm not going to any police station! I've done nothing wrong. If my patients got wind . . ."

"Hold on, Charles." The lawyer's voice bled in and out as his words crossed with the doctor's over the speaker. "I can't leave the office just at the moment, but . . ."

Anger stained the doctor's cheeks an alarming scarlet and Claudia felt a flicker of concern. He was a total jerk, but after what had just happened to Ivan, she wasn't anxious to witness him having a heart attack.

"Why the hell do I pay you that fat retainer every month if you aren't here when I need you?" the doctor growled at the speaker phone.

Gershman had certainly danced this two-step many times before, and he had the routine down pat. His tone was conciliatory but firm. "Charles, I have another client here at the moment, but I can be there in about a half-hour. We'll meet in your office at one o'clock. Detective?"

"Sorry, sir," Jovanic said, keeping tight control of the interview. "I have another appointment. We'll see you and Doctor Bostwick at Wilshire Division at . . ." he consulted his watch, "five o'clock. Shall I send a black and white to pick you up, Doctor?"

Bostwick cast a baleful look at the phone. "Dammit, Myron," he muttered. "You useless sonofabitch." He ended the call and brought his hard stare back around to Jovanic. "I'm not going to any goddamn police station. What do you want from me?"

"You do understand that you are going against your legal counsel's advice if you speak to me, and that you don't have to answer any questions?"

"Yes, yes, goddammit . . . get on with it. Ask your questions. It won't do you any good because I don't know anything."

"Did you meet with Lindsey Alexander on Saturday, September twenty-third?"

Bostwick sucked air through flared nostrils—a bull ready to charge a red cape. "Yes, I saw her. It was a pre-surgery visit. She was scheduled to come in on the following Monday for a procedure."

"What kind of procedure?"

"Blepharoplasty."

Jovanic gave him a thin smile. "I'm sorry, doctor. Would you mind translating?"

"Eyelid lift. It's done with sedation, either IV or general anesthetic . . . in this case, general. She was scheduled for both upper and lower lids."

"I see. Okay, so she was scheduled for surgery on Monday. Where did you see her on Saturday?"

Bostwick hesitated and his gaze shifted to the left, toward the window. He was giving them less than the whole truth. "I met her here, here at the office. She was nervous about the procedure, very stressed. Kept calling me at home."

"Do all your patients get your home number?"

Bostwick reddened again. "It depends on the patient. Lindsey was . . ." Whatever he was going to say stayed on his tongue. "I ended up telling her I'd meet her here and give her some medication to alleviate the anxiety and help her get through the weekend."

"Wouldn't it have been easier to just call in a prescription to the drug store?" Jovanic pressed, edging closer to the desk.

"My patients get more personalized care than that. Ms. Alexander required my reassurance."

And that's what they pay for.

Claudia cast a glance at the hand-carved chairs, the Persian rugs covering the floor. Plastic surgery for the affluent evidently included a far higher level of care than she was accustomed to.

"What's 'PS,' doctor?" Jovanic asked.

"PS?"

"There was a note in Ms. Alexander's calendar that she was meeting you at PS."

Bostwick blinked at him, the color leaching from his face. "I . . . don't . . . know . . . what . . . you're . . . talking . . . about."

"You have no idea what she was referring to?"

Bostwick picked up some papers from his desk and riffled through them, not looking at Jovanic, obviously discomfited by the question. "I just said I didn't. Weren't you listening?"

"Okay, then. Did you supply Ms. Alexander with Blue Heaven?"

"Blue Heaven? Are you talking about Amytal, detective? I don't use street names."

"Did you give her Amytal?"

"I gave her some to help calm her."

"Enlighten me, but isn't Amytal a rather outdated drug, sir?"

Bostwick looked Jovanic in the eye, in his element now. "You have a medical degree, do you, detective? I gave my patient a legal sedative to help her with anxiety before surgery. What's the problem?"

"What time did you see her?"

"Sometime in the middle of the afternoon. I don't remember exactly. I'd have to check my records."

"You'll need to do that, sir. Now, perhaps you could tell me where you were between eight o'clock on the night of the twenty-third and six o'clock the next morning, the twenty-fourth?"

"Home in bed with my wife," Bostwick answered quickly. Too quickly. "Just ask her." He removed the granny glasses, carefully folded them before dropping them into his coat pocket and heading for the door. "Your time is up, detective. I have patients to see, and I've had enough of your interrogation."

Jovanic dogged his steps. "Thank you for your time, sir," he said as they passed Bostwick at the door. Then, in a classic Columbo move, he stopped abruptly and turned back. "There *is* one more thing, sir."

"What *now?*"

"I understand you have a particular fondness for Labrador Retrievers."

Chapter 18

"I think we shook old Bostwick up pretty good," Jovanic drawled, looking smug as he leaned on the elevator button.

"Did you see his face?" Claudia said in disgust. "I thought he was going to have a stroke."

They stepped into the cab and Jovanic punched the Lobby button, unwrapping a toothpick. "He certainly knows bestiality is a crime. I'm gonna get him for that, even if nothing comes of this Lindsey business." The cool grey eyes found hers. "So, you got time to stop by Lindsey's penthouse? I want to start looking for that tape Ivan told us about."

Claudia hadn't been able to rid herself of memories of the blood-spattered kitchen and what had happened there, but she wouldn't tell Jovanic how much she did not want to return to the Wilshire Boulevard apartment. She gave a casual shrug. "Sure, let's go."

Jovanic said nothing, but he bumped his elbow against hers, letting her know that he understood. Telling herself she was being stupid didn't stop her from taking comfort from the contact.

Security had tightened since the attack on Ivan. A guard in a spiffy uniform manned the door at the Wilshire Boulevard building, and they had to show their IDs before meeting with the property manager who gave them a key to Lindsey's penthouse.

Jovanic ripped away the yellow crime-scene tape that

criss-crossed the entry to the apartment and unlocked the door. Before they stepped inside, he took two pairs of latex gloves from his pocket and handed one to Claudia. "Wear these," he said.

"Do you always carry rubber gloves in your pocket?"

"I got them out of my kit while I was waiting for you at the hospital."

"You have a kit?"

"Crime-scene kit . . . gloves, plastic and paper bags, stuff like that. I keep it in my car." They moved through the foyer into the living room. "Don't touch anything unless you absolutely have to. If you see something you think is important, let me know."

Claudia nodded and pulled on her gloves. The latex slid on easily over her hands, powdery inside, loose against her fingers. "My, what big hands you have, detective," she said, stretching her right hand out and wiggling her fingers in the glove. Jovanic matched his glove to hers. The top joint of his fingers reached well past her fingertips.

For the space of a second or two there was silence, apart from their quickened breathing. Claudia snatched her hand back, suddenly awkward with the intimacy that had invaded the moment. She glanced around, looking anywhere but at Jovanic. "So, where should we start?"

"Uh, let's uh . . . the kitchen." He sounded as disconcerted as she felt. "I want you to show me where you found that flash drive."

She followed him along the service corridor but stopped at the kitchen doorway. She'd expected to find the blood and gore gone, the room sanitized, but the remnants of savagery remained undisturbed. The rusty stains everywhere and the lingering smell of congealed blood still nauseated her.

"He was over there, on the other side of the island. Like I told you, he was lying on top of the flash drive." She gulped and drew a ragged breath, unable to continue.

"It's not your fault," Jovanic said softly.

"Dammit, maybe if I'd gotten here five minutes sooner, maybe the guy would have been spooked, or . . . I could have done something heroic, or . . . At least I could have gotten a better look at him."

"You could have been another victim," Jovanic said, the momentary warmth in his eyes giving way to his usual pragmatic toughness. "If you'd arrived five minutes sooner, you might be dead, too." His penetrating gaze took in every inch of the gourmet kitchen. "If Ivan brought the videotapes in here, the suspect got them, but since he still had the flash drive, we'll check it out. You start at that end."

Claudia said no more about her flight of fancy. Jovanic was much too practical to waste more time with what might have been. She moved as far away from the site of the attack as she could, unable to think of any man who possessed the power that Jovanic had to simultaneously attract and exasperate her.

They had no luck in the kitchen. Claudia informed the detective that she would start on Lindsey's office, and went upstairs.

Seated behind the queen-sized glass-top desk, she opened the first drawer and stared at the flotsam and jetsam that Ivan had not yet packed into moving boxes. Little bits of a life that now meant nothing.

Two lives.

She sifted through the contents: utility company envelopes, bank statements, a small bottle of Elmer's glue, a staple remover. Nothing different than someone searching her own desk drawers would find. Until she came upon a plastic bag filled with multi-colored pills and capsules.

"Find anything?" Jovanic's voice interrupted from behind.

"Are you trying to give me heart failure?" she said, annoyed that he'd made her jump. "I found a bag of pills and capsules. No videotapes, no references to tapes."

"Nothing downstairs, either. Let's try her bedroom."

"Best little whorehouse in Brentwood," Claudia murmured, feeling like a voyeur as they entered Lindsey's most private space together.

Modern four-poster bed on a six-inch platform. Black satin tethers attached to each post waited to bind a willing victim. A wild zebra comforter turned back on glossy black satin sheets, a black negligee carelessly draped. On a pillow, a leather mask and nylon-thonged whip. Vividly erotic paintings from the Kama Sutra decorated the walls. Dozens of candles on virtually every surface, waiting to be lit.

Jovanic jerked his chin upward. A spray of peacock feathers framed a six-foot gilt mirror on the ceiling above the bed. "The lady liked to watch."

"With a capital W," Claudia said, moving around the room and looking into the largest bathroom she had ever seen. French doors led to an enclosed deck with the full-sized Jacuzzi where Lindsey's life had ended.

By her choice? Or someone else's?

Jovanic called her back into the bedroom and pointed to a small dark globe high up on the wall opposite the bed. "See that?"

"What is it, a camera pretending to be a light fixture?"

He nodded. "Maybe we're getting hot."

Claudia was getting hot, but not in the way he meant. The bedroom's raw readiness for sex aroused fantasies that surprised her, and Jovanic's proximity was getting to her. She wondered if he felt it, too.

She was relieved when he went to check out the camera, disappearing inside a closet. She could hear him tapping on the walls.

"There's a locked door," he called out. "Camera's gotta be hidden in back of it. Have you seen any keys?"

Claudia strolled into the closet and collided with him as he was coming out. "Oh, come on, be a big bad cop, break down the door."

He gave a snort that she thought might have been a chuckle. "You're a real wiseass, you know that?" he said. "Just add keys to your list."

Keys.

Claudia stared into the past.

*   *   *

A couple of weeks after their lunch at the Great Wall, Lindsey had summoned Claudia and Kelly to the patio at Spago in Beverly Hills. She'd just wanted company, no special occasion.

"Let's see your key rings," Claudia had said when the conversation lagged. "I read an article that says your key ring tells a lot about you."

"Where'd you read that?" Kelly had asked.

"The International Handwriting Journal. Richard Koko-chak says the more keys you carry, the more entanglements you draw into your life."

Lindsey had squinted over the top of her menu. "The fewer entanglements the better is my philosophy. It's why I don't wear underwear."

Kelly rolled her eyes and slapped her menu on the table. "Who do you think gives a fuck what you put on your skinny ass?"

Heads twisted around to see what had made the tall blonde laugh so loud.

"We were talking about keys," Claudia had interjected before the two of them could get going.

Lindsey took her key ring from her Coach purse and jingled it: a brass L with only three keys attached.

"One for the car, one for the penthouse, one for my bedroom."

Claudia said, "You lock your bedroom *with a key?"*

"Always." Lindsey had swallowed a mouthful of wine and set the glass down a little too hard, splashing a few crimson drops on the damask tablecloth. "You never know who might show up in the middle of the night."

"Yeah, you mean like someone's wife?" Kelly had asked.

"Now, there's the pot calling the kettle black," Lindsey had retorted, and they were off again, bickering and sniping at each other the way they always did.

Lindsey hadn't locked her bedroom door on the night she died. Had she perhaps admitted a trusted visitor?

"Did you find anything in there?" Claudia asked.

"No tapes, just a ton of commercial DVDs. Come on, I'll show you."

Jovanic led her into the cavernous closet. A center-island dresser held a dozen drawers on each side. Built-in racks covered three walls filled with enough designer clothing to stock I Magnin. On the fourth wall, more DVDs than Blockbuster Video.

"Looks like she was a big Mickey Rourke fan," Claudia observed, browsing the titles. "Personally, I never could get into him."

"Too rough for you?" Jovanic's voice was soft, sensual, close to her ear.

Alarm bells went off in her head and Claudia backed up a step, doing her best to resist the magnetism she felt emanating from him. "Er, no, just . . . er, too, er . . ." She broke off, stumbling over her words.

He looked amused. "Let's look for Ivan's tapes and a key."

They divvied up the bedroom and began the search.

Less than a minute later, Claudia found an address book in the bottom drawer of Lindsey's night stand.

"Maybe we'll find the names on the spreadsheet," she said, flipping through the pages.

Jovanic glanced over from the armoire he was examining. "That'd be a nice break. Let me know if you recognize any."

"They're all girls' names: Breanna Anderson; Kandy Boots—if that isn't a hooker's name. I wonder if they all worked for her." She turned a few more pages. "Toni Giardina . . ."

"Hey, I know her," Jovanic interjected. "Toni Giardina. She's a pro. She was, anyway."

"A pro? As in prostitute?"

"I busted her a couple of years back when I worked Hollywood Vice."

Claudia gave him the cocked-eyebrow. "You remember the names of all your busts?"

"No, but this is one bust you couldn't forget." He grinned sheepishly at his pun. "She was a teenage Dolly Parton.

Sixteen, a real looker, even under a ton of makeup and a crazy red wig. My partner and I got her into the Children of the Night program. Supposed to help her turn her life around. Maybe it didn't take."

"I wonder if Lindsey recruited . . ." She broke off, staring at the next name. "Oh, man . . ."

"Whatcha got?"

"Ivan kept saying something that sounded like 'brand.' And that word he wrote that we couldn't decipher? This is it! Look . . . *Brandi* Jones. He was trying to tell us her name. Maybe this Brandi has the tapes, or at least knows where they are."

Jovanic crossed the room and took the address book from her. "Ever thought of changing careers?" he asked with a wink. "You can be my new partner."

Chapter 19

Claudia arrived home around eleven after dropping Jovanic back at his Jeep, which he'd left at Cedars-Sinai Medical Center. He had followed her most of the way back to her house, turning onto a side street just before she'd reached Ballona Creek.

Friday night, and she'd spent it at a murder scene, trolling for a mystery video.

A real hot date.

Kelly would get a laugh out of that. Claudia locked the door behind her, kicked off her shoes with a groan of relief and peeled out of her suit jacket. The pantyhose went next, landing on the couch in a heap beside her purse. Without the protection of her outer clothing, goose bumps pebbled her flesh. The warmth she had carried home with her from the evening spent with Jovanic receded a little as she shivered, wondering why the air temperature inside the house was so cool.

For a moment she considered building a fire, but the hour was late and a hot drink would be easier. Padding to the kitchen, she froze in the doorway. Across the darkened room, the soft glow of the outside porch light shone through the back door, which stood ajar.

She crossed the room in slow motion, not wanting to admit the obvious—that someone had entered her home while she was away. She checked the doorframe. No splintering, no sign that the lock had been jimmied.

Had she checked to make sure the door was all the way

closed and locked when she'd left that morning? Of course she had. There had been a rash of burglaries lately in the Marina area, and she was always careful about locking up. She thought back over her early-morning activities. After the phone call from Jovanic, she had showered and dressed for her meeting with Lillian Grainger, leaving the house around nine.

Returning to the living room, she stood statue-still, tension tightening her stomach. Listening to the silence. Ears stretching for the faintest sound. Absorbing the atmosphere. Would she sense an unwelcome presence?

Moving stealthily to the coat closet, Claudia opened the door, cringing at the loud click it made. Holding her breath, waiting for any telltale answering sounds from upstairs, she grabbed her baseball bat from behind the box of Christmas gift wrap. She had never been much of a ball player, but a woman living alone needed some kind of protection, and a gun would be her last weapon of choice.

The adhesive tape wrapped around the handle of the heavy wooden bat felt rough in her hands. She eased her way up to the second floor in bare feet, taking care to avoid the treads that creaked.

In her bedroom, she checked inside the closet and under the bed, never doubting that she would swing the bat with all her might if she had to face down an intruder.

She made a rapid assessment of her small stash of heirloom jewelry, a legacy from her grandmother. The ruby ring and the emerald necklace were nestled safely in their carved wooden box.

The guest room appeared undisturbed, but when she crept into her office and over to her desk, she knew immediately that something was wrong.

The screen saver should have been active on her computer monitor, but the screen was black. The CPU had been switched off. Her mind ticked automatically through the facts: she always left the computer on; if there had been an outage, the clocks would be blinking; the clocks were not blinking; therefore, no power outage.

The semi-organized chaos on her desk looked just as

she had left it, but someone had been through the stacks, she knew it in her gut. Quickly riffling through the piles of paper, she satisfied herself that nothing had been taken. The envelope Earl Nelson had given her containing the exploitive photos of Lindsey was where she had left it.

Claudia threw on sweatshirt and pants, then headed back downstairs. She closed the back door and snapped the deadbolt into place, then went back through the living room and out on the deck to study the street.

About halfway down the block and across the street she could see a van with a florist's logo on the side. Had it been there when she'd arrived home? She didn't think so, but she'd been busy thinking about Jovanic and it was possible that she had missed it.

Claudia didn't believe in coincidences. Not that week, anyway.

"Give me ten minutes," Jovanic said, answering his cellular. "I'm on my way."

"Nothing's missing, but someone was here."

"Get me the license plates on the van, in case he leaves. I'll run them on the way over. Your name and picture were on the news, and it's not hard to find out where you live."

With that less-than-comforting thought, she stayed outside until his Jeep turned the corner. He slowed to a stop behind the van and sat there for a couple of minutes until a black and white patrol car arrived and parked behind him. He exited the Jeep, his weapon in his hand. After speaking to the uniforms, he strode over to the van.

Jovanic stole along the fender and peered cautiously into the driver's window. He veered around the back, circling the vehicle and reappearing at the front end. He went back to the patrol car again and leaned in the window for a moment, talking to the uniforms.

As they drove slowly down the street, he got back into the Jeep and parked it in Claudia's driveway.

Inside, he stripped off his leather bomber jacket and laid it next to the clothes Claudia had left on the couch. "I've asked for a cruiser to drive by a couple of times during the night," he told her as they sat together at the kitchen table, going over the details.

"Thanks, that makes me feel a little safer."

Jovanic rose and went to the service porch. Crouching on his heels, he peered at the door. "Do you have a magnifying glass? I want to take a closer look."

Claudia ran up to her office, returning with one of the powerful lenses she used to reveal the hidden details in handwriting. She aimed a flashlight over his shoulder while he examined the lock through the magnifier, drawing her attention to some very fine scratches.

"Get the locks changed right away, Claudia; the suspect could have made himself a key."

"Shit! I'm having an alarm installed."

"Got anything to help you sleep tonight?"

"A glass of wine sounds mighty appealing right about now. Care to join me?"

"Sure, thanks." Jovanic locked the door and followed her into the kitchen. He leaned against the counter while she poured the wine. "You got an extra blanket? That couch in your office looks pretty comfortable."

He must have fallen asleep as soon as his head hit the pillow. Through her bedroom wall, Claudia heard his breathing even out and the sound of light snores. He'd been at the hospital with Ivan since last night, and investigating the attack late the night before that. It must have been the first real sleep he'd had in forty-eight hours.

Even after the bottle of Merlot they had shared, sleep didn't come so readily for Claudia. A jumble of images rolled around in her head: Lindsey's funeral; Lindsey's brother, Earl Nelson; Zebediah's revelations about Lindsey's childhood. And Ivan Novak, a man she had scarcely known, but who had suddenly become the focus of her life.

Before she had arrived at complete consciousness the next morning, Claudia's nose caught the fragrance of freshly brewed coffee. Momentary confusion was followed by embarrassment when she realized that Jovanic must have introduced himself to her kitchen. Her modern single woman's nearly-empty refrigerator wasn't stocked for guests.

She took a quick shower and came downstairs to discover that he had made himself at home. Coffee and a toasted bagel awaited her. He must have made an early morning trip to the bagel shop in town.

Jovanic drew out a chair for her at the kitchen table. In yesterday's wrinkled shirt and trousers, and with the rough stubble of a five o'clock shadow more than twenty-four hours old, he looked slightly sinister. And intensely attractive.

Kind of like a Jane Austin hero, Claudia mused, taking a sip from the mug he set before her. *Or a twenty-first century Maxim de Winter.* She looked up at him and smiled. "A man who can make good coffee. I'm impressed."

"The least of my talents," he said with an enigmatic lift of his brow.

Opting for the safe route, she changed the subject. "So, what's next on the agenda, Columbo?"

"I have an appointment with Senator Heidt later this morning." He dumped a couple of heaping spoonfuls of sugar into his coffee. "I'll rattle his cage a little. If he's as slimy as Doctor Bostwick, I'll have to dig harder."

Claudia got up and rooted around in the pantry for a jar of marmalade, wondering whether he would invite her along. "If you can believe it, he's even slimier." She spread jam on the bagel and offered him the jar, which he declined. "In my opinion, he's the *worst* kind of slime because he's two-faced. He's being appointed as co-chair on a presidential committee to address *women's issues.* A customer on Lindsey's spreadsheet, for Chrissake! How hypocritical is that?"

Jovanic showed mock surprise. "You don't think he's sincere in his appreciation for women?"

"Sincere my ass. After Lindsey's funeral, there was this woman at the reception. She was all over him. He couldn't push her away fast enough. Pretended not to know her. It was pretty obvious he did, and she mentioned Lindsey."

Jovanic made the connection. "You think this woman is part of the sex business?"

"Could be. At the funeral I overheard her say that she didn't believe Lindsey killed herself. I wish I could remember her name. I know it was unconventional, but it wasn't Brandi."

He glanced at his watch. "Speaking of Brandi, I called her earlier and left a message. I've got an hour before I have to go home and clean up for Heidt. You up for a walk on the beach?"

They turned in the direction of Marcia's house in time to see the Chevy van with the florist logo being hoisted onto a flatbed tow truck.

"One of yours?" Claudia asked.

"Yeah. They'll impound it and forensics will go over it for prints and any other evidence . . . hairs, fibers. Maybe we'll get lucky and find some DNA evidence that links it to Ivan."

"I wonder what happened to the guy who left it here."

"Probably realized the van had been made . . . you know, identified."

Marcia came to the door in a terrycloth bathrobe, her head wrapped in a striped towel, turban-style. Her jaw dropped when Claudia told her about the break-in. "Oh, no! Are you okay?"

Jovanic stepped forward. "Marcia, did you see or hear anything out of the ordinary yesterday?"

Marcia tightened the belt on her robe, a frown creasing her forehead as she thought about it. "You know, come to think of it, some guy was knocking at your place yesterday, Claudia. I came outside to get the newspaper and Flare started going nuts when she saw him, so I brought her back in. Man, I thought he was just selling something."

"What time was that?" Jovanic asked.

"I'm not real sure, maybe around nine-thirty."

Nine-thirty. Shortly after Claudia had left for her appointment. He must have been watching her as she left.

Jovanic jotted on his notepad. "Did you notice the van parked down the street?"

"What van?"

"The one that's being towed right now."

Marcia stepped out onto the porch and saw the tow truck. "Oh, hey, no, I didn't."

"Do you think you could describe the man you saw yesterday?"

Marcia delved in the side pocket of her robe and took out a pack of smokes and a lighter. "Jeez, lemme think." She lit up, turning her head to blow the smoke from the corner of her mouth. Claudia noticed that Jovanic turned his face in the direction of the smoke and breathed in. He searched his pockets, but apparently had used his last toothpick.

"I wasn't paying that much attention." Marcia pursed her lips, eyes narrowing as she recalled the visitor. "I got the impression he was young, maybe early twenties. Dark hair, average height, kinda hefty. I'm sorry I can't be more specific."

"How was he dressed?"

"Hmmmm. Levi's, I think, and a dark shirt . . . long sleeves."

Claudia's heart banged against her ribs like a trip hammer. A stranger had gained entry to her home almost without leaving a trace. If he hadn't been careless about closing the kitchen door, she would never have known he'd been there. What had he wanted? Had he accomplished what he set out to do?

"Try not to worry too much," Jovanic said, as they went down the path to the beach with Flare padding ahead of them. "I doubt he'll come back. He had all yesterday to look around."

Is that supposed to make me feel better?

"What if he planted a bug or something?" Claudia said, expressing a concern that had been forming in her mind.

"I can have a tech come out and sweep the place."

"Yes, please," she said gratefully. "It would definitely make me feel better."

They took off their shoes and let the sand crunch between their toes as they walked. Off the leash, Flare bounded off in pursuit of a flock of seagulls and sandpipers skittering around the shore. The air smelled of salt and seaweed.

"Do you think he was looking for the tapes?" Claudia asked, unable to leave the subject of the intruder. "Or the flash drive? He couldn't have known that I took it, could he?"

"Assuming this is the guy who attacked Ivan, and he knew you were at the penthouse that night? Sure, he might have thought you had it. But it's all guesswork. We don't know if whoever attacked Ivan even knew about the drive, or whether he was looking for the tapes."

"Why would he mess with my computer?"

"It might be a coincidence. Maybe this was someone looking for your personal financial information, you know, identity theft. You'd better alert your bank, in case." Jovanic picked up a small rock, tossed it overhand into the waves, walking backwards a few steps, so he could look at her as he spoke. "So, what do you do when you're not discovering bodies and getting your house broken into?"

Claudia stuck her hands in her pockets, hunching her shoulders against the brisk wind that had kicked up. "Mostly, I analyze handwriting for clients, I write articles, do TV appearances once in a while. Pretty dull."

"Shit, no. I don't know many people on TV."

"Doesn't mean anything. Testifying in court is a lot harder."

"I don't much like it myself." They walked along in silence for a while, then he blurted, "You ever been married?"

She glanced at him sharply. Was this Detective Jovanic, or Joel, the private citizen asking?

"Once. Didn't last too long, but we're still friends. We've been divorced six years. You?"

"Divorced. She didn't like my job, wanted me home more."

There was more to that story, she was certain, but the way he said it didn't encourage questions. Still, she pushed a little. "You're not on friendly terms?"

He didn't speak for a moment, and looked as though his thoughts were giving him an acid stomach. "I hear from her when she needs money. It wasn't enough that she took every-thing we had . . . house, furniture, bank account. Everything, in exchange for a promise that she'd never contact me again. She never was any good at keeping promises."

"Any kids?"

"No. I was away a lot." Brief and sharp. Claudia didn't push it; it was a prickly area for her, too.

After that, they walked in silence for a while, detouring around the rocky peninsula that jutted into the marina until they reached the Venice Boardwalk.

Back on the leash, Flare strained to explore a new path, but by that time the merchants were beginning to open their stalls and arrange displays of assorted beach gear for the tourists.

Jovanic left to get ready for his appointment with Senator Heidt without suggesting she go with him. Claudia went upstairs and downloaded her e-mail. Fifteen new messages popped up on the monitor. Running her eye down the list, she saw a name that made her heart skip a beat: lindsey6969@pinups.com. The subject line said *be careful*.

Maybe it was true; maybe Lindsey was really alive and playing a horrible practical joke on them all. Thinking that nothing would surprise her anymore, she opened the e-mail.

Chapter 20

The fine hairs rose on the back of Claudia's neck.

Pixel by pixel, a graphic embedded within the e-mail came into view: a white Jaguar parked in a driveway facing a brick-edged garage door that had recently been painted the color of bittersweet chocolate.

Omigod. Omigod.

The edges of the picture were curled and charred, as if someone had held a match to it before scanning it into the computer.

Claudia clicked on the View menu and zoomed the magnification. Long before the figure in the driver's seat became clear, she knew who it was. Someone had snapped a picture of her sitting in her own driveway.

A stranger had watched her; entered her home and her computer; pawed through her things; threatened her security.

"I'm sorry, ma'am. We can't give out a user's name, that's confidential information."

She knew she must have misheard. Her internet provider couldn't be refusing to help her. "What do you mean, *it's confidential*?" she asked, her nerves jumping. "Someone sent me a threatening e-mail! Isn't that against the rules?"

"Yes, ma'am, it is, and we've already closed down the account."

The customer service rep's patronizing manner angered

her almost as much as his refusal to cooperate. "You're telling me I have no recourse?"

"The user opened the account with a fictitious name and false credit card information, ma'am. As soon as the system caught it, the account was closed."

"So I'm basically up shit-fucking-creek?"

"Ma'am, I don't have to listen to . . ."

Claudia slammed the handset back into its base. Her body had gone hot all over and she was short of breath. Too much was happening, too fast. Something evil had oozed into her home along with the mocking e-mail.

"Been seeing a lot of burglaries lately," the locksmith said with a portentous shake of his head as he deftly unscrewed the thirty-year-old doorknob. "Not too many 'round here, though. Usually kids looking for cash, guns. For drugs. Know what I mean?"

Kids on drugs are the least of my worries.

"Just make sure no one can get in, okay?" Claudia urged. "I've ordered a security system, but they can't install it for a couple of days."

"You'll be safer than Fort Knox with these babies," the locksmith said with pride.

At least the new locks should slow down the housebreaker if he returned.

Jovanic arrived shortly after the locksmith's departure.

Staring out the front window, wondering who was behind the assault on Ivan and the incidents in her own home, Claudia watched the Jeep turn into the driveway. Jovanic climbed out, looking stylish in a navy pinstripe suit and dark tie, the grey-flecked hair neatly groomed. He'd dressed up for the Senator.

She closed her eyes and let relief wash over her, thankful that she wasn't in this mess alone. The thought was followed by the loud clanging of alarm bells in her head. She wasn't ready for that level of involvement.

She went downstairs and met him at the door.

"Can I talk you into lunch?" he asked, trading his dead-pan expression for a smile.

Before she could answer, he read her face. "What happened?"

She pulled him inside, unwilling to stand at the front door, where she felt vulnerable and exposed. "You'd better come upstairs and see for yourself."

They went up to the office, where she seated herself at her desk. While Jovanic watched over her shoulder, she rolled the mouse across its rubber pad to turn off the screen saver, and instantly, the graphic threat filled the screen.

"It's the guy who broke in here," Claudia said. "It has to be."

Unspoken words hung in the air like the smell of something rotten: *The guy who assaulted Ivan.*

Jovanic studied the photograph, his brow wrinkled in concentration. "The flash drive you found is in the evidence locker. We still don't know where the tapes are, so unless there's something you haven't told me, they probably didn't find what they were looking for."

"There's nothing else. Unless . . ."

"Unless what?"

She could feel his eyes boring into the back of her head. After the incident with the flash drive she'd probably already lost all credibility. She swiveled her chair and looked up at him.

"Ivan sent me to see Lindsey's brother, Earl Nelson . . . who's really foul, by the way. Ivan thought he might have some of Lindsey's printed writing that I could compare to the suicide note."

"Did he?"

"No. He had some old photos of Lindsey with printing on the backs, but the writing was done too long ago. He demanded money for the photos. Ivan paid."

"What kind of photos would be worth money?"

"Kiddie porn. I wonder if the break-in had anything to do with that?"

Jovanic looked skeptical. "You think this Nelson did

the break-in here? If he sold Ivan the photos, why would he need to retrieve them?"

"I'm grasping at straws." She picked up Nelson's envelope from her desk and offered it to him. "I'll gladly give you the photos."

He flipped through the stack of photographs, his eyes hardening at what he saw, but he offered no comment on them. "I think the video is the key," he said, replacing them in the envelope. "Once we find it, maybe we'll have some answers. Let's get out of here."

Outside, he removed his suit coat and folded it, tossed it onto the back seat of his Jeep. He loosened his tie and laid it on top of the coat. The opening chords of Rachmaninoff's *Rhapsody on a Theme of Paganini* began to play as he fired up the engine.

"I wouldn't have pegged you for a classical buff," Claudia said in surprise.

"Why? Because I'm a guy, or because I'm a cop?" He ejected the disk and put on his best redneck accent as he snapped it into the jewel case. "Aw shucks ma'am, some of us got cultshah."

"I didn't mean it like that. I love Rachmaninoff, and that's one of my favorite pieces."

Jovanic grinned. "Don't get too excited, Garth Brooks is pretty high on my list, too."

They drove down to the Shack, where sawdust covered the floor and the patrons perched on red plastic-covered bar stools at tall tables.

The Shack's cheeseburgers were arguably the best on the West Side, but Claudia chewed hers with little enthusiasm. The gnawing anxiety of the past few days topped off by the break-in and the threatening e-mail had put a damper on her appetite.

"What happened at your meeting with the slimy senator?" she asked in an attempt to distract herself.

Jovanic squeezed a puddle of ketchup onto his plate and dunked a couple of fries. "Whole lot of nothin'. His attorney was glued to his hip. He met Lindsey through some friends and hired her to help with his campaign PR; she was the greatest, yada yada."

"I'm sure he couldn't imagine how his name got on the kinky sex list?"

"There's been a terrible mistake, Detective," Jovanic said in a fair imitation of Senator Heidt's sonorous baritone. "I'm a respectable family man, a devout Christian."

He dropped back into his normal voice. "That's all his attorney would let him say. But, just between us, I snagged this for you." He took a paper from his pocket and handed the folded square to Claudia.

She put down her burger and wiped her fingers on a napkin. "This is his handwriting?" When she opened the paper, it appeared to be the draft of a speech.

"Yeah. Don't ask how I got it."

"I wouldn't dream of it."

It was the handwriting that interested her, not the legalities of how Jovanic had obtained it. Moreover, he was offering a test of her skills. She unfolded the paper.

"Holy shit!" The senator's signature on the sign-in sheet at Lindsey's funeral reception was nothing compared to what she saw here.

Jovanic grinned at her reaction. "That the technical term?"

She glanced up. "It's so ornate! See these hooks and convolutions and twists in the lower loops? It's worse than I imagined."

Jovanic managed to look both interested and wary. "Okay, you got me. Now, would you mind translating?"

"It's dishonest; it's vulgar. What you see is not what you get. He's definitely got perv potential."

"How the hell did you get all that out of *this*?"

"Would you like a quickie basic lesson?"

He folded his arms and gave her a nod and a sly smile. "Sure, I like quickies."

Ignoring the double entendre, she held the paper up in front of him. "Look at the writing as if it were a picture, rather than a bunch of letters and strokes. Look at the way it's arranged on the page, the margins, the spaces between words, lines, letters. Heidt's writing is big, but it's cramped, the words are crowded together. That means he doesn't respect boundaries.

"The style is flamboyant, it's overdone." She pointed with her fingernail. "Look at these oval letters, *o's* and *a's*, for example. They show how clearly the writer communicates.

"The cleaner the ovals, the more up-front and direct he is. When there are little hooks or circles inside them, as we see here, it interferes with clear communication. Look at this stroke . . . it looks like a *v* inside the *o*. People who do this are often liars." She paused and looked straight at him, drawing his eyes to hers to make sure he was listening carefully. "It's dangerous to make assumptions about any one stroke or letter, but in the context of this particular writing, *liar* is a fair assessment."

He took a swig of his Coke and gave her a dubious look. "You get all this out of a few loops?"

She shook her head. "No, I get it from the whole picture. But some of these characteristics are big red flags. See this weird twist in the lower loops? No one *taught* him to make the letter *g* that way. After the circle, the stroke should move down, then back up to the left and finish at the baseline. Heidt puts a twist in the upstroke."

Jovanic looked confused. "You're losing me."

"Everything in handwriting is symbolic. Among other things, lower loops symbolize the drive for food, sex, money. So, when the loops twist around like these do, it means that something is 'off' with his basic drives. They aren't satisfied in the 'standard' ways."

Claudia watched him struggle with the concept. "Don't get me wrong," she added. "I don't mean *everyone* who makes this kind of stroke is a sicko, but combined with all the other negative indicators in *this* handwriting, it's a big red flag."

Jovanic shoved a couple of fries into his mouth and thought about it while he chewed. "It's fascinating, but he won't be convicted based on loops and swirls. We need something tangible. Maybe something to connect him to blackmail. Let's drop in on Miss Brandi. She called right after I left Heidt's office."

"What did she say?"

"She sounded pretty nervous and said she's not seeing anyone."

Claudia laughed. "But that won't stop you, will it, Columbo?"

He smiled at her and she felt her spirits lift. "She lives in Hollywood," he said. "I got her address from the reverse directory."

"God, I hope she has Ivan's tape."

"I hope it's helpful if she does."

Brandi Jones lived in the rear unit of a rundown duplex off Selma in the heart of old Hollywood. In the dusty yard of the front unit, a pair of toddlers in grubby diapers squatted in a dilapidated sandbox long since depleted of sand, pounding on clods of dirt with plastic shovels.

They made their way past a weeping willow that looked as sad as its name, and up the cracked, oil-stained driveway. A spanking-new red Beemer parked next to the rear unit struck a false note.

Jovanic checked his shoulder holster before rapping on the door. "Maybe she got a new pimp," he murmured.

After a lengthy pause, he stepped back from the porch and took a good look around. Bent and broken miniblinds, cranked open, hung crookedly at the windows. The drapes behind them were drawn.

Jovanic returned to the front door and banged on it with the side of his fist until the scrape of a chain lock sounded.

The door cracked open an inch, revealing a bloodshot blue eye. "The fuck you want?" a young female voice demanded.

"Hi, Brandi," Jovanic said in a friendly tone that belied the ferocity of his assault on the door. "I'm Joel. I called you a while ago."

Dirty fingerprints at eye level marked the door. It inched open on a patch of pasty facial skin.

"I tol' ya, I'm not workin' right now." Her voice was slurred, maybe from sleep. Maybe from using. Something about it tickled the edges of Claudia's memory, but it wouldn't come into focus.

Jovanic's six-two form loomed over the girl. He put his hand on the door, leaning on the frame. "We need to talk to you. It won't take long. Can we come in?"

The door started to close. "Get the fuck outta here," the girl mumbled.

Jovanic jammed his shoulder into the doorway, forcing it open. A girl with blonde-tipped black hair stood there, her jaw slack with surprise. A red tattooed heart peeped over the top of her wife-beater T-shirt.

Memory cleared. "Wait a minute," Claudia blurted, pushing in front of Jovanic. "You were the Goth girl at Lindsey's funeral!"

Brandi frowned at her as if trying to recall her face. "Who are you?" she asked with suspicion of one who was no stranger to hard times and bad people.

"I'm a friend of Lindsey's. We need to talk to you."

"I got nothing to say. Go away."

"Wait . . . I heard you talking to your friend. She said Lindsey didn't kill herself, but you thought it was an accident."

The girl's eyes grew round and terrified. "Go away," she whispered hoarsely. "Just go."

Jovanic flipped her his badge. "Brandi, we're not here to hurt you. We need your help."

The girl stared back at him, her pupils dilated to the outer rims of the irises. She crossed thin arms over her flat chest, holding herself with hands that trembled. "I don't know jack. Leave me alone, pleeeeeease."

"I guess you know that Ivan is dead," Jovanic said.

His words struck her like physical blows. Brandi slid down the doorpost and collapsed in a heap on the floor. A high-pitched keening arose from somewhere deep inside her, breaking loose into uncontrollable sobs.

From behind her, a new voice spoke over the wailing; a voice with a faint Caribbean lilt.

"I think I'm smellin' cop."

The door opened wide and Brandi's beaded companion

from the funeral stood there, one hand resting on a curva-
ceous hip. *The woman who had so thoroughly unnerved
Senator Heidt.*

Her name suddenly came back to Claudia.

"Why donchu come on in, officers," Destiny Cardoza
said, tossing her braids with a sassy smirk.

Chapter 21

In her champagne Dana Buchman suit and braided hair, Destiny Cardoza might have been at home in a corporate office, but in Brandi's dump she looked as out of place as perfumed toilet paper in an outhouse. The place reeked of the kind of mustiness that resulted from age and poor housekeeping.

A heavy-duty vacuum might improve the stained, thread-bare rug, Claudia thought as she surveyed the small dark living room and its thriftshop furnishings. She wanted to stride over to the windows and flip open the blinds.

Jovanic showed Destiny his badge. "Detective Joel Jovanic, LAPD."

She turned her sexy smile on him before narrowing her eyes at Claudia. "This is a reunion for you and me, am I right, girlfrien'?"

"Looks that way."

"We're here on a murder investigation," Jovanic began again, but Destiny ignored him, her gaze boring into Claudia as if they were alone in the room.

"Is that what you was doing at that funeral, girlfrien'? Investigatin'?"

Claudia shook her head. "I knew Lindsey a long time ago. The investigation came later, after Ivan was murdered."

Brandi picked herself up off the floor and flung her slim frame onto the sagging couch. Hugging her knees to her boyish chest, she buried her head in her arms, rocking herself like a five-year-old in need of comfort.

The image of a feral cat came to Claudia again, as it had at the funeral, and she sat down near the girl, just close enough to offer contact. "Ivan sent us to see you. He said you have a . . ."

"Brandi," Jovanic interrupted. "We need to talk to you."

Brandi's head snapped up, the mistrustful glare back on her tear-stained face. "I didn't do anything!"

"We're not here to hurt you, Brandi."

"There is nothing for you here," Destiny said coolly before the girl could answer.

Jovanic stepped toward her, a slight hint of menace in the way he used his height and broad shoulders. "Brandi can answer for herself."

The girl cut her eyes at Destiny, but the older woman's expression was one of warning, and she remained silent.

"Listen, Brandi," Claudia spoke in a soft voice, approaching the girl as gently as she would a child. "Ivan told me he wanted to give me some tapes. I don't know where they are, but before he died, he gave me your name, so I figure *you* know."

"Brandi," Jovanic said. "We're not Vice and I don't give a shit how many johns you've serviced, or what you . . ."

"Hah! You think *that* is the problem?" Destiny Cardoza interrupted with a harsh laugh.

"What then?" Claudia asked. "What's on the video?"

"Not what," Destiny said. *"Who."*

"He'll hurt me if I tell," Brandi said in a small voice. She might have been talking about the neighborhood bully.

"Who'll hurt you, Brandi?" Jovanic asked, but the girl kept her face turned down, shaking her head.

How long has she been on her own, selling the only asset she has?

The contrast between the two women's wardrobes, and the condition of the duplex, told Claudia that whatever Lindsey had been paying her, it hadn't come close to what Destiny might earn.

Jovanic crouched in front of the couch, the grey eyes masked. "We can protect you, Brandi. I'll make sure you're okay, I promise."

"What you gonna do, put her in the Witness Protection Program?" Destiny scoffed. "You gonna get her killed, too, dat's what. So, what is it worth to you, dis *video*, mister big-time detective mon?"

Jovanic's jaw hardened, all tough cop now. He rose to his full height and went eye-to-eye with her, his voice chilly enough to make ice cubes. "Lady, what's it worth to *you* to stay out of jail?"

Brandi started wailing again. "Noooo, not jail!"

Destiny swung around and lashed her hand across the girl's cheek, staining the white skin with a bright-red palm print.

Jovanic grabbed Destiny roughly, twisting the fine fabric of her jacket as he jerked her away from the girl on the couch. He gave her a little shove that made her beads swing. "You want me to arrest you right now for assault?"

She stared at him for a moment, her chin jutting defiantly. Then she gave a low laugh. "Give de mon de tape, Brandi. Go on, give it to him."

Brandi looked up at her, petulance marring a face that would have been pretty with a little care and attention. Destiny gave her the slightest nod. If Claudia hadn't been watching so closely, she would have missed it.

The girl pulled herself off the couch. With the enthusiasm of a death-row inmate headed for lethal injection, she led them to a pocket-sized kitchen.

She looked at Destiny, a question on her face. "But, there's nothing . . ."

"Just do what de man say," Destiny interrupted. "Give him de tape."

The refrigerator must have been forty years old. The little door to the freezer section creaked loudly against crusted ice as Brandi reached in and retrieved a plain-wrap ice cream carton. She handed it to Jovanic with a pout.

The label read *Rocky Road*. "What's this?" he asked, frowning.

"Inside."

Jovanic lifted the sticky lid and took out a plastic bag containing a mini digital cassette tape.

Buried Treasure, Claudia thought, remembering a favorite treat from the Good Humor ice cream truck of her childhood. She and her brother would race each other to eat the ice cream off the top and find the plastic toy embedded inside the sugar cone.

Brandi scuffed her foot against the refrigerator door, her eyes suddenly awash with tears. "What are we gonna do now?"

Jovanic had to do a little tango to switch places with her in the cramped kitchen. "Pack up some clothes," he said. "I'll arrange a place for you to stay until this is over."

Going to the sink, he pushed up his shirt sleeves and rinsed the bag under the faucet. He tore off a couple of paper towels from the roll on the countertop, dried off the plastic, and turned to Destiny. "What about you?"

She gave him a look that was halfway between a leer and a grin. "No need you worryin' 'bout me, sugar. I can take care of *my*self just fine."

Brandi, Claudia, and Jovanic drove to the Wilshire Division station, where he handed the girl over to a female officer, with instructions to find her a temporary safe house. If he'd hoped for gratitude, he was disappointed. She slouched off without a backwards glance.

"Think she'll be okay?" Claudia asked as Jovanic steered her into a small interview room that he'd commandeered.

He shrugged and popped the tape into a combination TV/VCR that stood on a side table. "We can protect her for now. After that, it's up to her."

The only other furniture in the room was a plain grey metal table bolted to the floor and two chairs, one facing a two-way mirror. Claudia took the other one and unpacked the coffees they'd picked up from Starbucks on the way in. She pushed one across the table and pried the lid off hers, blowing gently into the cup while Jovanic fiddled with the controls.

He glanced at her over his shoulder with the raised brow. "You sure you're over eighteen? This show is likely to be triple-X."

She showed him the tip of her tongue, getting into the banter. "If anyone asks, I'll just say you're a dirty old man trying to seduce me."

He turned back to the player with a quiet chuckle.

After a few seconds of static the screen went blank, then Brandi, unfamiliar in blonde pigtails, was mugging for the camera in a parochial school uniform with a skirt short enough to show off her white lace panties. Black patent Mary Jane shoes completed the outfit. With her small breasts and slim body, she could have passed for a ten-year-old, if it hadn't been for the world-weary eyes in the young face.

She climbed onto a wrought iron-framed bed like the one in the photos Earl Nelson had sold Claudia, and began jumping up and down, playing trampoline.

"What the hell?" Claudia said. From the background came a raspy male voice that she'd heard before.

"Hey, knock it off and lay your ass down. I gotta get the lighting right."

Earl Nelson.

The girl laughed and threw herself onto her back, spreading her knees wide, mocking him.

"Goddamn it, Brandi, he's not your fucking gynecologist."

A chill ran through Claudia. "That's Lindsey," she breathed.

There was something eerie about watching the subject of their investigation step in front of the camera. Skintight jeans clung to long, slender legs, and she wore a sleeveless shirt that showed off her tanned arms. An untidy mass of blonde hair tumbled over her shoulders as she strode over to the bed and whacked Brandi on the leg.

"Come on, get serious. He'll be here in an hour. I want everything set up and ready."

"Yeah," Earl Nelson called from behind the camera. "Get that cute little ass in gear."

Lindsey whirled on him, her lip curled derisively. "Shut up, dumbshit. You're only here to operate the camera. Don't forget it."

The screen went black for a moment, and Claudia wondered about the exchange between the siblings. Had one of them become violent? Earl was resentful that he had been cut out of Lindsey's will. Had he known before her death that he was to be disinherited? Or could his resentment have triggered her murder?

The picture flickered back on.

Destiny, in a black leather bustier laced in front with a leather thong. She turned and gazed into the camera lens through half-closed eyes, running her tongue slowly over seductively parted full red lips. Her legs were encased in polished black boots that ended at mid-thigh. The exposed areas of her amber skin glistened with oil.

The camera zoomed out to reveal a naked man spread-eagled, handcuffed to the headboard and footboard of the bed, his head and face concealed by a leather hood. A zipper had been left open across the lower section to allow him to breathe. Clamped between his teeth was a rubber bit.

"That makes me want to throw up," Claudia exclaimed.

Jovanic banged his fist on the desk in frustration. "Shit, we can't ID him from that."

"I bet that's Senator Heidt. It's his build."

"That won't cut it with the DA. Maybe if he had a tattoo on his . . ." Jovanic broke off, a dull red flushing his cheeks.

Claudia laughed, surprised at his embarrassment. "Don't mind your language on my account, Columbo. You can say 'dick.' "

"Jee-eez, Claudia, do you always talk like a sailor?"

She returned her attention to the monitor, where Destiny Cardoza was slowly screwing nipple clamps onto her squealing client.

Claudia winced. "I can't believe he actually paid for that."

"Pleasure and pain, it's all the same," Jovanic said, pointing the remote at the television. He fast-fowarded through the bondage session, stopping, finally, at a frame that showed Destiny loosening her client's bonds.

He hit Play, and they watched Destiny help the man sit up

on the edge of the bed. Brandi pranced over and straddled his lap. She pulled off the hood, but her body blocked the camera's view of their client's face. The tape ended here.

With a fed up sigh, Jovanic hit Rewind and leaned back in his chair. "That might be Heidt on the tape, but even if we could prove it, it doesn't mean he had anything to do with Lindsey's death, or Ivan's, either."

"The girls can testify it's him, can't they?"

"A couple of call girls against the kind of lawyers his money can buy? Who would *you* believe? Anyway, this tape doesn't connect him to murder or blackmail."

"What about his finances? He must have paid Lindsey a ton of money."

"We'll be looking into that."

"Do you think this is the tape Ivan wanted us to have?"

Jovanic shook his head. "Doesn't make sense. It doesn't incriminate anyone." He dug a fresh toothpick from his pocket and unwrapped it. "Lindsey's assets listed a house in Palm Springs. With Ivan dead, I need to find out who the legal owner is."

"Palm Springs?" Claudia sucked in a sharp breath. "That note on Lindsey's calendar said *'Remind Bos—Blue Heaven—PS.'* Holy shit! Do you think she was meeting with Bostwick in Palm Springs?"

Jovanic contemplated it, his mouth twisting thoughtfully as he crumpled the plastic toothpick wrapper and dropped it into his empty coffee cup. "Maybe. You could be onto something."

"I could go out there and look around," she offered. "If you can get the keys to the place."

He eyed her curiously. "You like to live dangerously, don't you? We don't know what's out there. We might need a search warrant. In fact, I'll get the paperwork started before . . ."

He trailed off, his face a blank, hiding his thoughts. Claudia didn't know him well enough to guess.

The small room was silent as he rewound the tape, then replaced it in its box and slipped it into an evidence bag.

"What aren't you saying?" Claudia asked when it became too uncomfortable to let it go any longer.

"What do you mean?"

"I'm an analyst. I analyze people. I think there's something you need to say."

"Damn, you're good." There was a hesitation before he blurted, "I've gotta go away tonight. I'm going to Phoenix on another case."

Claudia's heart sank. Just when she'd begun to feel safe, the rug was being pulled out from under her. He kept talking, as if filling the gap with words would somehow make it okay for him to leave when she felt so vulnerable.

"We'll be in touch by phone. I'd feel better if I could keep an eye on things myself, but I don't have a choice. Something's breaking and I have to be there." He toyed with his trash, crushing the paper cup, straightening it out. "Is there someplace you can stay until I get back, or can you get someone to stay with you?"

"I don't need anyone to stay with me, and I'm sure as hell not letting some scumbag force me out of my own home." Her attempt to keep the letdown out of her voice made her sound truculent. She tried again, softening her tone. "Look, Joel, whoever this guy is, he knows the police are involved; he's not coming back. You said so yourself, he can't get in with the new locks, and I'm getting an alarm system."

Jovanic scowled. "Come on, Claudia, we're not dealing with some street punk here. This asshole broke into your house. He's probably killed twice already. We know he's been watching you . . . he photographed you, for Christ's sake! He threatened you by e-mail. What more do you want, a fucking gun in your face?"

Why was she arguing with Jovanic? He was right. She knew she would be jumpy alone in the house. But something kept her fueling the debate. Her privacy had been violated by the intruder, but she was drawing the line at letting some anonymous criminal steal her independence, too.

She rose from her chair and reached for the empty coffee cups. "I have a business to run. I get handwriting samples almost every day. All my equipment is at my house."

"You have a laptop computer you could use, don't you?" he said, his voice tight. "Why are you being so stubborn?"

She shook her head decisively. "I'm not leaving my house."

A muscle jumped in his cheek. "Hey, you're a big girl and I'm not your keeper. If you want to stay alone, stay alone."

Chapter 22

The next few days passed quietly. No more threatening e-mails. No strange vans parked outside. No further break-in attempts when Claudia left the house to run errands. Life started to slip back into its familiar routine. She could even go fifteen minutes without thinking about Jovanic.

The days were spent analyzing handwriting samples for clients, the evenings watching the news, chatting with Kelly or Zebediah on the phone, and catching up on the pile of professional journals she'd been neglecting. First thing Monday morning, she would ship Lindsey's boxes to Jovanic's office.

By the time Saturday rolled around, the case and the upsetting events attached to it had begun to recede comfortably into the background. The loud knocking at her front door late in the evening shook the foundations of her newfound complacency like an earthquake.

A shakeup that was compounded when the unwelcome presence of Earl Nelson met her gaze through the peephole. How had he come by her home address?

Claudia's heart was still thumping unpleasantly as she yelled through the door. "What do you want?"

"Open up." Nelson rapped urgently. "Come on, open it."

"Yeah, I don't think so."

"You have to, lady, I got somethin' for ya. Come on!" He held up a manila envelope so she could see it. "You'll wanna see this."

Claudia stared at the closed door, asking herself how stupid she would be to open it to him. She had already discarded the notion that Nelson had anything to do with Lindsey's death. For him, it would have been a case of killing the golden goose, and she couldn't see him doing that, nor being clever enough to set it up to look like suicide.

Almost without consciously making the decision, she unlocked the deadbolt and opened the door a crack, ready to slam it if he tried anything. He was still as smelly as he had been the day she visited his apartment. She breathed through her mouth to avoid having to inhale the musty miasma of drugs and alcohol that oozed from his pores.

"What is it you want?" she asked sharply.

"You gonna let me in?"

"No."

Nelson held up the five-by-eight manila envelope and waved it at her. "I heard you was lookin' for a tape."

Destiny must have told him about the visit Claudia and Jovanic had paid Brandi.

"I told you before, what I'm interested in is Lindsey's handwriting."

Nelson snickered. "I gave you what I got. But this tape . . . you're gonna want it. Mr. High-and-Mighty himself threatening to put a hit on me."

"Who're you talking about?"

"I figure you already know."

"If you're here to waste my time, I'm shutting the door." She started to follow through on her threat, but Nelson stuck his foot in the opening, stopping it.

"Who ya think it is? Mr. U.S. Senator, our biggest customer. I told him how it was, now little sister's out of the picture. *I'm* the man."

Claudia rolled her eyes. "Oh, I get it. You told him you planned to continue blackmailing him, and you thought he'd be fine with that?"

Nelson shrugged. "Hey, it's an insurance policy. Protect him from public embarrassment."

"And he's threatening you on this tape? Why bring it to me?"

"It's *my* insurance. There'll be someone else who knows."

"I guess you can't very well call the police with that story, can you? Okay, give it to me." Claudia reached through the opening in the door to take the envelope, but Nelson snatched his hand back.

"This ain't a bunch of baby pictures, lady. This is *gold*. A measly thousand bucks won't cut it this time. Whaddya say?"

Fury rose in her throat like hot acid. As far as she was concerned, even though he might not directly have caused his sister's death, he was every bit as responsible as the killer.

"What do I *say?* I say get the *fuck* off my porch before I call the cops." Without another word, she slammed the door in his face. She could still hear him.

"Lady, you don't know what you're doing! Come on lady, it's your last chance. *Hey, lady?*"

Then, next evening, a phone call out of left field.
Unknown caller.
Nursing a small hope that it would be Jovanic, Claudia picked up the handset. He had been deafeningly silent and the silence rankled. But it was the mocking voice of Destiny Cardoza that quickly shredded the safe little cocoon in which Claudia had wrapped herself.

"How did you like the *tape* we give you girlfrien'?"

Her throaty laugh stung, but Claudia kept her voice casual, not allowing the other woman the satisfaction of knowing that she was riled. "Where'd you get my phone number?"

"You are not the only *one* playing detective. It is not so *hard* to find you."

"What do you want, Destiny?"

"Listen, girlfrien', I *need* to see you." The Jamaican accent thickened as she spoke.

"Why didn't you give us the tape Ivan wanted us to have?"

"Why would we give something to de cops that somebody else is willing to pay plenty for?"

Claudia drummed her fingers on the desk impatiently. Everyone was trying to sell her something, but no one was offering what she really needed—a good sample of hand printing done by Lindsey as an adult. She brought her attention back to her caller.

"Destiny, you're playing with fire. The guy on the tape is a dangerous sonofabitch." Jovanic's warning buzzed in her head. She had ignored it herself. How could she expect Destiny to listen?

But the other woman surprised her.

"I *have* been thinking a lot," Destiny said. Despite her jaunty manner, a thin edge of fear sliced through her words. The kind of fear not easily faked. "I have sometin' to give you."

Suspicion sharpened Claudia's tone. "What changed your mind?"

"Hidin' out in my apartment all *these* days, thinkin' about every*t'in'*, it made me feel all disheveled. Dat is not an enjoyful *feelin'*."

"Why don't you call Detective Jovanic?"

"You t'ink I want to deal with *cops?*"

"Where are the tapes Ivan told me about?"

"In *Palm* Springs, at de house." A pause. "I *don'* want to talk on de phone. Meet me at de Grove, by de Farmer's Market on Fairfax."

Claudia hesitated. No way in hell did she trust the other woman to be straight with her. But if Destiny was willing to part with evidence that incriminated Heidt or another of Lindsey's clients, and she could get hold of it, she would succeed where Jovanic had failed.

She glanced at her watch. Ten-thirty. "Where are you now?"

"Hollywood, near de *Magic* Castle. I will meet you at de fountain in de Grove at quarter to twelve."

Claudia replaced the phone in its cradle, wondering whether she was about to make a monumental mistake. What if Destiny were setting her up with this phone call, using her promise of evidence as bait?

*   *   *

She made it forty minutes early, shunning the parking structure to park the Jag a half-block down the street behind a big black Ford Expedition. The SUV provided a shield, but still allowed a clear view of the entrance to The Grove, the trendy open-air shopping mall in the heart of Los Angeles, next to the old Farmer's Market landmark.

Cutting the engine, Claudia slid down low in her seat. *Like a cop on surveillance,* she thought with a secret smile. She'd dated a PI a few times, keeping him company when he needed to serve a summons on someone hell-bent on avoiding it. Her company made the endless dreary hours more bearable, he'd said. She'd kept him awake when even hi-test mocha no longer did the trick and the need for sleep had grown from a vague threat into a scream.

Tonight, staying awake was not a problem for Claudia. Adrenaline rushed through her veins until she drummed her fists on the steering wheel to dissipate the excess energy. She stuck her hand in her pocket and stroked the nasty little folding baton with which she had armed herself. She'd never had occasion to use it, but its presence gave her a sense of security. The PI had given it to her one night when they'd gone to a particularly unsavory neighborhood. It was illegal for a civilian to carry one, but who was going to tell?

Despite the lateness of the hour, Fairfax Avenue teemed with vehicles in both directions and garish neon signs lit up the night. Still, the lipstick-red Beemer was hard to miss. When it slowed at the parking lot next to the CBS television studios, preparing to make the turn, Claudia slumped lower in her seat.

An arm reached from the driver's side window to take a ticket from the machine. At the lot entrance, a streetlight shone brightly on the car, outlining Destiny's statuesque profile in the driver's seat. She appeared to be alone. The gate arm rose, then fell behind her.

Claudia started up the engine and pulled into traffic, drove around the block, and found a place to park in the bank lot next to The Grove. She might be on a fool's errand, but crossing Fairfax on foot near midnight would be more dangerous than any trick Destiny might have up her sleeve.

She found Destiny standing in front of the eighteen-foot high *Spirit of Los Angeles* statue at the entrance to The Grove.

"You look like Catwoman," Claudia said, admiring the way the skintight black jumpsuit and high-heeled boots clung to the other woman. It was no surprise that men were willing to pay big bucks for her services; she exuded sexuality. "So, what is it you have for me?"

Destiny's eyes darted this way and that, intensifying the impression of a feline on the prowl. She unzipped the front of her jumpsuit and reached inside, taking out a small envelope. "Lin'sey's brother send me sometin'. He got scared."

"Earl Nelson? He came to my house the other night and tried to sell me a videotape."

"Well, sometin' got him *scared* bad. He call me and say he is leaving town, and he will mail me sometin'. This was in *my* mailbox today." She shook something from the envelope and stretched out her palm, showing Claudia a flat metal locker key.

Claudia frowned at her, puzzled. "What's this for?"

"I t'ink it is a locker combination." Destiny slid a scrap of paper from the envelope, on which was written a number: *AA243, 65843 - LAX.* "He put de tape he tell you about. At de airport."

"Why give this to me?"

"Lin'sey brother is *big* trouble," Destiny said, and her voice was strained with anxiety. "But I got dis feeling sometin' bad has happen. You give dis key to de cop. Maybe he will know *what* to do with it."

"Blackmail is a dangerous business," Claudia said, dropping the key and the combination into her jeans pocket. "Earl said he had the Senator on tape, threatening him."

Destiny shuddered. "Girlfriend, you got no *i*dea of his power. Lindsey thought she be safe, but *she* is dead now."

"You think the senator had her killed?"

"What *else* can I t'ink? Listen to me, girlfrien', I don' want him comin' *after* me." Destiny wiped her hands together, a symbolic cleansing. "If you can stop him, de better for me. But I tell you one t'ing: I will not be hangin' around, waitin'."

Suddenly, Destiny stiffened and swung around. Claudia had heard nothing, but she saw a stocky figure slip out of the shadows at the side of the building and come toward them at a run.

His face was covered by a leather hood like the one worn by Lindsey's client on the videotape. But this one had eye holes, and the eyes that burned through them were flat black disks. He wore baggy khaki work pants, slung low over his hips, and a black T-shirt.

"Move and you're dead meat," he hissed, swinging a pistol back and forth, covering them both. Claudia had no idea what make the gun was, nor what bore. It just looked big and black, and the barrel was pointed at her chest. "Where's the fuckin' video? Tell me where it is, and you can go home, nice and safe."

Safe like Lindsey? Safe like Ivan?

Claudia stared at his hands. Even in the low light of the street lamp she could see that they were covered in dark curly hair that reached almost to his knuckles. Clutching her purse tight under her arm, she stole a glance at Destiny, who had recovered and was trying to cajole him.

"Come on, sugar. You don' need a gun. Let us *talk* about money. We can work together. I *can* give you whatever you want."

Through the open zipper the man's lips twisted. "Forget it, bitch, I'm already getting paid plenty for this job. Just tell me where the tape is."

"We do *not* have what you want."

Keeping her eyes fastened on the gun, Claudia edged her hand into her pocket. Her fingers curled around cold steel. Maybe with his attention on Destiny, she could . . .

Sensing her movement, the man pointed his weapon at her face. "Hey, what the fuck!"

The momentary distraction was all Destiny needed. Moving faster than Claudia could visually track, she landed a vicious kick on the man's weapon arm, knocking his elbow upward. The gun crashed to the sidewalk. Destiny swept around in a half-circle, kicked again, catching the back of his knee. His feet went out from under him and he went down, grabbing for her leg.

Claudia whipped out the baton and snapped it open to its full, lethal length. She smashed it against the man's forearm, heard the sickening crack of metal meeting bone. But his first scream of pain was no match for the second as she drove the end of the club into his groin.

Destiny snatched the gun up from the ground and started to run in the direction of the parking garage. Abruptly, she stopped and swung around. Returning to the man, who was dragging himself up, groaning, she delivered a savage kick to his head. Soundlessly, he hit the sidewalk, unconscious.

"Was that necessary?" Claudia asked, feeling slightly sick from the sound of boot meeting flesh.

"At the *dojo*," said Destiny with a touch of pride, "we are taught to *leave* an attacker incapacitated."

Claudia strode over to the prone figure on the ground. She leaned down and gingerly tugged off the hood. Olive complexion, black hair, a broad, flat nose. She pegged him as being of middle eastern descent.

"Do you recognize him?" she asked Destiny.

Destiny nodded, her features taut with fear. "I have seen him. He is one of de senator's cleanup *boys*. I do not know his name."

Claudia began to punch numbers on her cell phone.

"What are you doing? *No* cops!"

"What are you talking about? Of course we have to call them."

"Hey!" The voice came from the avenue that separated The Grove shops. "Hey! Stop!" One of the green-jacketed Grove guards was coming toward them.

Destiny spun around and made a beeline for the parking garage.

Instinctively, Claudia ran, too. As she fired up the Jag and hit the road, she saw the red BMW race up the ramp and out onto Fairfax toward Third Street.

Driving away from the scene, she asked herself why she had run, as if it were she and Destiny who had done something wrong, when they were simply defending themselves against an attacker. She knew she should have stayed and made a police report, but would the police have believed her?

The adrenaline rush began to ebb as reality set in, leaving her insides quivering like a bowl of jelly. She had no doubt that the man would have killed both her and Destiny if they hadn't rushed him like a pair of Charlie's Angels.

Chapter 23

"Look, darling, you're an anonymous celebrity."

Zebediah Gold, clad only in a pair of white tennis shorts, a curly thatch of graying hair sprouting from his chest, thrust the newspaper at Claudia as she entered the tiny kitchen, rubbing her hair with a towel. "You've made the front page again."

She had called him after leaving The Grove, and asked to spend the night. A long time had passed since they'd been lovers, but he was always there when she needed a friend, and after the experience she'd just had, she was more than willing to follow Jovanic's suggestion to stay away from home.

She took the newspaper from him, wrinkling her nose at the black liquid in the carafe on the Mr. Coffee. "What is this stuff? Looks like mud."

"So don't drink it. God, I don't know why I put up with you!"

Claudia ignored him and scanned the article, reading parts aloud.

"Two women, caught on surveillance cameras, left the scene after an apparent mugging. The male victim, who was unidentified, also left the scene before police arrived." Claudia put down the paper and stared at Zebediah in amazement. "Oh my God, they think *we* mugged *him!* And he got away, too."

Zebediah rolled his eyes in disgust. "You know the media. When things aren't exciting enough, they make it up."

She dropped into one of the two chairs at the table and jabbed her finger against the newsprint. "If it's on camera, they can see he attacked us. *Shit!* And I left my baton there, too. *Shit!*"

With an uncomfortable sense of a noose tightening around her neck, Claudia produced the key Destiny had given her. She'd been too overwrought to give it any attention the night before. She showed it to Zebediah.

"I'll have to give this to the cops. I hope they can find the locker. LAX is a big place." She stirred sugar into her coffee thoughtfully. "Nelson said he got the senator on tape. And of course, he secretly taped the bondage sessions."

"Kinky sex isn't illegal, dearest."

"But blackmail is," she reminded him. "And blackmail provides a motive for murder. You can bet our sanctimonious senator wouldn't want this stuff to get out."

"Oh, I don't know; might help his next campaign."

"This is serious, Zeb. He obviously believes that Destiny or I have the tapes of him, and he's going to do whatever he has to, to get it back. She's probably in Jamaica by now."

Zebediah took off his glasses and rinsed them under the kitchen faucet. He sat down at the table, leveling his gaze at Claudia as he blotted them dry with a paper towel. "Do you realize you could be in trouble with the police for leaving The Grove without giving a statement?"

"Yes, Zeb, I do know that. When Destiny took off, I lost my head and ran, too."

"What about that detective you've got the hots for? He surely can help you with that?"

"He went to Phoenix last week and I haven't heard from him. I don't even know when he'll be back." Claudia stumbled, heat rising in her face. She looked away, uncomfortable with the feelings that thoughts of Jovanic brought up in her, not ready to put them into words.

Zebediah shot her a knowing look. "Don't tell me you've already pissed him off?"

"What are you, a psychologist? What makes you think he's pissed off?"

"I'm psychic, too." His brow curved into a stern arch. "What did you do to the poor fellow?"

She shifted uncomfortably in her chair. "Nothing! He didn't want me to stay at my house while he was gone."

"Ahhh, and you, my independent friend, said no, which made him feel you were rejecting his efforts to protect you."

"If you say so. Then, when Destiny called, I thought I could help by getting the evidence from her." Claudia couldn't suppress a nervous giggle. Well, *destiny* had called all right, and she had answered.

Zebediah had known her far too long and refused to be diverted. "You mean you thought you would win if *you* got what this woman had, rather than handing it right over to the cops."

"Okay, fine. I probably shouldn't have gone to meet her, and Joel's going to find out about it." Claudia made a face at him and poured an extra-heavy dose of creamer into her coffee. "It was all over with him before it began, anyway."

"Are you sure about that?"

She was saved from having to answer by several notes of a Bach fugue playing. "Is that your purse ringing?" Zebediah asked as Claudia reached for her cell phone.

"You had to start without me?" Jovanic's voice instantly set her heart thudding.

"Bad news travels fast," she said. "How did you . . ."

"I saw the news, recognized you and Destiny. Dammit, Claudia! I've been calling your house, you didn't answer your cell."

"My phone was turned off and I stayed over at a friend's last night. Like you suggested."

"Kelly?"

"No, another friend." There was a long moment of silence while the unasked question hung between them. She felt him wondering who the friend was.

Let him sweat.

"Looks like you kicked some serious ass," he said when she didn't offer any further explanation. "A broken arm *and* busted his nuts. They even showed the surveillance tape on Phoenix TV. How's it feel to be a fugitive?"

She couldn't keep the grin off her face, suddenly confident that he would fix it for her. "That jerk will probably need at least a couple of ice packs today."

"Remind me not to piss you off," Jovanic said.

"Too late. But I left my baton at the scene, so you're safe."

"I'll get it back for you."

"Is that a peace offering?"

She heard him sigh. "Yeah, Claudia, a peace offering. What are you offering in return?"

"The location of the real videotape and a key."

"Don't say anything else," he said quickly. "Cell phones are too risky. I'm flying back tonight on Southwest. Can you meet me at LAX?"

Chapter 24

If the amount of junk mail that ended up at Claudia's house were any indication, the rain forest was in bigger trouble than anyone knew. In the batch she picked up from the post office on the way home from Zebediah's house, the only mail that interested her was a letter from her mother (who steadfastly refused to learn how to use e-mail) and a small envelope, her name and address splashed across the front in calligraphic script.

The envelope contained an invitation. Martin and Lillian Grainger requested the pleasure of her company at a Halloween party aboard their yacht for an evening cruise two weeks hence. Claudia had forgotten about the party, but now she remembered that Lillian Grainger had mentioned it at their first meeting.

Tucked in with the RSVP card was a handwritten note from Lillian, urging Claudia to come to the party and bring a date. The handwriting was pure Palmer copybook. *I*'s perfectly dotted, *t*'s crossed precisely mid-stem. The only distinguishing feature was the overblown lower loops on the letter *f*, which was an expression of physical urges.

Claudia grinned to herself, remembering Kelly's remark about the size of Martin Grainger's sexual apparatus. Considering the uptightness that the handwriting revealed, those *f*'s suggested Lillian had found an outlet for her pent-up drives.

The party invitation followed the junk mail into the trashcan under the desk. Partying with the rich and famous might have excited Lindsey, but Claudia couldn't care less.

Halfway through a cup of strawberry yogurt, she remembered that Senator Heidt was on the guest list, and reconsidered. Deciding that an opportunity for some gentle interrogation of the senator was too good to pass up, she retrieved the invitation. She would ask Jovanic to be her date, and find costumes that would conceal their identities. In a party setting, Heidt wouldn't be suspicious.

She began to imagine how she might elicit a confession from someone whose proclivities stretched to S&M, when an unexpected phone call jolted her out of her fantasy.

"Ms. Rose, this is Doctor Bostwick."

The doctor's tone was entirely different than it had been at their in-person visit. More formal; charm without the arrogance. "I have some information I'd like to pass along that I believe might be helpful to your investigation."

Your investigation. He thought she was Jovanic's partner.

Bostwick cleared his throat. "Er, I'd like to apologize for my abruptness the other day. The confidentiality issue. Please understand, as a plastic surgeon, I get patients who aren't entirely realistic in their expectations. They think I can make them young and beautiful and usually I can, of course, but I can only work with what I've got, and, well, occasionally there are lawsuits and I've learned to be . . . shall we say, *circumspect,* when it comes to legal matters."

"Did Lindsey threaten a lawsuit, doctor?"

"Well, no; I was just explaining why I felt upset with the police showing up. I mean, surely, you have to agree that your partner was damned offensive."

So that's why he had called her. He thought she was a softer touch than Jovanic. She kept her voice neutral. "You said you have some information?"

"Yes, yes; I thought it might be important." He hesitated. "I was thinking about my contacts with Ms. Alexander, and I recollected a conversation we had the week before her death. She told me she wanted the eyelid lifts done because she had someone new in her life . . . a younger man she was serious about. She . . . she wanted to impress him."

Claudia's interest accelerated, but she kept her tone casual. "Do you have a name for this mystery man?"

"She never mentioned him by name, but there must be phone records or some such. You can look that up, can't you? *That's* who you need to find."

"Why's that, doctor?"

"Obviously, he could be the killer." He was sounding desperate.

Claudia rocked back in her chair, glad he couldn't see her Cheshire Cat smile. "Lindsey's death was ruled suicide. What makes you think there was a killer?"

Too late, Bostwick realized his error. "But . . . but isn't that why you came to my office? That detective implied there was something irregular about her death." Panic raised Bostwick's voice to a near-squeak. "Ms. Rose, is her death suspicious or not? I can't afford to have my name dragged through the mud."

"Sorry, doctor," she said. "That's something you'll have to take up with Detective Jovanic. I'll give him your message. In the meantime, if you think of anything else that might be helpful, you know where to reach me."

How *did* he know how to reach her?

She rang off without saying goodbye. And without confessing that she wasn't officially involved in the law enforcement aspect of the case. He wouldn't be interested in talking to her if he knew she had no clout, and it seemed a sure bet that Bostwick was doing his best to divert suspicion from himself. But was it because he really had something to do with Lindsey's death, or because of the sexual implications? She wished she knew.

In the early evening, too restless to work, Claudia searched her closet for something to wear when she picked up Jovanic, settling on an outfit midway between sexy and businesslike: a black knit top with a deep V-neck that she hadn't worn yet; silky slacks and jacket. A skirt would have been better, but was too dressy for a quick trip to LAX.

She hooked a pair of gold hoops in her ears, brushed on blush and mascara, applied a light lipstick, and surveyed herself critically in the cheval mirror in the corner of her room.

Not bad.

LAX was just a ten-minute drive down Valle del Mar. Claudia cruised into the Southwest terminal pickup lane just as Jovanic's plane was scheduled for arrival, and parked at the curb to wait for him. As she watched several flights take off, she couldn't help thinking of Destiny Cardoza and the near miss they'd had at The Grove the night before. Destiny was probably sipping piña coladas on a beach in Jamaica by now. What had happened to their assailant? Claudia wondered. He must surely have sought medical attention for the injuries they had left him with.

Jovanic was among the first group of passengers to come through the baggage claim doors, a suit bag slung over his shoulder. His slightly rumpled look was already endearingly familiar. A better-tailored, taller Columbo. He stood on the sidewalk, looking around.

When he saw Claudia's wave, his face lit up for an instant. She might have thought she'd imagined it if she hadn't been watching so closely for his reaction.

Just having him back made her feel safer. "How did your trip work out?" she asked.

"Pretty well." He ran a hand through his short-cropped tawny brown hair, leaving a few tufts sticking up. "But I hate flying; you're at the pilot's mercy."

"You don't like not being in control, do you?"

He flipped her a glance, brow arching. "You psychoanalyzing me, grapho lady?"

She grinned back at him. "Your handwriting is mostly block-capital printing, which suggests control issues. I'm just extrapolating that to air travel."

"Well, I don't like being analyzed." The words were curt, but he didn't sound serious and her step lightened as she went around to the passenger side and offered Jovanic the driver's seat.

"So, you want to know about the new evidence?" she asked as he slipped behind the wheel and started the motor.

"Go ahead. I can see you're dying to tell me."

They drove through the parking booth and Claudia filled him in on Earl Nelson's visit and her adventures with Destiny.

"Ivan's tape is in Palm Springs," she finished. "The key belongs somewhere here, at LAX."

"Where's this key now?" Jovanic asked, making the turn into traffic and driving north on Sepulveda Boulevard.

"Locked in my safe at home."

He threw her a sidelong glance. "I must not have been clear when I gave you the 'tampering-with-evidence' lecture. Now you're *withholding* evidence, too? You don't take the law very seriously, do you?"

"Yes I do, honest." She gave him what she hoped was a winning smile, thinking, *God, he's attractive.* "I'm trying to distract you so you won't take me to jail."

"I should," he said, shaking his head. "I really should."

Claudia unlocked the deadbolt and disarmed the alarm, all the while grousing about living in a fortress.

"Welcome to LA," Jovanic said, following her into the kitchen. He came up behind her, until they were almost touching. She stood very still, catching the faint scent of his aftershave—*Eternity,* she thought. He was so close, and she was suddenly aware of how much she wanted him.

Then he stepped back and the moment was gone.

Why hadn't he seized the opportunity to kiss her when she knew he'd wanted to? Well, she hadn't seized it, either. She got two glasses from the cabinet and a bottle of Merlot she'd bought on the way home from Zebediah's, giving Jovanic a questioning look. "Glass of wine?"

He accepted and she handed him the corkscrew and bottle. "You any good at this? I'm not. Do you think Earl's tape will be enough to arrest Heidt?"

Jovanic shrugged. "We don't know what's on it yet. I doubt it's proof that he had anyone killed, *or* that he sent anyone over here to break in. We don't even have proof that Lindsey didn't kill herself."

Claudia thought of the note Ivan had hired her to analyze. *"It was fun while it lasted."* Lindsey's philosophy of life.

"I'm thinking out loud," she said, leading him back to the living room. "Let's assume Lindsey *was* murdered. Maybe the killer forced her to write the note."

"Was there any evidence of coercion?"

She pondered that for a long moment. "Mmm, not really."

"So, what do you think?"

"I'm still looking for good comparison writings. Nothing so far disputes that it *is* her handwriting." She gestured at Lindsey's stack of boxes in a corner of the room.

"We need to tie a suspect to Lindsey the night she died, as well as to Ivan, and to the break-in here. That takes means, motive, and opportunity. We haven't found any hard evidence against Senator Heidt or anyone else. It's time to go to Palm Springs." Jovanic fiddled with unwrapping a toothpick, as if he were conflicted between the polite amenities and comfort. "Feel like taking a ride out to the desert?"

Claudia answered without hesitation. "Absolutely."

"Good. We'll head out first thing in the morning."

They sat on the couch, lamps turned low, reviewing the case and talking desultorily, drinking wine, the stereo providing mood music in the background. Rod Stewart's *Great American Songbook* gave way to *Billy Joel's Greatest Hits,* then a sensuous sax disc.

Finally, the music ended. The conversation ran down, too, until the only sound was the ocean sighing through the half-open balcony door.

Claudia leaned her head back against the cushions, viewing Jovanic through half-closed eyes. The wine was making her drowsy and she wasn't sure what he expected, if anything.

"Uh . . . we're getting an early start, you've got your travel gear here . . ." She broke off, embarrassed in case she had completely misread him.

Jovanic sat forward, reaching for her hands and enclosing them in his. A warm tingle ran all the way up her arms. He cleared his throat awkwardly.

"We don't know each other very well yet, but I think you know that I like you a lot, Claudia. I just have to warn you, my work is pretty much my life. It's hard on a relationship." He released her hands and sat back, staring at the floor, chewing on his lower lip. "You know that my marriage didn't work out. Well, I walked in on my wife and found her in the shower with my best friend. How's that for a cliché? Sleeping together while I was out protecting and defending." Flint hardened his voice. "I was gonna kill them both . . . actually had the gun in my hand. I wanted to. God, I wanted to. But when I saw her eyes, I couldn't do it. She was terrified."

His sigh weighed a ton. The weight of guilt. "It was my fault and I knew it. I left her alone too much, she got lonely. But I couldn't forgive her, so . . . I got a divorce instead of twenty to life."

Claudia felt a pang of sympathy, he looked so bereft. "Don't be so hard on yourself. My ex played second fiddle to my work, too. He stuck it out for nearly five years, then he found someone who was happy to just cook and clean house for him. Nothing wrong with that, but it wasn't for me."

It felt like a confession.

"So, I'm gun-shy myself," she added, reaching out to touch her fingertips to his cheek, rough with a day's growth of beard.

Jovanic turned his face and kissed her palm. He smiled, a tiny flame of hope flickering in his eyes. "So, we'll have to tread lightly."

He stood up, reached down and drew her up, folded her into his arms. She rested her head against his chest and felt his accelerating heartbeat. He stroked her hair, her face, her neck, let his fingertips travel lightly over her breast, searing her skin through the fabric. Her breathing quickened, her body responding instantly as his hands reached her hips and pressed her against him.

Chapter 25

Moonlight poured through the half-open blinds, casting long shadows across the bedroom. Claudia rolled over and squinted at the red numbers glowing on the digital clock on her nightstand.

Three-thirty.

She couldn't have slept for more than a half-hour, but something had awakened her. Beside her, Jovanic's breathing came deep and steady.

Unfamiliar.

Maybe that was it. She smiled to herself in the darkness. They'd made love for hours, at first tentatively exploring, leisurely acquainting themselves with each other until passion had finally consumed them; coupling wildly as if they had something to prove. Lying back on her pillow, she closed her eyes, savoring the warmth of his bare skin against hers.

Is getting involved so fast a mistake?
Probably.

But it felt very, very good. She resolved to just let go and enjoy the sensation. Plenty of time later for self-recrimination. She drew the blanket up over them both and closed her eyes, fending off the question of where this might lead.

Jovanic shifted in his sleep, threw his arm over her and pulled her close, spooning her against him, fitting her form to his so that his breath warmed her neck. She dozed off.

And snapped awake.

There it was again—the noise that had roused her. She sat up on her elbows, listening hard until she was able to identify the sound: the French doors, quietly rattling.

Had she armed the alarm system?

No!

Setting the burglar alarm had been the last thing on their minds when they'd climbed the stairs, leaving a trail of clothing behind them

Real smart, Claudia, right after spending the money for a new alarm system.

She rolled out of bed and grabbed her kimono from the floor, pulling it around her as she tiptoed out to the landing.

I should wake him.

It might just be a possum or raccoon. They prowled the beach neighborhood at night, foraging for food.

Let him sleep.

Quietly descending the staircase, her toe hooked on the bra Jovanic had removed from her on the way up to the bedroom. The dark carpet rendered the black lace invisible and she stumbled. Grabbing hold of the railing in time to catch herself from tumbling down the stairs, she ended up half-sitting on a step.

As she started to rise, a movement below caught her eye. Across the living room, through the French doors, a glimpse of a dark figure outside.

Claudia raced back to the bedroom and touched Jovanic's shoulder. "Joel, wake up! Someone's trying to break in."

"Call nine-one-one," he said, instantly alert and on his feet. "Tell them there's an off-duty officer here with a weapon." He retrieved his trousers from the landing and returned to the bedroom before he had finished speaking. "Tell them what I'm wearing."

"What you're *wearing*?"

"So they don't mistake me for the suspect." He pulled on his T-shirt, then went for his weapon in the shoulder holster hanging over a chair. Pointing the nine-millimeter at the floor, he started down the stairs.

Claudia watched him go, her heart in her mouth. "Be

careful," she whispered. A useless caution, but she had
to say something. A prayer almost, a benediction to keep
him safe.

Taking the cordless phone from her office, she dialed
911, watching from the landing as Jovanic crept around the
periphery of the living room.

He stood to one side and looked out the French doors
before opening them and moving onto the deck. Through
the early morning semidarkness, Claudia could see the asparagus fern on the deck, the pot toppled on its side. The
intruder must have jumped over the side and gone down the
outside steps, probably leaving the way he had come.

Hugging herself, she tried to control the trembling that
shook her from the depths.

*Who is doing this? Senator Heidt? Doctor Bostwick?
Someone else?*

Jovanic reappeared and motioned her to stay where she
was. He eased open the front door, gun first, and stepped
onto the porch with practiced movements, flattening himself
against the siding as he descended the steps.

Claudia ran into the office and went to the window, in
time to see him round the front of the house and take off
down the block. He soon disappeared in the pre-dawn fog
rolling in from the ocean. Thank God she'd awakened.
Thank God Jovanic had been with her.

Less than five minutes later, a black and white patrol car
slid silently out of the mist and came to a halt outside the
house, blue lights strobing on the roof.

Three more cars followed. One made a quick U-turn and
returned the way it had come. The others continued up the
street and turned at the corner, where the alleyway behind
the houses offered any number of escape routes.

Two patrol officers climbed out of the parked car and
came up the walk, radios clipped to their shoulders crackling with chatter. A Mutt and Jeff pair, both wearing bulky
green nylon jackets over their uniforms.

If the neighborhood isn't awake yet, it soon will be, Claudia thought, shivering in the doorway.

Mutt came halfway up the stairs. Jeff waited below, scanning the street, his hand on the butt of his weapon. Not that he'd be able to see anything through the fog. "You okay, ma'am?" he called up to her.

"I'm fine. Did you see him?"

"We saw Detective Jovanic around the corner. He thought the gentleman went over a back fence."

The cop-speak irritated her. As far as she was concerned, the creep who had tried to break into her house was no gentleman.

"Did he get inside?" Jeff asked. "You want us to check the house?"

"That's okay, thanks. He never got in."

"You'd better go in and lock the door now, ma'am. We're gonna go give them a hand. Just wanted to make sure you were okay."

He was staring at her with frank curiosity, and Claudia suddenly became conscious of how short her kimono was, and that she was naked beneath it. She thanked them again and stepped hastily inside, locking the door behind her. If they were wondering how it was that Jovanic happened to be in the neighborhood in the middle of the night, her appearance was enough to fire up a red-hot rumor.

She sat on the couch waiting for Jovanic to return, hugging her grandmother's blue and white crocheted afghan around her, trying to keep her mind blank so she wouldn't freak out. But the unwelcome thoughts kept intruding: *What if something happens to him?* The intruder probably had a gun, too.

Just what she needed—a cop for a lover. How many nights like this could she look forward to—waiting for him to come home from a dangerous pursuit, wondering if he would come home at all? That's not what she wanted from a relationship.

You're getting ahead of yourself. So far, it's just sex.

But she knew there was more to it. Even when they were sniping at each other, electricity sparked between. There was definitely something worth taking the time to explore; something for which it might be worth letting down her precious need to be independent.

A tense fifteen minutes crawled by before she heard him on the stairs.

She ran to the door and flung it open. "What happened? Did you catch him?"

Jovanic was breathing hard, from adrenaline, not exertion. "No, goddammit, we lost him." He reached up to the lightbulb in the porch light, which the intruder had loosened, and tightened it until it glowed yellow. "Twenty-five officers falling over each other like fucking Keystone Cops, and nobody sees him." He went inside and examined the lock on the French doors. "They're checking license plates on the next couple blocks. Tomorrow . . . today, that is, while we're in Palm Springs, I'll get someone to test the deck for prints. There might be a shoe print in the dirt that spilled from the pot."

"Too bad you couldn't have just shot the bastard."

"Oh, now you want me to shoot him? I thought you were a pacifist."

"You could at least yell, 'Stop! Police!' or something like that."

Jovanic gave a derisive snort. "Yeah, he's going to stop because I yell at him. More likely some unsuspecting taxpayer hears, comes outside and gets in the way of a bullet. Shit, it's freezing!"

Claudia rubbed his bare arms, which were damp with ocean mist. "Did you get a look at him?"

"Not good enough for an ID. He was wearing a watch cap."

"The man who attacked Destiny and me wore a leather mask."

He shook his head. "Different guy. You probably broke that joker's arm. One thing's sure. Whoever is behind these attacks has plenty of resources."

"A senator does. So does a plastic surgeon."

"Yeah, we're checking them both out, and everyone else on Lindsey's list." Jovanic set the alarm, cursing himself for a fool that he hadn't made sure it was armed earlier.

He pulled off his T-shirt and hustled her upstairs. "There's nothing more to be done down here tonight. Back to bed, grapho lady."

"Is that an order, detective?" Claudia mugged. "Or are you just happy to see me?"

Chapter 26

Palm Springs was more than a hundred miles east, out the
San Bernardino Freeway. Jovanic's foot mashed the accelerator and they blasted up the on-ramp. The Jeep wasn't
exactly top of the line when it came to comfort, but that
morning, the old Jaguar, temperamental at the best of times,
had steadfastly refused to respond to Claudia's curses, and
they'd taken a cab to the police station where Jovanic had
left his ride while out of town.

Heading away from the beach, they soon left the marine
layer behind. By the time they zipped past Monterey Park
doing eighty-five, the morning overcast had given way to
smoggy haze. Sixty miles out, beyond the Banning/Beau-
mont exit, brilliant sunshine and clear blue skies replaced
the clouds.

In the desert, only a few scraggly trees and the burned-
out shells of an old house or two dotted the wilderness
landscape with long stretches of nothing between them. A
prickly pear cactus appeared here and there. Not like the
Arizona desert Jovanic had just left, where groves of saguaro
raised spiny arms to the sky in supplication.

Claudia yawned and stretched, raising her voice over the
sound of the wind-whipped ragtop. "What do you s'pose
we'll find?"

"If we're lucky," Jovanic yelled back, "maybe evidence
of the phantom boyfriend Bostwick told you about."

"I wonder if that was for real. He sounded sincere."

"Yeah. Sincerely wanting to cover his ass."

They fell into a silence intermittently broken by the rattle of the Jeep bumping over uneven spots in the road. Morning had brought with it the awkwardness that often assails new lovers. But the connection felt good. Maybe *too* good for someone afraid of being hurt.

Nearly two hours after they'd hit the road, the wind farms loomed. Alien-looking propellers harnessing ecologically friendly energy; bringing life to once barren land. Twenty miles to go. The propellers heralded the northernmost edge of Palm Springs.

They exited the Interstate at Highway 111, which merged with Palm Springs' main drag. Jovanic asked if she were hungry, and when she admitted she was, he pulled into the lot at the Flower Drum on South Indian Canyon.

Before climbing out, he leaned into the back seat and launched a search for his Thomas Guide to help them locate Lindsey's house.

"I could've looked it up for you on MapQuest," Claudia said as he pawed through the coffee-stained Starbucks cups, Milky Way wrappers and assorted McDonald's debris littering the floor of what appeared to be his mobile home away from home. "Ever thought of getting a trash bag?"

He gave her the beetle-brow over his shoulder. "You aren't going to try and change me, are you?"

"No way. It's your car, your life."

The words came out sounding more snippy than she'd intended, but he didn't seem to notice. With a triumphant, "Ha!" he hauled out the battered guide. They strolled into the restaurant, his arm around her shoulders.

The restaurant had just opened for lunch and they were the first customers. Black lacquer and red leather figured prominently in a spacious dining room that featured a rock garden and a waterfall. The host, an elderly Asian man in a gold embroidered vest and shiny black trousers, bowed in welcome all the way to a corner booth. His broad smile as he enumerated the day's specials exposed a set of gold-tipped teeth.

They both had a good appetite, and while they made

the mu shu vegetable and lemon chicken rapidly disappear, Jovanic asked Claudia about her family.

She smiled. "It's a pretty standard dysfunctional family. My parents have been married forty years and barely tolerate each other. My brother's a widower with a wonderful daughter, and my sister is a moderately successful stand-up comedian. She's on tour most of the time, so we don't have a lot of contact."

"I have a sister, too," Jovanic said, and Claudia remembered the story of his father's violent death. "She's a big-shot in a Silicon Valley firm, so she doesn't have a lot of time for family socializing, either. I have a couple of teenage nephews." He got that hooded look and said, "They've had their share of problems."

They chatted until the waitress cleared away the remains and brought the check with two fortune cookies. Insisting on paying, Jovanic pushed the plate of cookies toward her.

"You're supposed to take the one closest to you," Claudia said, picking one. She snapped it in half and extracted the slip of paper wound inside. "What's yours say?"

Jovanic laid aside the map book he'd begun thumbing and picked up the second cookie. " *'You will be successful in your endeavors.'* What about yours?"

" *'Beware of sexy involvement with good-looking cop.'* "

He snatched the paper from her, shaking his head. "Didn't your mother teach you not to lie? Let me see that. *'Your mind is filled with good ideas,' "* he read aloud, his left brow hiking wickedly. "I just hope those ideas involve massage oil and a hot shower."

She sent him a sultry look from under her lashes that held a promise, and he looked pleased as he returned his attention to the map.

"Cahuilla Trail isn't in here," he concluded after poring over every page for the Coachella Valley.

"We can ask," Claudia suggested. "Maybe the host knows."

"He doesn't speak English any better than the waitress.

I'll find it. It's probably a side street off Cahuilla Drive, or Cahuilla Parkway. They're not all that far from here."

"What is this thing men have, that you can't stand to ask for directions?"

He jammed a toothpick between his lips and started for the door, beckoning her to follow.

After a fruitless forty-five minutes of exploring every street on the map with *Cahuilla* in its name, they concluded that Cahuilla Trail wasn't among them. Jovanic's grumbled profanities became more explosive with each wrong turn until, with a final, defeated, "Fuck it!" he turned the Jeep into a Shell station and parked at a pump.

Biting her tongue on the temptation to say, "Told you so," Claudia followed him into the convenience store.

They got lucky with the pimply-faced attendant minding the counter. "Cahuilla Trail?" the kid repeated, scratching at the scrubby growth on his chin. "Yeah, dude, I know where that is. It's way the fuck out there, is where it is." He jerked his head in the direction of the desert.

"Yeah?" Jovanic put both hands on the counter and leaned across it so the kid had to step back. "So, how the fuck do we get there?"

The kid proceeded to draw the directions in the air with his finger—go left, left, and then right, then just keep on going. "You sure you wanna go out there, dude?" he asked. "Nuttin' there 'cept crazy people."

"Crazy people?"

"Yeah, dude. Don't you know . . . the further out in the desert you go, the crazier people are. It's a fuckin' fact, man."

The kid's voice followed them out the door. "You gotta really watch for it, dude. You get to Indian Wells, you went too far."

They almost missed the turn.

Just in time, Claudia caught sight of a wooden signpost in the dirt that read "Cahuilla Trail." And painted underneath in faded lettering: "Private Road." It wasn't a road in any paved sense of the word, she realized as Jovanic wheeled onto it.

They bounced along what was, in fact, little more than a dirt track. The Jag's shock absorbers would never have survived the assault, and Claudia was glad they had not driven in it. She raised her voice to make herself heard. "Feels like we're in the Old West."

"We *are* in the Old West," Jovanic shouted back.

They drove a couple of miles before the house came into view, standing alone in the desert landscape: a low-slung, boxy structure, hiding behind a pink concrete-block wall nearly as tall as Jovanic himself. The road ended there.

Claudia appraised the wall. "I hope she didn't have a Rottweiler."

Jovanic switched off the engine and slipped the keys into his pocket. "If she did, I hope someone's been feeding it, or we could be lunch."

Once-white gravel covered the yard on their side of the wall. It was tan now, coated in desert dust. Only a few palm trees and yucca plants grew around the house, and the weeds poked through the rocks. The property seemed to have been minimally maintained. Just a house, not a home.

Jovanic had picked up a search warrant to allow them to enter the house. He took it from his pocket, adjusted his shoulder holster and kissed Claudia on the tip of her nose, which made her ridiculously happy. "Wait in the Jeep until I check it out."

For once, she didn't feel like arguing with him.

The wrought-iron gate was fastened with a heavy padlock and chain; spikes topped the fence. Jovanic rattled the gate loudly. "Hellooo, anybody home?"

No snarling guard dog bounded out to greet them; no one appeared at the door to see who was making all the racket. In fact, the place had a distinctly deserted air. Jovanic returned to the Jeep. He opened the tailgate and grabbed a pair of bolt cutters and a crowbarlike tool from behind the back seat. He applied the bolt cutters to the chrome-steel padlock and the lock body fell to the ground, allowing the gate to swing open.

"Helluva lot easier than climbing over that fence," said Jovanic, picking up the bolt cutters and motioning Claudia to join him.

She followed him inside the yard with an amused laugh. "Now, that's a sight I'd like to have seen."

Aside from the modern wooden shutters at every window, the house had a certain fifties retro look. They took the cement path around back.

Claudia circled the pool and climbed up on a rock at the rear of the yard, gazing over the top of the block wall. Miles of sand and tumbleweed stretched in every direction, bounded by the San Jacinto Mountains to the north.

"No neighbors anywhere close," she noted.

Jovanic was looking at the scattering of insects and dead palm fronds floating lazily on the surface of the murky blue water. "I don't think she came out here to host block parties."

The modern design of the spa and its rock grotto placed it as a much newer addition to the house. "I bet it's romantic at night with the spotlights on," Claudia remarked. "When it's clean, of course."

"After what probably went on in this pool, I'd want all fresh water."

"I could've gone all day without you planting that thought in my head."

They circumnavigated the house and found it sealed tight enough to frustrate the most enterprising peeping tom. Arriving back at the front door, Jovanic took his weapon from its holster and waved Claudia behind him.

"Let's make sure no one's home before we go barging in."

Claudia backed up to give him room to retreat. He hammered on the front door, his knock booming like thunder in the silent desert. After a few moments of total silence, he holstered his weapon, took the crowbar tool and went to work on the door.

It swung open almost immediately, and holding the Smith & Wesson in front of him with both hands, he slipped quietly into the house.

It wasn't until he called out to her, after he'd cleared the place, that Claudia realized she'd been holding her breath.

A short hallway opened onto a spacious living area with wood-beamed ceilings and mission-style furnishings. The house smelled as musty as an unsealed tomb. Jovanic immediately pulled back the shutters and opened the patio door. A warm breeze wafted in with the light, freshening the air and giving them a better view of the room: whitewashed walls and a glass-enclosed fireplace, woven Native American rugs. Not quite what she had expected, Claudia thought with surprise.

There was an enormous flat screen, high-definition television system with speakers big enough to provide surround sound for an entire theater. DVD and VHS players suggested that Lindsey usually brought along her own entertainment.

Jovanic laid the search warrant on a side table and reholstered his gun. "What do you think?"

"All it needs is a bunch of out-of-date magazines on the coffee table. Feels like a waiting room."

"Yeah, but waiting for what?"

"I'm not sure I want to know."

They toured the renovated kitchen, where the stainless steel appliances looked new and expensive. Claudia began opening cabinets and drawers. A small stack of hors d'oeuvre plates, a few silver forks. A rack of wine glasses under a cabinet. "I hope there aren't any bugs in here."

"I'd be looking for snakes and scorpions if I were you," Jovanic countered, putting an immediate end to her exploration.

She opened the refrigerator and looked inside with a low whistle. " *'Champagne wishes and caviar dreams.'* Beluga, no less."

"That's good?"

"At least a hundred bucks a pop. French champagne, too. Moët Chandon."

Jovanic leaned over her shoulder, taking the opportunity to nibble her ear. "I guess Lindsey took good care of her guests."

"As long as they didn't get too hungry."

"They couldn't overstay their welcome, anyway."

"My dad always says that guests and fish start to stink after three days."

"Maybe Lindsey shared his philosophy. Let's hit the boudoir."

Not much to see. The guest room was furnished with an antique-style metal bed. Scroll work and scallops on the headboard and footboard; a rust-colored damask bedspread and pillows to dress it up. A matching nightstand with a small lamp. No dresser; empty closets.

In the larger bedroom, framed prints hung on walls painted a calming tan color. White accents. Desert-theme rug. A mahogany bedroom set the color of espresso. Original charcoal line drawings of nudes by an artist whose name Claudia didn't recognize. Tall windows, drawn shades hiding views of the back yard lanai.

There was nothing of Lindsey's personal character stamped on the place. Perhaps, as with her Brentwood apartment, it had taken its color from her flamboyant personality and only came to life when she was present. It seemed a sad commentary on her life.

Unlike the one in the guest room, the king-sized bed in the master bedroom had been stripped of linens. A stain roughly the shape of Africa defaced the mattress. Claudia turned away, repelled. Remembering the photographs Earl Nelson had shown her of the young Lindsey lying next to Preston Sommerfield, she couldn't help feeling pity for the woman who had once been her friend. As much as Lindsey'd had the capacity to be a friend to anyone.

A walk-in closet held a selection of desert wear and a range of provocative outfits. A black spandex cat suit similar to the one Destiny had worn at their ill-fated meeting at The Grove. Skimpy leather dresses. Chain-ornamented leather, merry widows, garter belts. Five-inch spiked heel shoes, black boots. Wigs in colors that didn't even pretend to be natural.

"Everything for the chic dominatrix," Claudia said, taking out a dress that was far too demure for the dark company it was keeping. Pink flowered fabric, a ruffled lace-up bodice and skirt. "I wonder what this is doing in here."

Jovanic glanced up from the dresser drawer he was searching. "Maybe one of her clients was into Little Bo Peep."

"Think there's a shepherd's crook to go with it?"

"I can guess where she'd put it."

"Please don't."

"Never saw Little Bo Peep in one of these."

Claudia looked over at the spiked leather collar he was holding and felt a pang. How callous were they, blithely digging into the outlandish belongings of a dead woman and making fun? She replaced the dress in the closet and told Jovanic she would check the bathroom.

The medicine cabinet held no secrets, only a bottle of aspirin, nail-polish remover and a half-filled box of cotton swabs. The old-fashioned claw-footed tub and freestanding pedestal sink offered no hiding places.

"Why would they come all the way out here?" Claudia wondered aloud as Jovanic joined her. "This place is nothing special."

He dropped to one knee and began probing the edges of the floor covering. "High-profile people like Lindsey's clients want to avoid being seen. This is about as far out of town as they can get."

"Lindsey once told me she was the auctioneer at a slave auction in San Francisco. I have to admit, I didn't take her seriously."

Jovanic unwrapped a new toothpick and sucked on it thoughtfully. "She took *herself* pretty seriously." He straightened and wiped his hands on his jeans. "C'mon, let's check the garage."

"Wait a minute." Claudia's eyes were drawn upwards. A faint rectangular outline in the ceiling, maybe eight by ten.

Grabbing Jovanic's arm for support, she climbed up

onto the toilet seat to get a better look. She reached up and
felt cold metal; a recessed ring for easy access. When she
pried the ring loose and gave it a sharp tug, a small door
dropped down.

She glanced down with a pleased smile. "Hey, Columbo,
I think we've got something."

Chapter 27

It took Jovanic's extra height to reach all the way inside the cache when they traded places. He handed down three videotapes and a notebook.

The authorship of the sprawling handwriting in the notebook was unquestionable.

"Lindsey," Claudia said, skimming pages written in her trademark green ink. "It's a journal." She could see Lindsey's need for control in the upright letters—no slant in either direction. Yet, it was the teardrop-shaped lower loops that told the truth about all the bottled-up emotion she had held. "Looks like she . . . hey, Joel?"

Jovanic wasn't paying attention. "It's a fucking pharmacy," he said, hauling a bundle of plastic bags from the ceiling cache. A bag of white powder dropped into the sink, followed by a bag of multicolored pills.

"Coke?" Claudia asked.

He tasted it and nodded. "I'll go get some evidence bags out of the Jeep. Maybe some of this shit can be tied back to Bostwick."

While he inventoried their find, Claudia curled up in a corner of the living room couch and read through the pages of Lindsey's journal. The first entries were dated earlier in the year.

> *Feb. 15—BH payments set up. He looked sick when he saw the tapes. I almost felt sorry for him.*

*Mar. 23—PF scared shitless the big shots will find out.
I haven't had so much fun in ages.*
March 25—BH could be big trouble.
*March 28—Got BH handled. He now knows better
than to fuck with me.*
*April 5—Have the condo in Z cleaned. Should be an
interesting trip.*
*April 10—Loosening them up takes some doing, but—
wow, what a weekend!*
*April 30—Bos is a pain in the ass. Have to find a better
way to control him.*

The next entry came several months later.

*August 19—That damn Bos and his dog. What a sicko.
But as long as he pays the bills and brings the pills,
I'll keep him cumming (haha).*

The entries became even more sporadic, but continued
in a similar vein. As Claudia read, she noticed changes beginning to emerge in the handwriting.

*September 2— Enough is enough. When it's not fun
anymore, it's time to call it quits.*
*September 21—Why did I start this shit? It was fun while
it lasted, but it's over and it needs to be ended.*

"That's the last one," Claudia said, tapping the date with
a fingernail. "Just a couple of days before she died. And it
says the same as what's written in the 'suicide note.' This
handwriting looks pretty stressed compared to the earlier
entries."

Jovanic glanced up from counting pills. "So, what are you
saying? Now you think she really *did* commit suicide?"

"No, I'm saying the handwriting looks stressed." She
heard the impatience in her voice and tried again in a gen-
tler tone. "I'm looking at her state of mind compared to
how it was earlier in the notebook. I don't know whether

she became suicidal, or she was tense because someone was threatening her, or something else. I'd need a crystal ball for that. What I do know is, there's a definite change over the last couple of weeks."

"What kind of change?"

"The writing rhythm was always tense, but later, the writing gets smaller and cramps up; the lower loops tighten; the slant starts leaning slightly to the left. That adds up to stress. There's also strong movement away from the right side of the page . . . the right margin is really wide here, see?" Her brows knit together as she considered what it might mean. "It's symbolic of pulling away from the future. People who are suicidal often write all the way to the edge of the page. The right side of the page represents the future, so writing all the way to the edge could be symbolic of moving toward the *'end of the future,'* which is death. She doesn't do that."

"So, what do you think it means, grapho lady?"

"It could be that she was afraid. After all, look at the hint of threats. She says BH could be a problem. That has to be Bryce Heidt. Or maybe Bostwick got to be a bigger pain in the ass than she could handle."

Jovanic put down the drug-filled baggies and came to look over her shoulder. He leaned down close, his cheek brushing her hair. "How about PF? Sound familiar?"

Claudia shook her head slowly. "Not that I can think of."

"Let's see who's starring in Lindsey's home movies."

Bondage and discipline: Games played by powerful, educated men adopting a submissive role—a role contrary to society's expectations; a role far removed from their everyday lives.

A string of famous faces figured among the cast of Lindsey Alexander's personal video collection. Each client addressed her as "Mistress Alexander" and meekly complied with her orders.

Bend over the spanking table and receive your punishment.

On your knees.

Lick my boots. The soles, lackey, the soles!

"Hey, do you recognize that guy?" Jovanic was staring at the television screen, his eyes narrowed in concentration and focused on the man who crawled on screen on all fours, a wickedly spiked dog collar encircling his scrawny neck. "I know I've seen him before."

The man wore only a wide leather belt cinched tightly around his midsection. Lindsey, in blonde pageboy wig and a skimpy blue vinyl dress with long matching gloves, rode him like a pony, her fingers laced in his white hair. When he cried out in pain, she jerked the old man's head up so that the camera caught his features.

Claudia drew a sharp breath. "Holy shit, it's Bishop Flannery! He's the guy who gave the funeral Mass. Jesus, that's more of him than I ever wanted to see."

Jovanic leaned forward, elbows on knees. "What the hell next?"

They watched Lindsey climb off the elderly cleric's back and point him toward a wooden cross attached to a frame—sturdy two-by-tens that formed an X. Ordering him to spread his arms and legs, she handcuffed his wrists and ankles to the device, then reached between his legs and began stroking him, teasing him until he cried out.

When she'd had enough of that, Lindsey made a dramatic display of selecting a leather cat o'nine tails from a wooden rack. Applied it to Flannery's back and buttocks while he begged her to stop and then begged her for more.

Claudia shook her head, scarcely able to believe what she was witnessing. Then it dawned on her. "Isn't his name Patrick Flannery? Lindsey's Journal . . . *PF!*"

Jovanic glanced over at her, chewed on it, then nodded. "I think you're right. The "big shots" she mentioned in the journal could be the Church."

Claudia made a face as if she'd smelled a bad odor. "The Church who didn't want to bury her in consecrated ground because she supposedly killed herself, but here's this nasty old pervert getting his naked ass whipped."

Jovanic removed the tape and slid in the next one. It opened with the camera panning to Senator Bryce Heidt strapped to a doctor's examining table, an IV pole beside him, his feet in the stirrups. No mask covered his head this time.

He doesn't look so commanding now, Claudia thought, measuring the mixture of dread and anticipation that distorted his features.

"Don't worry, babe," Jovanic said, misconstruing her smirk of satisfaction for something else. "If she *really* hurts him it's because he wants her to."

She snorted. "That probably costs extra."

Destiny came into the scene wearing a nurse's uniform a couple of sizes too small, and hung an enema bag on the IV pole.

"I think we can pass that up," said Jovanic as he grabbed the remote and fast-forwarded the tape.

The scenes rolled on. A series of clients, some famous, others unknown to Claudia, submitting to whatever torture satisfied their fantasies.

The final video featured Charles Bostwick bound to a chair with a short seat and high back. Big black plastic clamps hung from his nipples. When Brandi approached him with a lit red candle and began to pour hot wax on the doctor's genitals, Claudia sprang up, palms outstretched in protest. "Enough! This is making me want to puke."

Jovanic grinned. "Ah, come on, you know it turns you on."

"Turn it *off*!" Nothing could stem her growing revulsion. "Just because I understand the psychology behind this kind of behavior doesn't mean I want to watch it."

Jovanic gave her a sly look. "But I bet I know what you're thinking right now."

"Oh, yeah? What's that?"

"You're wishing you could get hold of those sicko bastards' handwritings."

She couldn't help laughing; he was right about that.

He slipped the last tape back into its protective clamshell box and gathered up the evidence they had discovered in the bathroom cache. "I think that about does it. Have we missed anything besides the garage?"

"We haven't checked the linen closet yet."

Back in the hallway, Claudia twisted the handle of the louvered door, surprised when it resisted.

Who locks their linen closet?

Jovanic fetched his crowbar and wedged the blade in the space between the doors, applying pressure until the lock began to yield. The wood gave with a cracking sound and the doors popped open.

Inside was no linen closet; just black emptiness leering back at them.

Jovanic reached inside and found the switch for a low-burning light bulb mounted in a wall sconce. Just enough illumination to reveal a spiral staircase that plunged into the darkness below. He glanced at Claudia with raised brows. "I think we just found the dungeon."

"We're not really going down there are we?"

Their eyes met and he grinned. "It's like one of those movies where the kids go into the house and everyone knows there's a killer waiting for them."

"Yeah, and you're yelling at the TV, *don't go down in the basement, you idiots.*"

"You can stay here and wait for me."

Claudia shook her head. "No way, Columbo. I'm sticking with you."

Jovanic patted his weapon in its shoulder holster, as if to reassure himself. "Okay, just stay close, it's dark down there."

As if she needed telling.

Chapter 28

He moved in front of her and they descended into the soundless basement. Thirteen steps, Claudia counted as the light from the dim bulb receded behind them. Thirteen steps on wrought iron risers, taking them into—what?

Sensory deprivation, she thought. Poor visibility; the cold brass handrail under their hands; the only sounds, their breathing.

"It smells musty," said Claudia, wrinkling her nose in distaste as she descended.

Jovanic shrugged. "Dead rat."

At the foot of the stairs, a small table held a butane lighter and a ceramic candle holder fashioned in the form of a human hand. A fat black candle sat in its palm.

The flame flickered eerily when Jovanic lit it, sending ghostly shadows skittering across the room. He swept the candle slowly from one side to the other, his eyes glowing like gunmetal above the flame. "Holy shit."

"Holy shit," Claudia echoed, still on the last stair. *"The Little Shop of Horrors."*

"Depends on your tastes, babe."

Lindsey's private dungeon had no electricity, but when Jovanic lit a few more wall sconces, they found themselves in a large room that ran the length and width of the house— about two thousand square feet, including a bathroom with Jacuzzi tub.

The dungeon had been sectioned off. The red area, where Lindsey had whipped Bishop Flannery on the cross. The medical examination area where Bryce Heidt's enema fantasies had been acted out. The green-painted area, dominated by a large wooden wheel with leather cuffs attached; a spanking bench, a twenty-seven-inch-high cage.

Claudia had researched paraphilias for a case she'd once been involved in, but reading about it on X-rated Web sites and even viewing Lindsey's videos hadn't prepared her for a firsthand experience. The fantastical implements of torture took on an even more sinister cast in this place of shadows.

Still, as she wandered from one strange contraption to another, she found herself fascinated by the sort of person who would get a sexual thrill out of being restrained and physically tormented. The air in the basement was dry, but the temperature felt much lower than upstairs in the main house. Shivering a little, she wished she'd brought a jacket.

"Come look at this," Jovanic called to her. He showed her a small metal box in the medical examination area. On top were dials and switches.

"What the hell is it?"

"It's for electrical fun. The dial controls the intensity of the charge." He shifted the candle to show her a glass wand. "Gotta be careful with this one. It's UV; gives off static electricity. You hold it on the same spot for too long, you get burnt."

"And people get turned on by that?"

"Takes all kinds, right?"

They toured the dungeon together, checking it out as if they were visiting a museum. Wooden shelves loaded with sex toys, flavored lotions, bottles of scented oils. Economy-sized bottle of Viagra. Bragging label: *makes you last for hours.* Drawers containing leather hoods and bridles, bits and red rubber balls.

"Gags," Jovanic informed Claudia, who promptly gagged at the concept. She eyed him with suspicion. "You know an awful lot about all this."

"I worked Hollywood vice, remember?"

"And it's all legal?"

"As long as no one's paying for actual sex. Then it's prostitution."

"Seems like splitting hairs to me."

"That's the law. Your tax dollars at work."

"Do you think anything we've found here will help make a case?"

Jovanic held the candle aloft and looked around at the paraphernalia of sexual submission and humiliation. "First we need proof that Lindsey was murdered." Frustration filled his face. "No doubt about Ivan Novak, though."

Claudia turned away, not wanting to think about that. A drape of red silk in a corner of the room caught her attention and she drifted over to the shadowy niche, trying to distract herself from visions of Ivan in the last moments of his life.

A black tassel dangled from the valance above the drape and she turned to see Jovanic watching her from across the room.

"Go ahead and pull it," he said. "Let's see what's behind Door Number One."

Claudia forced a laugh. "I hope there's not an iron maiden back there."

With a swish of silk, the curtain swept aside to reveal a door. Half-expecting it to be locked, as the stairway to the dungeon had been, she was surprised when it opened easily.

A nauseating odor hit her and she staggered backward, gagging.

Watching from across the room, Jovanic saw her reel. He sprinted over and threw a protective arm around her, drawing her away from the closet. She turned her face against him, breathing into his shirt, trying to rid her nasal passages of the smell of feces and vomit that now permeated the dungeon.

In the wavering flutter of the candle flame that Jovanic directed at the closet, a tall, narrow cage took shape. There was no doubt as to the condition of its occupant.

Claudia told herself that she needed to be strong, forced herself to turn and look. But she couldn't control the trembling that shook her whole body. "It's a tomb," she whispered hoarsely.

Jovanic let go of her and moved closer to the corpse, all police business now.

The candlelight illuminated a black form-fitting leather hood that entirely covered the head. The mouth was zippered shut. *"Jesus,"* he muttered. "He probably suffocated."

"Oh my God, I wonder how long he's been here."

"Not too long." Jovanic swept the candle slowly downward. "He's still in rigor."

"What does that mean in terms of timing?"

"Rigor is at full stiffness somewhere around twelve hours after death, releases after about seventy-two, depending on the conditions."

The fine hairs on the back of Claudia's neck rose. "You're saying he was killed in the last *few hours*?"

Jovanic nodded grimly. "I'm no medical examiner, but that'd be my guess."

"I wonder who he is."

Aside from the hood, the body was nude, arms stretched and handcuffed to the top of the cage, which was suspended from the ceiling. All over the flat, bony chest were the bloody abrasions of a flagellum. Electrical wires were clipped to the purple-mottled genitals.

"They hit the poor bastard with some ball-shock," Jovanic said, directing the candle flame higher, to the corpse's manacled wrists.

Claudia felt the blood drain from her face. "That tattoo." On the dead man's forearm, the faded turquoise scales of a cobra slithered among the scabs and old needle scars. Malevolent red eyes stared back at her.

The Chinese food they'd had for lunch curdled in her stomach; rose into her throat. Turning, she ran blindly for the staircase.

"Claudia, what the . . . ?"

She heard Jovanic's voice, his running feet as if from a long distance. Shadows danced all around her as she collapsed on the bottom step, gasping.

"Earl Nelson! Omigod, it's Earl Nelson."

* * *

The afternoon sun finally warmed her as she sat in the Jeep, waiting for Jovanic to finish giving his statement to the Palm Springs police. He had called the local department from his cellular phone to report the discovery of Earl Nelson's body. Lindsey's desert house was now a crime scene and outside his jurisdiction. He would fill in the local cops and turn over the fruits of their search. Then he and Claudia would return to LA empty-handed.

"But they'll cooperate," he said, climbing into the driver side. "Their department is small enough to appreciate the help we can give them."

"When is it going to end?" Claudia asked bleakly. "Lindsey's dead, Ivan's dead, Lindsey's brother is dead. *Nobody* should have to die like that. Even a creep like Earl Nelson."

Jovanic reached over and squeezed her hand. "You're really getting a snootful, aren't you? But you know what? You're . . ."

"Don't tell me I'm a real trooper, or I *will* throw up."

The corner of his mouth lifted slightly. "Okay, no clichés. Let's just get the hell outta here."

Chapter 29

On Friday afternoon, three days after the grim discovery in the desert, the offices of Grainger and Grainger, Inc. were as hushed as a library at closing time.

"Where is everyone?" Claudia asked Yolande Palomino as she accompanied her through the deserted hallways.

"Staff retreat. Every few months, Mr. and Mrs. Grainger give everyone a day to rest up and relax while they work on the schedule for the next period."

"But she's here at the office, and you are, too?"

Yolande smiled, which smoothed the anxiety lines around her eyes and made her look younger. "Don't worry, I'll be leaving in a little while."

Lillian Grainger was seated at her desk, dwarfed behind a large stack of papers.

She pointed at the stack, shaking her head at Claudia as if in amazement. "Honest to Pete, since our advertisement came out in the *Times*, the résumés just keep on proliferating like . . . like bunnies!"

"I hope you're getting some better applicants than this one," Claudia said, taking a seat. She opened her briefcase and withdrew the handwriting analysis report she had prepared on Lillian's candidate. "He's someone I wouldn't have recommended for you."

Lillian's perfectly penciled eyebrows lifted a fraction before they settled into a frown. "His references are impeccable; what's the problem?"

Claudia passed her the report, noticing Bryce Heidt's

well-scrubbed face beaming from a glossy brochure on Lillian's desk. He stood in the midst of a crowd of factory workers in his hand-tailored suit. A photo from his recent senatorial campaign, she guessed. This was the man being considered for an appointment to the president's committee with Lillian Grainger.

What would Lillian say if she knew about Heidt's fun and games in Lindsey's desert dungeon?

"You can read the details later," said Claudia. "I'll just give you a summary. He has some good qualities of course, but he has a lot of hidden resentment toward women. The potential problem is, if he has to work under female supervision . . . which would be you . . . and if you didn't see eye-to-eye on something, he's going to undermine your authority, or he'll instigate a *major* blowup. There are some other things, too, but that's the big one."

Without a word, Lillian laid the report on her desktop and leaned forward to read it, her mouth pulling into a tight little moue.

Claudia tried not to fidget, but her mind was filled with too many disturbing thoughts for her to sit quietly and wait for Lillian to respond. She crossed and re-crossed her legs, wanting to get up and pace the long room, to dissipate some of the energy that had been building.

When Lillian finally glanced up from the paper, she was nodding. "Claudia, you've really saved our bacon on this one. This is *exactly* the kind of information we need."

"I recommend that you don't make hiring decisions based on the handwriting analysis alone, but I think you'll find it confirms whatever other background you do on him."

Lillian turned her eyes skyward. "My lord, can you imagine what might've happened if we'd hired this guy and he turned out to have a murky past! The confirmation hearings are right around the corner . . . everything could have been ruined. *Resentment toward women.* That would be the absolute worst! I can't have anyone in my camp that's going to be a problem."

Claudia's glance fell on Heidt's brochure again.

Should I tell her?

Would it compromise the investigation to let Lillian know that Heidt was being looked at by the police in Lindsey's death? Heidt himself was aware, so it wouldn't exactly be spilling the beans. Besides, it might lead to further revelations about the senator that would prove helpful to Jovanic's investigation.

Claudia cleared her throat. "Without getting into specifics, Lillian, I think you ought to know that Senator Heidt may be in for some public embarrassment, if not worse."

Lillian gave her a sharp glance. "What are you talking about?"

"It has to do with Lindsey. She was using a certain videotape to blackmail him."

Claudia quickly realized she had made a serious tactical error when Lillian jumped to her feet, her small face pinched and pale with shock. "Bryce Heidt . . . Lindsey . . . *blackmail?* That's insane! A story like that could *ruin* him if it got out."

"Don't kill the messenger, Lillian," Claudia said. "We were talking about potential scandal, so I thought you'd want to know."

Lillian plopped back down in her chair, looking as if she'd bitten into a Hershey bar and found a worm. "I don't believe it. There *has* to be an explanation." Her fingers drummed an angry little dance on the desktop. "It's utterly ridiculous. What on earth could she have blackmailed him with? Bryce Heidt is a devoted family man. We attend the same church. He was at last Sunday's service with his grandchildren, for pity's sake!"

The lady protests a bit too much.

"Let's just say that what he did wasn't illegal," Claudia said, closing her briefcase. "But it was of a nature that could come back and bite you."

The woman whose cool head and southern charm had built an empire in the celebrity event business actually wrung her hands as she worked herself into a tightly controlled frenzy.

"He's on his way to the White House!" Lillian's voice

rose to a higher pitch. "He can't afford even the *breath* of scandal."

And denial is a river in Egypt.

The truth was, Lillian couldn't afford a scandal any more than Heidt could. Yolande Palomino had made that abundantly clear. Any political hopes she might be nurturing could be on the line if it turned out she had allied herself with a soon-to-be pariah.

"I've sacrificed too much to have it all go down the drain over vicious gossip," Lillian said in a tight voice as she pressed the intercom button on her phone. "Yolande, get my husband on the line, then see Ms. Rose out."

"Just give me a moment to put this call through," Yolande said, as Claudia closed Lillian's door, glad to be leaving behind the electric tension that crackled in her client's office.

"Don't bother, I know the way by now."

The executive assistant gave her a thin smile as she picked up the receiver and began to punch buttons with a long, slender finger. "Not at all. I'll be happy to see you out." Something in the way she said it suggested that the escort wasn't optional.

After connecting the Graingers' phone call, Yolande walked Claudia back to the foyer. She stopped suddenly as they approached the reception area. "I felt so bad about Lindsey," she said unexpectedly. "She was such a . . . an interesting person."

Claudia's ears perked up. "Did you know her well?"

"We had coffee a few times when we were helping her with events for her clients. They were the big celebrities, so Mrs. Grainger always handled them herself. That gave us a chance to talk some."

"Talk about . . . ?"

"Oh, this and that. Personal things, mostly."

How personal?

"Have you heard the rumor?" Claudia plunged in, throwing caution aside. "Some people don't believe she killed herself."

"I've heard something about it."

"What do *you* think?"

Yolande's eyes turned away, looking everywhere but at Claudia. "I have . . . some thoughts."

"I'd like to hear them. How about meeting me for coffee later?"

"No!" Yolande said sharply, her shoulders bunched with tension. Keeping an eye on the receptionist, who was watching the exchange with obvious interest, she lowered her voice to a near-whisper. "I mean, Mrs. Grainger wouldn't like it. She has to be very careful about her image. Everyone around her has to be absolutely above reproach. She wouldn't want her name connected to any kind of scandal, like if Lindsey's death were . . . you know."

"Yes, we just had that conversation. But we're not talking about Mrs. Grainger, we're talking about you."

"Well, it extends to her employees and she's very strict about it. Everyone who works here signs an agreement not to do anything that will reflect badly on Mrs. Grainger or the company. You know, like get involved with drugs or . . . or, sleep around or anything. She only hires churchgoing Christians."

"But this is an entirely personal matter; nothing to do with her business."

"Nothing here is considered personal." Yolande smiled. "You look shocked, Ms. Rose. Don't be; it's our own choice. None of us is *forced* to sign the agreement, but if we want to work here, we sign it."

Claudia rearranged her face into a more neutral expression. She wouldn't get anywhere by criticizing this woman's employer. "Yolande, if you have some information about Lindsey's death, don't you think you're obligated to bring it forward?"

The woman shook her head emphatically, her dark eyes intense. "I don't. I mean, I don't have any information. Just . . . just some thoughts about it."

"I'm sure you'd feel better to get them off your chest, whatever they are."

"Ms. Rose, I'm raising four kids on my own. I need this job. I can't . . . I can't risk it."

Yolande took her past the reception desk in silence and accompanied her out to the elevator. Something was on her mind and Claudia wanted to know what it was. She stepped reluctantly aboard the empty elevator car feeling frustrated at her inability to break through Yolande's defenses.

She punched the Lobby button, but Lillian Grainger's assistant abruptly thrust her hand between the elevator doors as they started to close. As the doors reopened, Yolande leaned in and spoke rapidly, *sotto voce*. "You need to check out Mexico."

Before Claudia could respond, the woman turned on her heel and practically ran back into the Graingers' offices. Through the narrowing space left by the closing doors, Claudia saw the receptionist pick up the phone, her eyes following Yolande as she hurried past. Coincidence? Or reporting the conversation to someone?

Lillian as Big Brother? The idea made her smile. Then she turned her thoughts to what Yolande had said.

Mexico. Now, why did that sound familiar?

On the drive home, Claudia phoned Jovanic and caught him at his desk, munching a taco. She reported on her conversations with Lillian Grainger and Yolande Palomino.

"Mexico, huh?" he mumbled, the tortilla shell crackling as he bit into it. "Lindsey had some accounts in the Caymans, but I haven't found any references to Mexico. You got any ideas about that?"

"I'm not the detective, Detective."

"Oh yeah, I forgot."

"Maybe after this case, I'll think about changing careers."

There was a grin in his voice when he answered. "Okay, Claudia, I admit it, you've been a big help. Now, how about those boxes of Lindsey's sitting in your living room? I need to pick them up. Maybe there's something in there."

"Come on over; you're welcome to them."

"I thought maybe you'd get started without me. You're so good at that."

*　　*　　*

Next, she dialed Zebediah's number.

You just had to know the right people to ask.

"Mexico?" he repeated. "Lindsey had a time-share there. She went down pretty regularly."

"What did she do there?"

"What do you think she was doing in Zi-wha, sweetie? She went to have fun."

"Zi-wha?"

"That's what the locals call it. It's really Ixtapa-Zihuatanejo, but they just say Zi-Wha."

"You enjoy saying it, don't you?"

"It sort of trips off the tongue, don't you think? *Ixtapa-Zihuatanejo.* It's about a five hour flight from LA. Pretty exclusive, but not as touristy as Puerto Vallerta."

An unpleasant memory flashed a warning. She didn't have to remove his letter to Lindsey from her safe and re-read it to remember the opening line: *"Mexico was a huge mistake."*

"Did you ever go with her?" Claudia asked, afraid of his answer.

"I went once, a couple of years ago, but I have no idea who else she might have taken. She was pretty quiet about the place."

At least he wasn't denying it, she thought with a surge of relief. "Do you think she might have been hiding something about it?"

"Mmmm." At the other end of the line, Zebediah paused to reflect on the question. "Maybe. Yes, I think maybe she was being a bit secretive. If something was good, she'd spread it around."

"So, maybe it was something *not* good she was doing down there. What do you think? Drugs, money laundering, white slavery? Come on, doc, you're the headshrinker . . . give it up . . . tell me what you know."

Zebediah gave a sly chuckle. "I love it when you get tough with me, darling. But sadly, I have no idea. She certainly never showed me a dungeon while we were there. I never knew she had one in the desert. Too bad."

"Zeb, what do you really think was going on?"

He sighed. "I don't know, sweetie, maybe she had a married lover and didn't want anyone to know."

Claudia turned the possibility over in her head. Mused about it aloud. "A married lover? She was never one to hide that sort of thing before."

"But what if her lover were a U.S. senator?"

"Heidt was a client, not a personal relationship."

"Bostwick told you Lindsey had a new boyfriend. I wonder if he was real, or just a good story to cover his own ass."

"That's the million dollar question."

Ending the call, Claudia made the decision to re-examine every piece of paper that she and Kelly had gone through before Jovanic removed the boxes. Maybe they had missed something.

She turned west onto Jefferson Boulevard toward the ocean. The north side of the road into Playa del Reina was flanked by wetlands whose endangered status made them the subject of semi-regular protests by the ecology-minded. On the south side, above the wetlands, condos and houses clung to steep cliffs on flimsy-looking stilts.

Few cars were on the road in the cloudy mid-afternoon. As she steered the Jag onto the ribbon of highway that ran past Ballona Creek and would take her into town, Claudia felt suddenly drained. She wanted nothing more than for the case to be resolved so that she could return to life the way it was before she had become involved in Lindsey's affairs. Ironic that without Lindsey, she wouldn't have met Jovanic.

Wrapped in her thoughts, she failed to notice the small white truck that pulled alongside her until the other vehicle slowed and was almost even with the Jag.

In her peripheral vision, she noticed the truck's passenger window being lowered and wondered if the driver was going to ask for directions.

Then she glanced over and saw the gun.

Chapter 30

In a fraction of the time it takes for conscious thought to register and process panic, Claudia stomped the accelerator to the floor. Tires squealed and the Jaguar sprang forward, as graceful as its namesake.

The sound of two loud reports; a hot spray of powdered glass that left the smell of heat in the air.

The white truck tried to come alongside her again, but was outclassed by the Jag's powerful engine.

Near the Italian restaurant at the beginning of the little town's main street, Claudia hit the brakes, narrowly avoiding plowing into a pedestrian crossing at the traffic light. Glancing away from the pedestrian's shocked gaze, she checked the rearview mirror. A quarter-mile behind her, the white truck hung a jerky U-turn and sped away.

With hands that refused to stop shaking, she reached for her cell phone and dialed 911. After reporting the assault, she called Jovanic, but his voicemail message said he was in court and could not be reached. Going home was out of the question.

Her heart was still pounding double-time as she turned into Cowboys' driveway and parked near the rear wall, as far away from the street as she could. For a few long moments she just sat there breathing rapid, sharp gulps of air.

Pinpricks of blood stung her arm when she tried to wipe away the powdery glass. At least she was alive and, she was pretty sure, not hit. She turned her head slowly from side to side, tested each of her limbs, satisfying herself that everything still worked the way it was supposed to.

The driver's side window was a web of cracks and breaks, with a quarter-sized hole in the center. When she saw the damage to the dashboard where the shell had lodged, she realized how close she had come to being hit; probably killed. She opened the driver's door and stumbled out. Little bits of safety glass fell from her skirt and crunched on the asphalt under her feet.

The Cowboys lunch crowd had thinned to a couple of customers sitting outside on the deck. Claudia ducked into the small bathroom and locked the door. She stared in the mirror at the red patch on her cheek. Heat from the velocity of the bullet. Running cold water over her arm, she murmured a little prayer of thanks that she had been spared. Then she went out to the bar and ordered a vodka tonic.

When she told him she'd been shot at, the bartender—big guy past seventy, with brilliant blue eyes in a craggy, weathered face, gave her a tube of ointment. "Slap some of this on," he said. "It'll take the sting out."

Claudia twisted the cap off with hands that wouldn't stop trembling, and smeared the cream liberally over the sore spots. "Thanks, Dooley. I'm counting on the vodka to do the trick."

She sat at the bar and called Kelly.

"Oh, my God!" Kelly shrieked. "You could've been killed!"

"No shit." Claudia pressed a damp paper towel against her left arm. As quickly as she wiped them away, the tiny red flecks continued to blossom on her skin. Her face stung like hell from the heat of the bullet, even with Dooley's first aid cream. "The good news is, I'm still breathing."

"Where are you? I'll come get you."

"Don't bother; I'm okay, really."

Kelly gave a rude snort. "Shut up, stupid, I need to see you and make *sure*!"

Claudia gave up on her makeshift first aid and switched

the phone to the other ear. She tossed back a slug of vodka, choking as it hit her throat.

"Fine, I'm at Cowboys. I figured I could use a stiff one. No sex jokes, please."

"I can't believe all the shit that's come down on you. Does Detective Joel know yet?"

"I couldn't reach him; he's in court. Not that I had much to tell. Two guys who looked like ten thousand other white guys on the West Side: dark glasses, baseball caps, generic white truck . . . one of those little ones. I don't even know what make. It all happened so fast, there's no way I could get a license plate. *Fuck*!"

The vodka had allowed the panic to subside a little and she was now royally pissed. There had to be a way to catch whoever was responsible, whether the malefactor was Bryce Heidt or someone else. Yet, if it wasn't Heidt, who was it? Bostwick? Bishop Flannery? One of the other men on the tapes? Not Earl Nelson, they knew that for a certainty. Someone they hadn't yet uncovered? Whoever it was clearly had a lot to lose, considering the lengths they had already gone to—for what? A videotape?

Someone was engineering all the threats and attacks. Someone with the wherewithal to plan and execute. *Okay, maybe execute wasn't such a good choice of words.* Someone who could plan and direct others to carry out orders. That had to mean big money. Someone Lindsey was blackmailing. Someone whose name was in the spreadsheet and Lindsey's journal.

And that brought her back to the videotapes. Every man Lindsey had taped stood to lose should the contents be publicized. Exposure would mean public humiliation, ruined careers, possible jail time for drug use or prostitution. Maybe even a murder charge if it could be shown that Lindsey had not committed suicide.

Claudia realized that she had come full circle and was asking herself the question she had started with: *Had Lindsey written the note?*

A patrol car was parked next to the Jag, and two criminalists in plain clothes who had arrived in their own vehicles were going over it, looking for ballistics. The cops had already interviewed Claudia as she sat glued to her barstool. She had refused to let go of her drink, as if her hold on the glass was the only thing keeping her from falling apart.

Now, waiting outside Cowboys for Kelly, a cool ocean breeze ruffling her hair and lifting the hem of her skirt, it crossed her mind that she was making herself vulnerable standing there. But the booze had boosted her confidence and left her pleasantly light-headed. She'd realized that if her reaction time had been a millisecond slower and her car a little less powerful, she might now be on her way to the morgue.

"Considering how many times I've called nine-one-one lately," she said to Kelly, "I should have a direct line to the police station."

Kelly's eyes glistened with unshed tears as she gaped across the parking lot at the Jag's shattered window. "Oh my God, Claud, look at it!" She started sobbing. "What would I do if anything happened to you?"

"Don't cry, you'll ruin your mascara." Claudia plunked into the Mustang's passenger seat. "My poor car."

"For Chrissake, who cares about the damn car? Thank God the bullet missed *you*."

"Let's go. I don't want to see them dig out the bullet." Claudia averted her eyes from the Jaguar as Kelly sniffed into a tissue, then put the car in gear and drove out of the lot, avoiding the yellow crime scene tape around the Jag.

On yet another day where normalcy had become a scarce commodity, Claudia's house seemed weirdly normal; the lacy white birch stood as ever in the neatly trimmed strip of lawn; the flagstone path still led to the redwood staircase; plants spilled over the ledge from flower boxes on the deck above the chocolate-brown garage door.

Chained in her neighbor's front-yard next door, Flare barked an enthusiastic greeting. Marcia had been spooked by the break-in at Claudia's house and had taken to leaving her dog outside while she was away from home.

There had been no walks on the beach lately and the big

dog whined as Claudia and Kelly crossed the yard to give her fuzzy muzzle a rub. They were rewarded with a warm, sloppy tongue on their hands.

Kelly laughed. "Some guard dog; she's just a big old softy."

"That's because she knows you. One day I was walking her on the beach and some guy tried to talk to me. She nearly bit his hand off."

"Maybe we could take her for a walk together," Kelly offered. "Safety in numbers?"

"Oh, so we can all be killed together? Thanks, but no thanks."

Claudia unlocked the front door and switched off the alarm. She wondered whether she would ever be able to return to her old life. A life where she could do the simple, everyday things. Like walking the dog.

"Will they be able to prove she was blackmailing these guys?" asked Kelly when Claudia told her about the video-tapes she and Jovanic had discovered at the desert house.

"Her clients apparently didn't know they were being taped. She must have saved that little bit of information until she was ready to extort money from them. According to that spreadsheet I found, she was getting a whole lot more money from some of them than from others. If that doesn't suggest blackmail, what does? Of course, those are the ones who are least likely to admit it because they have the most to lose."

She hadn't told Kelly who all the men were. Even though she now was sure that her friend was innocent, Kelly had all but indicted herself with the account of her own visit to Lindsey on the night of her death.

The issue of Zebediah Gold's letter had yet to be resolved, too.

Yolande Palomino had told her to check out Mexico. She wished she had thought to ask Yolande about the phantom boyfriend Bostwick had mentioned. Even if she had refused to part with any further information, maybe she might at least have confirmed or denied his existence. And, if he really did exist, whether he was the Mexico connection.

Mental note: Call Yolande.

                                    *   *   *

An hour later, the living room looked like a paper factory after Hurricane Katrina. The floor was covered with file folders, the couch littered with scraps that they had set aside for later examination.

Jovanic phoned.

"I'll be there as soon as I can get out of here," he said in a tight voice. "Don't leave the house, and stay away from the windows."

Just knowing that he was aware of what had happened made her feel better. She lowered her voice to an intimate murmur. "Call me when you're on your way. I'll order pizza and we can hole up for the evening."

"Ask him if he's interested in a threesome," Kelly chimed in.

"Shut up," Claudia hissed, but she couldn't help laughing when Jovanic said, "That woman scares me." He admonished her again and rang off.

"Look for any references to Mexico," Claudia said, folding herself cross-legged on the floor. "It's something Jovanic is following up on."

Kelly dove into one of the file boxes and came out with Lindsey's leather-bound appointment book. "I'll go through this again. Maybe I missed something before."

"Look for anything that might point to a boyfriend, too. Bostwick could have been trying to throw us off-track with that, but it's possible there really is someone else we need to look at."

"Isn't it strange that if she did have a guy, he didn't show up at the funeral?"

"Isn't everything about this situation strange? Besides, how do we know he *wasn't* there? He could easily have been in the crowd, but not wanted to reveal himself for the same reason Lindsey wanted to keep him secret. If he exists."

"If we find him and he's cute, maybe I'll grab him for myself," Kelly said, only half-joking. "Poetic justice, wouldn't you say?"

"She's dead, Kel, why don't you drop it?"

"Being dead doesn't change how I feel about her. I *still*

hate her, and if I had a chance to steal her boyfriend like she stole mine, I'd do it in a heartbeat."

At a loss for an answer, Claudia got up and selected a Norah Jones disk, sliding it into the player.

It didn't take long for Kelly to discover several Mexico references that she had overlooked before. The first, in the previous January, was marked simply, "Mex."

"There's a flight number with this one. American Airlines. Nothing the other times. Maybe she drove."

"Too far to drive. Maybe someone else made the reservations for the other trips. What are the dates?"

"There's a note on January thirteenth, another on March twenty-fifth, and one on July fifteenth. Quarterly."

"How about October? Anything there?"

"Duh," Kelly said. "She died in September."

"Duh . . . even Lindsey might have planned ahead. Look in October."

Kelly flipped through a few pages and looked up with a sour face. "Okay, smartass, October fourteenth, with a flight number again."

"I bet Joel can find out if she booked two seats," said Claudia, getting excited. "Maybe the boyfriend will be revealed at last." She felt suddenly positive that they were about to solve the case. "Let's go upstairs. It's time to do some handwriting analysis."

Chapter 31

"Here goes nothing."

Claudia flicked a switch on the optical handwriting comparator and the exhaust fan began to whir. The screen flickered once and blinked on, transmitting bright light from behind the Plexiglas plate.

She clipped the suicide note under one of the hold plates and a specimen of Lindsey's uncontested handwriting on the other. Having failed to unearth any printed samples that would have allowed for a direct comparison, and the handprinting on Earl Nelson's photos had been done too long ago to be of any real value, she had selected the best of what was available—a page of notes Lindsey had written about a client.

After fiddling with the dial on the comparator until the two handwriting samples were magnified six times their normal size, Claudia stepped back a few paces and narrowed her eyes, blurring the focus. "It's a tough call, but I think she wrote it. The word spacing is similar. So's the pressure and the letter proportions."

She picked up a pen and pointed to one of the on-screen samples. "Look at that dented area in the tops of the o's. It shows up in both samples and it's idiosyncratic. It's her writing."

Kelly directed her gaze at the two handwritings projected onto the screen and blew out a gusty sigh of relief. "The note's genuine. It had to be suicide."

But Claudia shook her head in disagreement. "It's her handwriting, but something still stinks. I can *feel* it."

"What are you talking about?"

"Either someone forced her to write that note, or she wrote it for some other reason and the killer made it *look* like a suicide note."

"You're grasping at straws, Claud. Let it go, for fuck's sake."

"It's kind of hard to let it go when people are breaking into my house and shooting at me," Claudia snapped. She flipped off the comparator and removed the handwriting samples, her movement jerky with anger. She wanted to yell at Kelly, *At least I don't think* I *killed her*—but what would be the use?

As if sensing what was in her mind, Kelly clambered to her feet and grabbed her jacket from the kitchen chair where she had hooked it. "Nothing good ever came of being involved with Lindsey. Good luck, honey."

Jovanic arrived just ahead of the pizza and shortly after Kelly's departure.

The moment he was inside the door, his arms went around Claudia, electric energy emanating from his body as he held her. He touched the tiny glass cuts on her arm and face with fingers more sensitive than she would have expected from a man his size. Holding her a little tighter, a little longer, until his solid warmth made her feel safe again.

Finally, he let go and stepped slowly away. "Not much to go on," he said over his shoulder as he walked over to the French doors to check the locks. "No license plate, but at least they got the bullet. That way, there'll be something to match if a weapon is recovered." He ran a hand through the unruly salt-and-pepper hair in the absent-minded way he often did.

He told her he was still waiting to hear from the airlines with information on Lindsey's Mexico trips. No word yet from the banks in the Cayman Islands, where he had called to investigate her accounts. And he had checked with the detectives who were assigned to handle the attempted break-in at Claudia's house, and the shooting.

"I think we both need a drink," Claudia said, taking him

into the kitchen. She got the bottle of Stoli out of the freezer and mixed them both a vodka martini. They bumped glasses in a silent toast, then carried their glasses into the living room and sat close together on the couch.

Claudia leaned back into the curve of his arm. "I'm so glad you're here." Jovanic put his glass on the coffee table and turned to look at her. He leaned forward and took her chin in his hand, turned her face up to his. His kiss was gentle—too gentle. Her heart started to thump.

He's got more bad news. She held her breath and turned her gaze on him, the question plain in her eyes.

Jovanic hesitated for a long moment then gave his head a reluctant nod, as if he had made up his mind. "I got my ass handed to me for taking you to Palm Springs the other day. I don't know how the captain found out, but—I got tossed off the case. He's assigned a couple other detectives to the Novak and Nelson murders."

Claudia sat up straight, nearly spilling her drink, and stared at him. Her lips were still warm from his kiss, but she felt cold all over. "But what about *me?*" Her voice rose and she couldn't seem to stop it. "Is he gonna wait until *I'm* a murder victim, too, to do something?"

His voice stayed level. "Barnes and Zuniga are good detectives. It's pretty obvious that what's been happening to you is directly related to Lindsey's videotapes." He reached for her but she shrugged away from him, angry at his captain; taking it out on him.

"So, people can shoot at me and it's okay?"

"No, goddamn it, it's not okay. Pacific Division is investigating the shots at you and the break-in here. They'll be working with Barnes and Zuniga. Look, someone wants me off the case—could be Heidt or Bostwick pulling strings, I just don't know. I'm not gonna give up the investigation, but I'll have to keep a low profile."

After that, it didn't matter what he said. She'd been counting on helping him to solve the case and get her life back. Now, his news had pitched her into a foul mood and she was too frightened to pull herself out of it, even though she knew she was being illogical.

Her humor didn't improve when he rose from the couch, reminded her to set the alarm, and said a curt goodnight.

She wrapped the uneaten pizza and shoved the box into the fridge. *Why couldn't he have been more understanding?*
Why couldn't I?

"What do you expect, sweetie?" Zebediah said over the phone. "He's a man . . . you know we're all lower than pond scum."

Claudia switched the phone to her other hand and stretched out on the office couch. She felt empty and alone, and ashamed of the way she had handled Jovanic's news. It wasn't his fault he'd been pulled off the case.

"Let's talk about Lindsey," she said. "Ivan claimed she never printed, but it's her handwriting in the note, I'm certain of it. There wasn't enough handwriting to determine her state of mind when she wrote it to say whether she might have been suicidal."

"Chances are, it was to get attention more than a genuine attempt to kill herself," Zebediah said. "She was a primary narcissist."

"You mean by the DSM IV definition?"

The Diagnostic and Statistical Manual of Mental Disorders was the publication used by mental health professionals to diagnose behavioral disorders and mental illness. Claudia rolled off the couch and went to get her copy from the bookcase across the office.

". . . a classic case," Zebediah was saying. "Grandiose sense of self-importance, requires excessive admiration, sense of entitlement."

Paging through the index to Narcissistic Personality Disorder, Claudia took up the litany of symptoms, reading down the list where he had left off, paraphrasing. "Exploits other people for their own ends. No empathy, think they're special."

"I was out of my mind to ever get involved with her." Zebediah's voice cracked. "I sent her to another therapist as soon as we'd had sex."

Claudia said nothing, waiting. For what—a confession? She thought again of the letter he had sent to Lindsey.

"Get out of my life," he had written. *"Don't force me to do something drastic. I don't want to hurt you."*

"Why did you do it, Zeb? Why did you sleep with her?"

"I could say she seduced me." He huffed a short, humorless laugh. "But I'm not *that* lacking in a sense of responsibility. She came to the office one night . . . she always wanted our sessions scheduled late in the evening. That night, she brought a carpet bag with her. Halfway through the session, she excused herself to the bathroom. When she returned, she was . . . well, let's just say she was wearing a very sexy getup.

"Of course, I knew I should stop her, but I felt . . . *paralyzed*. She sashayed around the office; lit some candles she'd brought with her; poured wine. She'd thought of everything . . . a little dope, a little Ecstasy. She absolutely fascinated me." His voice trailed off, lost in that moment when he had made the choice to put his entire career in jeopardy.

Claudia caught her breath, staggered by the enormity of his confession. "Didn't she care that you'd lose your license if you were found out?" *Dumb question. Of course she hadn't cared.*

"I told her I wouldn't see her as a therapist again. She was furious." Zebediah's voice held a note of regret tinged with something else. Anger? Frustration?

"California law forbids a therapist to date a patient for two years after discontinuing a therapeutic relationship. For a long time, I couldn't stop myself from seeing her, even when she would torment me, threaten to expose what I'd done . . . it was the biggest lapse of judgment in my life. Finally, I couldn't stand it and put a stop to the whole thing."

Claudia's stomach turned over, stricken with fear. "Zeb . . . *what are you saying?*"

"Losing my license because of a chronic blackmailer would have been the end for me. Frankly, for a long time, I was terrified . . . I thought she might follow through on her threats. But I came to realize that having her hold it over my head was worse than if she had just reported me to the licensing board."

"What . . . did . . . you . . . do?"

"I told her I no longer cared; to do her worst. She just laughed at me and that was it. God, how stupid I was to let her get at me that way."

It felt like a reprieve, and the feeling left Claudia dizzy. Her eyes went to the Egyptian wall hanging that hid her safe. "I saw the letter you wrote her, telling her to leave you alone."

"What? Where on earth?"

She heard the shock in his voice, imagined the crow's-feet around his eyes creasing as he tried to figure it out. "Ivan found it. He seemed to think . . . he thought it implicated you."

"I don't understand . . . implicated me?" Zebediah went silent. "Good God, you aren't saying he thought *I* killed Lindsey?"

"He couldn't accept her committing suicide, so he tried to deflect the blame."

"Onto *me*? Why didn't you say something sooner? Sweetie, don't tell me you thought it was true?"

"Of course not." The lie came too quickly, but she couldn't stand to hurt her old friend that way. She should have known better than to doubt him.

"Who else knows about this?"

"Nobody else. Zeb, about the note . . . it's Lindsey's genuine handwriting, but I'm not convinced she intended it as a suicide note."

"Few narcissists actually complete suicide," he mused, allowing her to distract him. "When it happens, they're trying to get someone's attention. Completion is usually by accident."

"What if she called someone for help . . . someone whose attention she wanted . . . but they didn't come?"

"Whom do you have in mind?"

"Bostwick told me Lindsey had a boyfriend. What if she called him and he didn't want to come, or . . . or he was married and couldn't get away. That could explain why he didn't make himself known at the funeral, if he was there."

"Or maybe he *wanted* her dead for some reason. If she called him after taking the pills, he could have seen it as a way of getting rid of her without having to do it himself."

"He could be rid of her that way and be scot-free."

"Interesting concept, darling, but what about the attacks on Ivan and you?"

"Jesus, Zeb, I don't know. Even if Lindsey did kill herself, anyone she was blackmailing would know there was a chance the videotapes would be found. *Someone's* trying to avoid exposure." Claudia gave a deep sigh. "I guess we're back to square one again."

Later, long after she'd rung off and night had settled over the house, Claudia remained on the couch. Hugging one of the big puffy cushions to her chest, she stared into the darkness, battling the urge to call Jovanic and ask him to come back.

The hour grew late. Around midnight, she convinced herself to get up and shake out the cramps in her legs; tour the house, check doors and windows, re-check the alarm system. Ready to jump out of her skin at the slightest creak.

What's he thinking now?

Her hand hovered over the phone. Had she killed the budding relationship by behaving like an immature brat?

After spending the past two nights lying next to him, listening to him breathe, feeling safe and connected to another human being, the thought of climbing into that big, cold bed alone was singularly unappealing.

Chapter 32

"Claudia, it's Joel. Please call me back on my cellular. I'd like to see you for dinner."

She played back the message on her voice mail three times before she dialed his number. She wasn't sure she believed in love at first sight, but the past few days had certainly been a wild roller coaster ride. The attraction she felt for Jovanic warred with her unease at becoming vulnerable again—she saw herself more as a merry-go-round person. Yet, if she would admit the truth, deep in her heart, she wanted to open herself to him. If only she could.

The restaurant's name, Shanghai Red's, must have been left over from some long-ago attempt at Chinese that didn't work out, as the current cuisine tended more toward California Fresh. Claudia and Jovanic were seated at a window table where they could see the lights from the condos across the harbor shimmering on the water. *Romantic*.

Jovanic appeared relaxed, enjoying himself. He hadn't raised the topic of their tense parting the night before, and neither had Claudia, who was more than willing to let it go. "So, tell me about this Halloween party," he said.

She smiled invitingly. "Among all the sparkly guests, our personal buddy, Senator Heidt."

That got his attention. "You sure about that?"

"Lillian Grainger said so, and it's her party. Maybe you'll get a chance to have a private chat with him. I don't suppose he'll have his lawyer in tow at the party."

"Seems like too good an opportunity to miss. What should we do for costumes?"

"I already rented some. We're going as Antony and Cleopatra."

He gave her a scowl of disbelief. "Aww, shit, Claudia, I'm not going in a dress!"

"It's not a dress, Columbo, it's a tunic, and with your legs, you'll look great; trust me."

"Yeah? In my experience, someone who says 'trust me,' usually means, *fuck you*."

"Come on, smile. You're going to the party with the Queen of the Nile. Besides, you'll get to brandish a sword. The important thing is that he not recognize us."

"If he does, I'll probably get fired."

"Then maybe you shouldn't go."

He gave up pretending to be irked, and grinned. "Are you kidding? I wouldn't miss it." Then he changed the subject. "I saw our young friend Brandi today."

Claudia searched the impassive expression for what might be hidden behind it. "This sounds like one of those coincidences I don't believe in."

"Let's say I was in the neighborhood, so I stopped by for a friendly chat." Jovanic took a rosemary roll from the napkin-covered basket, breaking it open and slathering on a thick curl of butter. He bit into it, sighing like a man who hadn't eaten in days. "Now she's had some time to sober up, Brandi confirmed that Bostwick brought dope with him to their sessions. Not that her say-so is gonna get him convicted, but it's a start."

The waiter arrived with rare prime rib and a stuffed chicken breast.

The candle in the frosted ginger jar sent shadows playing across Jovanic's face, lending him a diabolical look. "I've been checking up on Preston Sommerfield," he continued, "the pedophile in those photos you gave me from Lindsey's brother . . ." He frowned at Claudia from under his brows. "By the way, you committed another felony when you paid Nelson."

"What?"

"You purchased child pornography. That's against the law."

Claudia groaned in mock repentance. "Oh Lord, that's my third strike." She counted on her fingers. "I took the flash drive from the crime scene, withheld the videotape, and now I bought dirty photos. I guess that makes me a career criminal."

"Yes, I think it does," Jovanic agreed. "I may have to arrest you yet."

He was being playful, but she suddenly felt as if cold water had been dashed in her face. "I think I had enough of handcuffs at Lindsey's dungeon."

Reaching across the table, he squeezed her hand. "Those photos really got to you, didn't they?"

"Yeah, they did. They explained so much about Lindsey's behavior. Between her brother and Preston Sommerfield . . . they just about destroyed everything good in her."

"Sommerfield is high on the suspect list. He wasn't on Lindsey's spreadsheet, but we know she blackmailed him." He picked up his fork and ate a couple of bites of baked potato, pushed a chunk of meat around on his plate. *Fidgeting.* He laid the fork on his plate and cleared his throat.

"Claudia, uh, there's something I want to say, and I'm, uh . . ." He glanced away, made a quick visual sweep of the room. She wasn't sure if he was checking his surroundings out of habit, or doing it to avoid looking at her. Then his eyes met her gaze and held it. "I know it's cliché, but this is the truth . . . you're not like any woman I've ever been involved with."

She stared at him in surprise.

"I know guys say shit like that, but this isn't a pickup line. Talking to you is like . . . talking to someone at work . . . no, wait," he protested, coloring up when she couldn't help laughing. "I mean, you're easy to be with. I don't have to watch what I'm saying all the time. I . . ." He trailed off, color suffusing his cheeks.

Claudia smiled gently. "Because a conversation about blood and guts over dinner doesn't upset me?"

Jovanic ran his hand through his hair, struggling to vocalize his feelings. "Okay, what I'm saying pretty badly is, you're really special. This past couple of weeks has been rough on you. I know that. Not everyone would handle it as well as you have."

It wasn't what she'd expected, and she was deeply touched, recognizing how hard it was for him to say what he'd said. She wanted to go around the table and put her lips to his ear, whisper reassurances; she wanted to show him how much it meant to her, too—to be with someone who understood and accepted her— someone who didn't complain about all the hours she spent working, or that she talked too much shop.

She reached across the table and laid her hand on his. He took her hand and turned it over, pressing his lips to her palm, a silent promise.

Chapter 33

"Please don't call me here again," Yolande Palomino said urgently in a low voice. "There's nothing more I can tell you." The line went dead.

Damn!

Yolande's home number was unpublished and Claudia had no other way to get in touch with her short of trying to catch her on her way to work. Pulling out the computer keyboard drawer, she keyed in the password to access her e-mail; cheered when no new threats popped up on the list. Maybe her pursuer, whoever he was, realized there was nothing to gain by intimidating her.

She ran through the list again. Heidt? Bostwick? Flannery? Someone else? Not knowing was driving her crazy.

Jovanic might be precluded from actively investigating the case, but Claudia wasn't. She picked up the phone and dialed.

When she entered the Bostwick medical suite, she was greeted with a big, plastic smile.

"Good afternoon," said the woman who looked like Donna Reed. "How may I help you?"

"I have an appointment with Doctor Bostwick. Claudia Rose."

The smile faded as recognition dawned. "But . . . I don't under . . . uh . . ." Donna Reed fixed an anxious stare on her computer screen, checking the appointments. "Why . . . yes, here you are . . . but . . . for a consultation? I thought . . . I thought you . . . that detective . . ."

Claudia patted her flat abdomen. "I'm considering liposuction, and since Doctor Bostwick is the best . . . well, the appointment secretary had a last-minute cancellation, so here I am."

It must have been fate. At least, that's how Claudia justified it in her own mind. Jovanic would probably have disagreed.

Donna Reed looked doubtful, but the lady had an appointment and she couldn't argue with that. She ushered Claudia into a small private waiting room. Oak paneling, dark leather side chairs. You could almost smell the pipe smoke.

A brag wall chronicled Doctor Bostwick's successes. Tastefully arranged gold-leaf framed certificates: Degrees and diplomas, framed articles and photos. An eight-by-ten black-and-white glossy: a young Doctor Bostwick, shaking hands with then-President Richard Nixon; the same handsome features, but white-haired now, glad-handing Governor Arnold Schwarzenegger. Bostwick must be a major campaign contributor to get so close to the top.

Did he put money into Bryce Heidt's campaign? Jovanic could probably find out easily enough.

"You!" Framed in the doorway, Bostwick suddenly seemed larger than life. "What are you doing here? I told you everything over the phone." Behind the granny glasses, his eyes narrowed to suspicious slits. "Frances said you were a consult."

"Oh, but I am," said Claudia, faking innocence. "Do you think liposuction would be a good idea for me?"

"If you're here about liposuction, I'm Santa Claus."

Claudia's smile was a mile shy of sincere. "Oh, doctor, is that how you dress up these days? You were wearing considerably less than a Santa suit when I saw you last."

Bostwick rounded the door in a flash, closing it sharply enough to rattle windows. "What do you think you're doing, coming here with your veiled insinuations?"

"Let's take the veils off. Your home movies might not win any Oscars, but I'm sure, if the tabloids got hold . . ."

The small room shrank as Bostwick moved forward, thrusting his face close enough to catch a whiff of his lunchtime tuna melt. "Are you threatening me? Because if you are . . ."

"If I am, then what? You'll get rid of me like you did Lindsey?"

"Like I did Lindsey?" He backed off, glaring at her. "What are you talking about?"

Claudia wagged her finger at him, feigning coolness. "Come off it, doctor, she was blackmailing you and you got tired of it."

He didn't even try to deny it. "She committed suicide, remember?"

"The cops know she was blackmailing you. Don't you think they'll put two and two together? Maybe even exhume her body?"

"Don't be ridiculous; they wouldn't find anything." Bostwick spoke bravely, but he plucked a crisp linen handkerchief from his pocket with a trembling hand and swiped it across his forehead where beads of sweat had begun to gather. "I won't deny I was glad when I heard she was dead. I thought the extortion was finally over, but . . . wait a minute . . . aren't *you* with the police?"

Claudia ignored the question. "What about the boyfriend you told me about? Was that for real?"

He removed his glasses, slipped them into his lab coat pocket and turned away, rubbing at his eyes. "I didn't *do* anything."

"You supplied her with drugs for those little parties in the desert."

Bostwick stiffened. All at once, he spun around, lunged at her. She pushed back, but she was no match for his weight and strength. He drove her hard against the wall, knocking the breath out of her.

"You bitch!" he cried in a low voice, clutching at her silk blouse. Pearl buttons flew in every direction as his hands fumbled her body. "You *bitch*! Are you wearing a wire?"

Grunting, Claudia twisted out of his grasp and sprang for the door. For all his bulk, Bostwick was faster.

"Get out of my way!" Claudia shouted, throwing herself against him, elbow first.

Bostwick stumbled, but kept himself between her and the door. As he righted himself she saw that his face was the shade of an overripe tomato; a vein throbbed wildly in his temple.

"I'm through paying," he panted. "You won't get a god-damn dime out of me!"

Without warning, his hands were on her throat, hot and heavy, squeezing. She clawed at his fingers, trying to scream, but his grip tightened on her windpipe until she couldn't breathe.

"Doctor? Doctor, is everything all right?" There was a timid knock on the door. *"Doctor?"*

Bostwick released his grasp, staring at Claudia as if coming out of a dream. She fell back against the wall, gasping, greedily sucking air.

"Go away!" the doctor shouted at the door, his voice shaky. "Everything's fine."

He looked down at his hands, which were trembling like those of a very old, sick man, as if he didn't understand how they came to be appended to his arms.

Claudia's throat hurt and the skin of her neck burned. Her knees wanted to fold, and only her back plastered to the wall prevented her from sliding to the floor. She pulled her tattered blouse closed, did her best to steady her breathing.

"I don't want money," she said in a hoarse whisper. "I just want the truth. And I want the harassment stopped."

He stared at her, nonplused. "What harassment?"

"My house has been broken into. I've been shot at. People have been killed. Did *you* send those lowlifes after me?"

"Why would I go after *you?*" He seemed genuinely perplexed. "I don't even know you."

"Because I had Lindsey's videotapes from the desert. The police have them now."

He stared at her for a long moment, desperation clouding the ice-blue eyes. "The *police* have them? My God, this will destroy me." Slowly, he sank onto a chair and dropped his head into his hands. When his eyes found hers again, they were glazed with tears. "I didn't do any of those things, I swear it."

Was he telling the truth? He sounded so earnest.

Claudia edged toward the door, desperate to put some distance between herself and Bostwick. "If you cooperate with the police . . . tell them what you know . . . you might be able to make a deal, keep it out of the newspapers."

"I had no idea she was videotaping the sessions until she invited me to her apartment and showed me the tape. She demanded the drugs as payment." He shook his head in despair, his eyes downcast. "Why should I have to go through this? I didn't hurt anyone."

Claudia opened the consulting room door. "Like I said, doctor, make your deal with the police. Who knows, you might come out looking like a hero, if you can give them something they don't already have." She massaged her bruised throat. "And as a bonus, I'll think about not having you charged with assault."

For a brief instant he looked cheered. "Would you talk to that detective for me? If you'd put in a good word, I could do something in return for you." He looked at her, appraising, a spark of the old fire flickering. "A breast reduction, or . . . or I could do something with your nose or . . ."

As if she'd let him near her with a knife.

Chapter 34

"Do you think I need a nose job?"

"What?" Jovanic threw a questioning glance over the tops of his sunglasses.

"My nose . . . do you think it's too big?" The day after her visit to Bostwick, his offer of cosmetic surgery still rankled.

"No, Claudia, I don't." He sized her up with healthy skepticism. "I don't suppose this sudden interest in plastic surgery would have anything to do with a certain doctor who just happened to show up at Wilshire Division?"

Claudia gave him a look of surprise. She'd decided to keep her visit to Bostwick to herself, and she wore a scarf to cover the marks his fingers had left on her throat. "Bostwick turned himself in?"

"Very interesting how he seemed to know what we had on him. Lo and behold, he suddenly decides he should help the investigation. In exchange for a consideration, of course."

Claudia tried to look innocent. "That day we were there, you came down pretty hard on him. He must have realized you weren't bluffing."

"Well, thanks to the doctor, I'm back on the investigation." Jovanic hefted two of Lindsey's boxes into his arms and carried them down Claudia's front steps, which were still damp from the morning dew.

She followed, jamming her hands in her pockets against the nippy early morning breeze coming in from the ocean. "You're joking. How did *that* happen?"

"Bostwick showed up demanding to speak with me and only me. Not that he loves me, you understand; damage control. Involve as few people as possible. My guess is, he leaned on the chief."

"But you said someone wanted you *off* the case."

"Being a big mucky-muck in the community doesn't hurt."

"What's he offering?"

"He'll cop to writing illegal prescriptions and get a slap on the wrist."

"What a foul bastard he is."

Claudia unlocked the Jeep for him and opened the back door. He shoved the boxes inside and turned to her. "There's something else . . . we got a break in Ivan's case. They lifted a good palm print and a partial thumb from the stairwell."

"A lot of people must have gone up and down those stairs and left prints."

"How many of them had Ivan's blood on their hand?"

"Good point." She tipped her head to one side, contemplating. "I wonder if he's the one who attacked Destiny and me."

"They're running the prints. If he has a record, we'll get a name."

"He would have had to get medical attention somewhere. I know his arm was broken," Claudia said. "Hey, if Bostwick hired him, he could have gone to him for treatment . . . nah, that would mean either Bostwick is behind all the attacks, or there's some kind of conspiracy. I don't think it's him."

"Why not?"

"The guy comes on strong, but he's basically a wimp. You know how bullies are. When you stand up to them, they back down."

"You sure know a lot about the guy after just one meeting," Jovanic remarked, fixing her with a suspicious stare.

She turned to close the Jeep's door so she wouldn't have to face him. "Oh, I got a look at some of his handwriting that day we went to his office. Sharp angles all over the place; strong right slant; super-heavy pressure plus red pen. It all adds up to angry man with short fuse. Still, it just doesn't seem likely behavior for him. He's more direct."

"He would have hired someone to do the dirty work."

"Maybe, but I don't really think so. Which brings us back to our favorite candidate."

"Heidt?"

"Yeah, or . . . what about Flannery?"

"Wouldn't the Church be delighted with that kind of publicity after the molestation epidemic," said Jovanic sarcastically. "Heidt's using his political clout as a shield, which is making it hard to get anywhere. Flannery also knew about the dungeon, and he knew Earl Nelson. He's a prime suspect."

"Someone's got to know *something,* and be willing to talk."

"I'm working on it. I'm going after his financial records." Jovanic ran a hand through his hair in a gesture of frustration, tousling it into a cowlick. "No judge will give us a search warrant on what we've got. So he paid for legal kinky sex. That doesn't tie him to anything else."

Claudia reached up and smoothed the errant hairs. "What's that F. Scott Fitzgerald line . . . *'the rich are different from you and me'*?"

"Yeah, *'they have more money.'* Okay, grapho lady, I've got a couple of angles I'm going after." He slipped his arms around her and backed her up against the Jeep, cupping her ass and drawing her close. "I'm gonna be up most of the night, working."

She leaned into him, tugging on his lapels until his face was close to hers. "Why don't you come back tonight?"

His lips pressed against hers, tasting her warmth, probing, lingering for a long moment before he pulled away with a regretful sigh.

He phoned around noon. "I've found Preston Sommerfield."

Sommerfield—the pedophile Earl Nelson had photographed molesting Lindsey. "So, give it up. What'd you find out?"

"Have you ever heard of Jordan Stanwyck?"

She thought about it. "Mmmm, sounds vaguely familiar. Who is he?"

"He's a big time children's advocate. You know . . . send your dollars to Timbuktu and feed a kid?"

She nodded, even though he couldn't see her. "Yeah, okay. I've seen the commercials with that actress. She's always holding some poor little ragged child, so you feel guilty if you don't send money. What's that got to do with Sommerfield?"

"Turns out his name is Preston *Stanwyck* Sommerfield." Jovanic paused, waiting for the penny to drop. "Jordan's an alias."

Claudia's hand flew to her mouth. "Holy shit, are you telling me that *pedophile* is a children's advocate?"

"He got a legal name change fifteen years ago. He's been operating a children's charity headquartered in Mexico."

"Mexico?"

"I haven't found any connection to Lindsey there yet. Still digging."

"What about his wife?"

"Drowned in a boating accident the year after Lindsey started college. Some coincidence, huh? Sommerfield was the sole heir."

"No shit," Claudia murmured, pushing her chair away from the desk. "His wife drowns, Lindsey drowns. Is there something wrong with this picture?"

"I pulled the file on the wife's death. *Looks* like a clean investigation."

"And Sommerfield is now Stanwyck, and he's involved with children? Joel, you've got to do something! After what he did to Lindsey, can you imagine . . ."

"Take it easy. As soon as we hang up, I'm heading over to SECU . . . that's the Sexually Exploited Child Unit to you."

"Do you think he could have killed Lindsey?"

"He's sure as hell made it onto my list of suspects."

Chapter 35

Jovanic's news about Preston Sommerfield kept Claudia tossing restlessly in her bed. Unable to rid herself of the images of children being exploited by the man whom she knew to be a monster, dawn had broken before she finally slipped into a sleep tormented by dreams that bordered on nightmares.

She awoke late, choking, fighting for air. Tossing back the covers, she sat on the edge of the bed until the panicky feeling subsided, then stumbled into the bathroom. She turned on the shower faucets full-blast, avoiding the mirror. Knew what she'd see there—dark shadows under her eyes; fine lines carving into her face more deeply than they had yesterday.

Setting the jet of hot water to pulse, she pushed the thoughts aside and indulged in a few minutes of fantasy— Jovanic lathering her body with French milled soap, massaging away the tension.

She dressed in sweats and dried her hair; made coffee and took her cup outside to the basket chair, where the combination of cool air and caffeine brought her fully awake. Had Jovanic actually pulled an all-nighter at the office? she wondered. Right on cue, the phone rang.

"You awake?" His voice dragged, gravelly with fatigue.

"I was just wondering the same about you."

"If I died at my desk they wouldn't find me for a week with all the paper. Hey, I got a question for you. Does the name Nasrin Kardosian mean anything to you?"

She frowned, concentrating, waiting for a prick of familiarity, not getting one. "Don't tell me it's another alias for Sommerfield?"

"Nah, nothing like that. We got a match on those prints they found at Lindsey's. This guy's got a jacket two feet thick: burglary, assault, dope, you name it."

Instantly, Claudia's hands began to tremble. Coffee slurped over the side of her mug, splashing onto her sweat pants as she jerked upright and set the basket chair swinging. She put the mug down on the mosaic-tiled garden table and shook coffee off her hands.

"This is the guy who killed Ivan? Are you sure?"

"Sure enough to get an arrest warrant. Uniforms are on their way to pick him up as we speak." Jovanic turned away from the phone and spoke in a low voice to someone in the background. When he returned he gave her the rest of the news. "You're gonna need to look at a lineup."

No!

The last thing on earth she wanted was to come face-to-face with the man who had attacked her and Destiny. But somehow, the words wouldn't come out.

"Normally, we'd use a photo lineup," Jovanic continued, filling the silence. "But I know you didn't get much of a look at him. Hey, even if you could get a feel for his general build and height it would help."

"That's not much to go on."

"Come on, you gotta do your civic duty. Anything that could identify him would help. The report said you noticed something about his hands."

In her mind, she saw them again, those hairy mitts clasping the dull black gun; she saw its deadly cargo aimed straight at her heart. "He had hands like an ape . . . hairy down to the fingers . . . but you said there was a bloody hand print. Do you really need me?" She hated the pleading quality that had entered her voice, felt powerless to make it stronger.

"A palm and a partial thumb," Jovanic corrected her. "We need to be able to link him to Ivan's homicide, *and* the attack on you and Destiny." His tone softened. "At least take a look at him, Claudia. He won't see you, he'll be on the other side of a two-way mirror."

"I know how it's done," she said, resigning herself. "I used to watch *Law and Order*."

The next time the phone rang, the caller was Zebediah, wanting to talk about the Graingers' Halloween party.

"I didn't know you were invited," said Claudia.

He pretended affront. "How could it be a party without me?"

"How do you know Lillian Grainger?"

"Same as you . . . met her after the funeral. I bowled her over with my charm and good looks."

Claudia had to laugh. "You dirty old dog, you do have a way with women. Who's your date?"

"Lillian confessed she needed single men who could dance, and I fit both categories. I'm going stag."

"Jovanic and I are going as Antony and Cleopatra. How about you?"

"Just look for the god in the gold thong, darling."

Before she could make a wisecrack in return, the call-waiting beep sounded. She said good-bye to Zebediah and clicked over.

"Our boys had a little trouble locating Mr. Kardosian," said Jovanic, sounding satisfied. "Slippery sonofabitch, but we got him."

"Okay, what do I have to do?"

"I'll pick you up in fifteen minutes. We're going downtown." Jovanic paused, did his Columbo thing. "Oh, did I mention that Mr. Kardosian was taken into custody wearing a cast on his arm?"

Debates continued over the nearly four-hundred million dollar cost of the proposed new police headquarters, but for today, their destination was Parker Center on Los Angeles Street. The building felt cold and unwelcoming to Claudia as Jovanic ushered her to the fifty-year-old elevators and they rode up to the fourth floor.

The room he took her to was plain to the point of ugly.

Ceiling tiles bore brown water stains and an electrical outlet was missing its cover, showing bare wires. It smelled of stale coffee and old french fries. Jovanic introduced her to Paul Barnes and Mario Zuniga, who were waiting for them there.

Barnes was the older of the pair. His hangdog, jowly face gave the impression of a jaded cop who had been around one block too many. Sandy brown hair was arranged in a pathetic comb-over, and the gut bulging over his belt could have used a few weeks with a personal trainer.

Zuniga seemed to be all arms. A tall, loose-jointed Hispanic in his mid-thirties who waved his hands around a lot when he spoke, his gaze bounced from Jovanic to Claudia with friendly interest. "Ready for the show?"

Claudia responded with a weak smile. "Oh, yeah, give me a ringside seat."

"Maybe you know how this works," Barnes said, stuffing an unlit cigarette behind his ear. Smoking was forbidden in the building, but a sprinkling of grey ash soiled his lapel.

He indicated the darkened two-way mirror. "We'll bring some guys into the room on the other side of this glass. They won't be able to see you. We want you to look at them all and tell us whether any of them is the person who assaulted you and Ms. Cardoza." He leveled a stern look at her. "It's important that you understand, the actual suspect may or may not be in the lineup, so don't feel like you *have* to pick anybody."

"I only saw his face for an instant."

"That's fine," Barnes responded, indicating an orange plastic chair that had been placed in front of the window. "Please have a seat. We want you to keep in mind that it's better for a guilty man to go free, than for an innocent man to be placed in jail."

Jovanic stood with the other two detectives, which left Claudia feeling isolated.

Them and me. She clasped her hands in her lap to steady them. The body holds onto past trauma and repeats the physiological response, even though the threat is past. That explained her dry mouth and rapid heart rate. Conditioned

Response, behaviorists called it—psychobabble that meant she'd rather lie on a bed of nails than come face-to-face with her assailant again.

Zuniga raised his brow at her and when she nodded that she was ready, he spoke into an intercom mounted on the wall. "Bring 'em in."

In the room on the other side of the glass the lights went on and five men trooped single file into the room.

Claudia stared at them, fully aware that they couldn't see her through the glass, but still utterly creeped out. Jovanic had earlier explained that there would be four fillers in the group and only one real suspect. All five of the men wore short-sleeved shirts. Four of them had been given a sling to put on their right arm to match the fifth.

Number One was a stocky African-American with a shaved head that shone under the glare of the overhead lights. The Number Two position was occupied by a brown-skinned youth who slouched against the wall in baggy corduroys that hung low on his hips. A pencil-thin moustache looked as if it had been drawn onto a face that was fixed in a permanent smirk.

Number Three was around five-nine, one-ninety with an olive complexion and dark, wavy hair. The backs of his hands and his right arm were covered in dark, curly hair. He gazed straight ahead, his face set in a carefully emotionless expression.

Number Four was a light-skinned Hispanic with an acne-pitted face, around five-eleven, medium build. Number Five had a long ponytail of matted black hair hanging over his shoulder. All of the men had a generally similar build and look, but only one commanded Claudia's attention.

"It's Number Three," she said, her mouth so dry she could hardly get the words out.

"I'm going to ask them all to repeat what the suspect said to you," Zuniga said, without acknowledging the identification she had just made. "Please listen carefully and see if you recognize any of their voices."

She muttered an assent and closed her eyes to help her concentration. Zuniga spoke into the intercom microphone.

"When I call you, step to the front, one at a time and say, 'Where's the fuckin' video?' Number One, step forward."

The first guy stepped up and in a bored, flat voice said, "Where's the fuckin' video?"

"Step back. Number Two, step forward."

Number Two marched forward, yelled, "Where's the fuckin' video, man? I fuckin' mean it."

Wiseass.

"Step back. Number Three, step forward."

The man in the middle sneered directly at the mirror and spoke the incriminating words.

"It's him," Claudia said, breathless, but trying to keep her voice level.

"Are you positive?" It was Jovanic who spoke up.

"I remember his voice and he has arms like a werewolf."

"We need you to hear Number Four and Five speak, to make sure," Barnes said.

She got to her feet and pointed at Kardosian. "There's no point. I'm telling you, Number Three is the guy."

Barnes flicked a glance at Jovanic, then back at Claudia. "Ms. Rose, we need you to listen to the others. We don't want anyone's attorney saying we stacked the deck against their client."

She plopped back down on her chair and listened with bad grace to Numbers Four and Five repeat the line. "It's Number Three." She got to her feet again. "Where'd the other guys come from?"

"Some come from the jail, and sometimes an undercover guy will fill," Zuniga said, opening the door and standing aside. "Hey, JJ, you wanna watch the interview?"

"Wouldn't miss it," Jovanic said. He'd been denied the collar, but at least he could participate at this level. *The privileges of membership.* All Claudia wanted to do was bolt.

Barnes said he would have Kardosian brought to an interview room next door.

The room to which they escorted her was scarcely larger than a broom closet, furnished only with a metal table and chairs; another two-way glass.

Through the glass Claudia could see a room that was a

mirror image of this one. A tape recorder had been set up on the table. A video camera mounted high up on the wall was focused on the chair where the suspect would be seated. The one bolted to the floor.

Barnes came through the door, followed by Zuniga, and a minute later Kardosian was brought in by a deputy who had to be at least six-five, built like a bull. No chance of Kardosian making a break for it with that guy standing guard, Claudia thought with satisfaction.

The suspect cradled his cast-wrapped right arm in his left hand and stared brazenly at the mirrored wall.

"Why don't you go in there with them?" asked Claudia, noting that Jovanic's body was straining toward the window.

"More than two of us at a time makes it look like coercion. I'll have a crack at him later."

Zuniga leaned against the door, his arms folded across his chest. Barnes hit the record button and spoke into the tape recorder, stating the date and naming all who were present.

"Mr. Kardosian, at the time of your arrest, were you advised of your rights?"

Kardosian stayed silent, his face a blank. They knew from the arresting officers that the suspect had already been given the Miranda warning, but Zuniga proceeded to read him his rights into the tape to ensure that everything was clean.

Barnes wedged his rear on the edge of the table, making himself comfortable. "You know, Nasrin . . . okay if I call you Nasrin? We've got your bloody prints at the scene of a homicide. It would go a lot better for you if you'd cooperate and tell us what happened."

Kardosian's body twitched ever so slightly.

Barnes was clearly the one in charge of the interview. He became more insistent. "You beat a guy to death, Nasrin . . . a Beverly Hills guy at that. Third strike, man. With your record, you're looking at lethal injection." He turned to his partner. "I think the DA will see this as a third strike, don't you, Zunie?"

Zuniga gave a big shrug. "No doubt about it."

"Look, Nasrin, we've got witnesses who can put you at the apartment building where you killed that guy. You got no alibi. You're fucked."

Kardosian twitched again, more obviously.

Claudia turned to Jovanic. "Who's he talking about? What witnesses?"

"He's lying," Jovanic replied. "We hoped the guard at Lindsey's apartment could ID him, but that flower arrangement hid his face; the guard assumed he was legit. There were plenty of flower deliveries after the funeral."

Claudia gave him a look of withering scorn. "How many of them delivered at nine o'clock at night?"

"Yeah, well, he wasn't much of a guard."

"You're not doing yourself any good, keeping your mouth shut," Zuniga said, continuing to press him. "We've got you, Kardosian, whether you talk or not. We've got plenty of evidence. We don't need a confession to convict you."

Kardosian met Zuniga's threats with stony silence, doing a fair imitation of a statue. The detective softened his tone persuasively. "Listen, dude, we know you were working for someone else; you were just doing a job. Give us a name, maybe we can talk to the DA for you."

Kardosian's dead eyes sparked with scorn. "You think I'm crazy, motherfucker? I want my lawyer."

Jovanic let out a groan. "Shit."

"What?" Claudia asked.

"Once he asks for an attorney we can't question him any further. These guys aren't about to jeopardize the case."

"You sure you want to do that?" Zuniga was saying. "Once the attorneys get involved we can't offer the same kinds of arrangements."

"Get me my fucking lawyer!" Kardosian screamed. "I'm asking for my lawyer, and you gotta let me see him. *Now!*"

Chapter 36

"He's not ready to deal," Jovanic said, stepping out of his grey flannel trousers and tossing them over the back of a chair, along with his shirt.

Friday evening, Kardosian's second day as a guest of the LA County Jail, Twin Towers.

Claudia took her Cleopatra costume out of the plastic bag hanging over the bedroom door and laid it on the bed.

Jovanic watched appreciatively as she peeled out of her stretch pants and T-shirt. "How about a quick shower?" he asked hopefully.

"We showered an hour ago. I don't get any cleaner than this."

"Cleanliness was not my first concern," he said, reaching for her. She ducked aside and started working her way into a pair of pantyhose. He gave up and sat on the edge of the bed, tugging off his socks.

"What are Kardosian's chances of getting off?" asked Claudia.

"Slim to none. With his prints at the scene and your ID, he's going down. We know he didn't act on his own, but until he cops to who's behind the whole magilla, we're basically fucked."

"Do you think he *knows* who hired him?" Her voice was muffled by the white silk sheath as she slipped it over her head. Next came a long linen dress, split up the front from hem to mid-thigh.

"There had to be a middleman, but Kardosian's at the

bottom of the totem pole. It's not in his best interests to spill his guts. DA's gonna have to come up with a damned attractive offer before he gives up anything interesting. Somebody's paying Kardosian a lot of money to keep his mouth shut. And somebody's paying a high-priced attorney to represent him."

Carefully draping a collar of fake lapis lazuli beads around her neck, Claudia planted herself in front of Jovanic, back-first. "Who's he got?"

"Robert Big-Ass-Money Sanders." He fastened the clasp for her and held her against him for a moment, burrowing his face in her hair before releasing her. "You *sure* we don't have time?"

"We board the barge in less than an hour, Marc. But if you behave yourself, your queen will make sure you're well rewarded tonight."

Jovanic eyed his Marc Antony costume with disfavor. "Lemme see this thing you're making me wear." Without much enthusiasm, he grabbed the red tunic and threw it on, tugging it as low as he could around the hips. The hem stopped about six inches above his knees. "It's a goddamn miniskirt!"

Claudia whistled. "Nice gams."

"That's supposed to be *my* line."

She laughed and helped him secure the clasps on his breastplate and cape. "Sanders is the next best thing to Johnny Cochran," she said, dragging him to the cheval mirror so he could admire the results. "I hope the DA doesn't let him plead out."

"Not a chance." He gave her a look of surprise. "Hey, I don't look too bad. What are the odds that Senator Heidt's actually gonna show up at this shindig?"

"He'll be there." Claudia bounced her eyebrows at him. "Maybe if we get lucky you can beat a confession out of him."

Jovanic twisted around with a scowl. "You think it's a joke? Listen, Claudia, I know I've taken you on some interviews with me, and to the dungeon, but I'm telling you, stay away from him. *I'll* do any confronting there is to be done tonight."

Throwing him a non-committal smile, she went into the bathroom and closed the door. She would need to tread lightly if she found an opportunity to get close to Senator Heidt. Remembering how Bostwick had ripped her blouse when she'd confronted him, she would guard against goading the senator as blatantly as she had the doctor. Bared breasts and buttons scattered on the deck was more drama than she desired that night.

Rummaging in the bag of cosmetics she'd picked up from the drugstore, she applied alabaster foundation, then dusted her cheeks with blush and glued on false eyelashes. A swipe of emerald eye shadow made her lids shimmer and brought out the green of her eyes. She leaned close to the mirror and outlined her eyes with thick black strokes, ending in a broad outward sweep that made them look enormous. Crimson lipstick completed her disguise.

Satisfied that she'd done a creditable job, she twisted her auburn mane into a ponytail and stuffed it under a nylon cap, which she clamped to her head with bobby pins. Last, she took the black pageboy wig from its Styrofoam form and slipped it on.

When she looked in the mirror again, Claudia Rose had disappeared, leaving behind an exotic Egyptian queen. The makeup was every bit as good as a mask.

Pleased with the results, she snapped on a coiled-snake bracelet and re-entered the bedroom. Jovanic looked up from buckling his sandals. His jaw dropped gratifyingly. "Holy shit! I wouldn't have recognized you, and I'm a damn good detective."

"As long as our buddy the senator doesn't recognize us, we'll be fat city."

"What about our hosts? They'll know who you are."

"But they don't know who *you* are, so they can't blow your cover."

Jovanic flared his cloak and pulled on the gladiator helmet Claudia had rented. The metal armor was designed to cover nose and cheeks, and offered a better disguise than a Roman officer's headgear would have.

She gave him an appraising look and put thumb and forefinger together in an OK gesture. "Got your sword, Marc Antony?"

He fiddled with his cloak to conceal his shoulder holster. "I'm not taking a goddamn plastic sword."

"Who're you gonna shoot at a Halloween party on a yacht?"

"My piece goes under the cape or you can count me out."

Wisps of mist floated close to the road, curling around the Jaguar like the cotton cobwebs the neighborhood children had draped over garden bushes. Passing Ballona Creek, Claudia lowered the window a few inches to breathe in the reedy scent of the wetlands at night. She did not bother to respond to Jovanic's grumbling about his helmet scraping the car's headliner.

Ten minutes later they arrived at the marina and found the parking lot alive with guests in designer Halloween costumes.

Joining the crowd making their way to the Graingers' yacht, *The Lilliana*, Jovanic and Claudia followed the music and laughter spilling from the boardwalk. Jack-o'-lanterns glowed above them along the bow of the yacht, their carved faces menacing in the moonless night.

Jovanic gazed at the yacht with frank admiration. "It's gotta be well over a hundred footer," he said as they strolled down the ramp to the gangway. "How many million you think this baby set them back?"

Claudia shrugged. "What do luxury yachts cost? Three, four? The party planning biz must be booming."

"Actually, Martin Grainger has his fingers in *several* profitable pies."

Somehow, that surprised her. "You checked out Martin Grainger?"

"It's what detectives do, honey," he replied smugly. "They detect."

It hadn't occurred to her to view Martin as a suspect. He

had behaved so clumsily at Lindsey's funeral reception when he'd stomped on her foot, she had never taken him seriously. "Well, what do you think about him?" she asked.

"Ask me later." They had reached the head of the red-carpeted gangway, where private security checked their invitations. Jovanic surreptitiously flashed his ID wallet and they were allowed to proceed without further question.

The Graingers stood at the head of the gangway dressed as Elizabeth I and Sir Walter Raleigh, welcoming their guests aboard. Despite her small stature, Lillian managed to look commanding in her bejeweled gown and a tightly curled red wig, a stiff lace ruff encircling her neck. Her husband, sporting a fake goatee, towered over her in puffy red breeches and green tights.

He could pass for a giant candy apple.

As Martin Grainger leaned over Claudia's hand in what he probably thought was a courtly bow, a blast of alcohol hit her. That explained his unhealthy plum-colored complexion.

Affecting a bad British accent, Lillian took Claudia's hand. "Cleopatra, Queen of the Nile, I greet you as one monarch to another. I'm delighted that you could attend our little party."

"Thank you, your majesty," Claudia said, dipping her head. "May I present Marc Antony?"

"Wait a minute, I know that voice." Lillian dropped the accent and lapsed into her usual lazy drawl. "It's Claudia Rose, isn't it? Bless your heart; I wouldn't have known if you hadn't spoken. You make a *fabulous* Cleo!"

Passed the first test.

Claudia introduced Jovanic simply as "Joel," and they exchanged a few friendly words with the Graingers before moving on to the lounge.

They got drinks from the bar and people-watched: Frankenstein and his Bride; a Roaring Twenties flapper with a fat man in a hula skirt and lei, a pink orchid tucked behind his ear.

Jovanic drew Claudia's attention to a two-legged black-spotted cow and milkmaid. She leaned close and spoke in his ear. "And you were worried about wearing a *tunic?*"

He tossed back a swallow of beer and reached up to adjust his helmet. "Just because he's making an ass of himself doesn't mean *I* have to."

"That's a cow," she teased. "Not an ass."

"Cow, ass, it's all the same."

"Lighten up, Columbo." She reached up and planted a kiss on the edge of his mouth. He rolled his eyes, but she knew he was amused. "I don't see anyone who looks like Heidt or Bostwick, do you?"

"It's a costume party, grapho lady; you're not supposed to recognize people." Jovanic jerked his head at a tall, black-robed figure standing by the bar. Edvard Munch's *The Scream* face chatting with Princess Leia. "What about that one?"

"Probably some little old lady on stilts."

"Maybe it's Doctor Bostwick, hiding his face behind that mask in shame."

"He *should* be ashamed."

Jovanic's cell phone rang.

Claudia's heart sank like a cement anchor. Even as she listened to him giving a couple of "uh huh's," and before he snapped the phone shut, she knew what he was going to say.

"Sorry, honey." He was suddenly jazzed, far more than he had been at the idea of a Halloween party on a yacht. "That was Zuniga. Kardosian's ready to deal and they want me there."

Suppressing a sigh, she mustered a rueful smile and got her car keys out of her evening bag and unhooked her house key. "Take my car, but you'd better hurry, we'll be setting sail any minute."

"I'll try and get back in time to pick you up, but . . ."

"I'll get a ride with Zebediah, or I'll call a cab."

He wagged a stern finger at her. "Promise you won't try anything stupid with Heidt."

The blast of the departure horn saved her from having to make a promise she was not sure she would keep. He delayed long enough to drop a light kiss on her cheek, then he was gone.

Claudia stood at the railing, watching Jovanic hurry back along the boardwalk, helmet under his arm as he disappeared between the shops that fronted the parking lot. This was what she could expect from a relationship with a cop—left at a party with no date.

She stood there, wondering what to do, when a man dressed as Merlin entered her line of vision and spoke in Zebediah Gold's voice. "Ancient Egyptian suits you, sweetie." He gave her a friendly kiss through the long white beard and touched her bracelet. "Nice asp."

She looked him up and down. The rich blue-velvet wizard's robe emblazoned with silver moons and stars, and even the tall, pointy cap, seemed to fit him. "Where's that gold thong you promised?"

"I chickened out. Merlin beckoned instead."

"Well, you do cast spells over women."

"You should know, darling."

"Don't push it, Zeb." The yacht rolled a little as it moved into the channel and she lurched against him.

Zebediah steadied her. "I'm glad you told me what you were going to wear, sweetie. It's a marvelous disguise."

"I wanted to introduce you to Joel."

"What have you done with him?"

"Didn't you see him take off like a bat out of hell? He got a call and that was that."

"Forget about him; let's walk like an Egyptian. Dance with me."

"Okay, but you have to help me figure out who Bryce Heidt is."

"Darling, can't you stop working for five minutes and just have some fun?"

His impatience was justified, but the truth was, she wasn't going to rest until she could prove that her suspicions about the senator were justified. For now, she acquiesced and stepped with Zebediah onto the parquet dance floor, where a handful of couples were dancing to the Monster Mash.

Twisting her feet and shaking her shoulders, she felt like a kid again. The steps didn't matter, as long as you were moving to the beat. She couldn't remember the last time she had danced, nor had so much fun.

She was enjoying herself immensely, when the Graingers bore down on them and cut in. Zebediah relinquished Claudia to Martin with a graceful flourish, and danced off with Lillian.

When the music stopped and the DJ called for a slow dance, Claudia thanked Martin Grainger for the dance and started to walk away.

He held onto her hand. "How about one more, if I promise not to tread on your toes?"

"Okay, last chance. Just remember, I'm wearing sandals."

He glanced down at her feet, then let his eyes roam slowly up the split in her dress, where her legs showed through to mid-thigh. "Nice," he said, and she knew he wasn't talking about her costume. "Say, what happened to your date? We had to hold up the departure for him."

"Unfortunately, he was called away to an emergency."

"Is he a doctor?"

It was an innocent enough question, but after learning that Jovanic had investigated Martin Grainger, Claudia felt uneasy with his curiosity.

"No, it was something else," she said, allowing him to draw her into his arms as the music started up again.

Martin leaned down, his alcohol-fumed breath hot on her ear. "I saw on the news that they caught the guy who killed Ivan Novak."

"Yes, they do have someone in custody." He was holding her too close, and Claudia pulled away, putting a few inches between them. Apparently getting the message, he dropped his arm and stood there looking ridiculous in his green tights and red breeches, his forehead damp with perspiration.

Martin reached into his breeches for a handkerchief and began mopping his forehead. "It's getting warm in here. Why don't we go out on deck so we can talk."

The music followed them, getting fainter as they stepped through the bulkhead into the cool salt air. The marina was far behind them now, and they were sailing into the open waters of the Pacific. Even without a moon, the yacht's lights left a golden wake behind them. A sight Claudia wanted to share with Jovanic, not Lillian's husband in that stupid getup.

"Let's go below, to my stateroom," Martin said. "So we can talk in private."

Claudia stared at him, surprised that he would make such a blatant overture. "I don't *think* so." She went to slip around him but he grabbed her arm.

"Wait! You've got it all wrong . . . wait . . . Lil told me about Bryce Heidt . . . what you told her about him."

That stopped her.

"Here's the thing," he said. "We've discussed it with the senator, and he denies those charges, absolutely."

Like he's going to admit it.

"There's video, Mr. Grainger."

"Call me Martin," he insisted, releasing her arm and mopping his forehead again despite the drop in temperature from the lounge. "Claudia, honey, you know we're in the entertainment business, and I'll tell you, these tapes can easily be dummied up. When someone gets to be big and important in political circles like Bryce Heidt, it's pretty much open season. And the closer he gets to the presidency, the more his enemies are gonna snipe at him. Hell, I wouldn't put it past 'em to hire a look-alike for those tapes." He stuffed the handkerchief back into his pocket and reached up to scratch at his goatee. "Bryce is a deeply religious man, a family man. Believe me, honey, he never would risk everything he's worked so hard for all these years . . . to do the kinds of crazy things you *thought* you saw on some tape."

Claudia met his gaze with a slight frown. "Actually, I never told Lillian that I saw the tape, nor what's on it."

His eyes widened. "Well, I'm just assuming . . . guessing, aren't I . . . anyway, Bryce wouldn't do *anything* that would get him blackmailed. He's smarter than that."

It wasn't worth it to debate what she had seen with her own eyes. She wondered whether his desire to protect the senator was more for Heidt's sake, or for Lillian's political aspirations.

"Is the senator on board tonight?" she asked.

"Of course." Grainger led her back to the lounge, his eyes darting from group to group until he found the one he sought. "Over there. See Abraham Lincoln and Mary Todd? You can't miss him in that stovepipe hat." He looked as proud as if he were the senator's campaign manager. He laid a heavy hand on her shoulder. "Now Claudia, I *can* count on you not to pester him, can't I?"

She mentally crossed her fingers. "Martin, you have absolutely nothing to worry about."

The band finished their set and took a break. Claudia kept an eye on Abe Lincoln, who appeared to be having a good time as he worked the room, always surrounded by an admiring group, laughing at something someone said, gesticulating as he expounded on some subject dear to his heart.

When the next slow dance started, Claudia elbowed her way through the crowd and moved in on him.

"Mr. President," she said, making her voice a little deeper, a little breathier. "Would you do me the honor of a dance?"

Heidt turned, the smile set to charm already in place. "Why, Cleopatra," he said, offering her his arm. "I'd be delighted."

He excused himself to his wife and the couple they had been chatting with, and gave Claudia his arm.

His hand felt warm and strong, closing around hers as they stepped onto the crowded dance floor. The other hand roamed down low on her back.

The band played early Beatles, and Heidt kept good time with the music, expertly gliding her around the floor. "Do I know you, Cleopatra? I feel as if we've met."

"Mmm, not exactly," she said, remembering to keep her voice low. "But I'm a big follower of yours, Mr. Lincoln."

"Really? I'm honored."

"Actually, I've been seeing quite a lot of you lately."

He leaned back so that his groin pressed against her, and looked at her searchingly. "And where would that have been? At one of my speeches?"

It took all her willpower to keep from pulling away from him; to give him a seductive smile from under her lashes; a little shake of the head. "I don't think so."

"Interesting. Was it . . . on TV?" Playful now, getting into the mood.

"Uh, you might say that."

"Okay, you've seen me. Have I seen you, too?"

Claudia shook her head. Over his shoulder, she saw his wife, Mariel Heidt, staring at them, her face tight, and not just from the nip and tuck of plastic surgery.

Heidt bent her backwards and swung her around. "You're making me curious, you little minx of the Nile . . . you've seen me, but I haven't seen you?"

Claudia moved her head so that the black wig touched his cheek, and softly lied through her teeth. "Your Lincoln costume can't hide your wonderful physique, Senator; I saw a lot of it in Lindsey Alexander's home movies."

Bryce Heidt's steps faltered. His hand tightened on her back and he dipped his head close to her ear. "What do you know about Lindsey's movies?"

As close as he was holding her, she hoped he couldn't feel the thudding of her heart against her ribs. "Lindsey and I went back a long way."

"Is that so? It's a shame about her death."

"Yes, a shame."

Heidt didn't pursue the topic and they danced in silence for a few beats. Then he said hesitantly, "So do you offer the same kind of services as Lindsey?"

"Well, Senator, that depends on what you're looking for."

"It sounds like you *know* what I'm looking for."

"I think I do. But . . . well, Lindsey got more than she bargained for, and that concerns me."

"Lindsey was greedy," Heidt whispered into her ear. "I'm sure you wouldn't put yourself in that position, would you?"

It couldn't be this easy. Surely, he wouldn't give himself away, just like that. Claudia made a rapid assessment of the situation. She wasn't threatening him, so he was unlikely to attack her as Bostwick had in his office. Not here, on a yacht in the middle of the ocean with dozens of people whirling around them. Still, she would make sure to stay away from the guard rail.

She smiled up at him from under her thick curtain of lashes. "Tell me, what position would you want me in, Mr. Lincoln?"

Heidt gave a little groan and she felt an unwelcome movement against her abdomen. "Your wife is watching," she cautioned, giving him a little push.

He twirled her away from him, trying to impress her with his dance moves. When he reeled her back in, his eyes were glazed with lust. "Let's go outside," he said.

Martin Grainger had been risky enough. The prospect of leaving the safety of the lighted salon and accompanying Heidt outside appealed to her about as much as swimming in a cesspool, but it was her one chance to get any information from him.

"How do I know I'm safe with you, Senator?" Her tone was coy, but the words came from the bottom of her heart.

"You have nothing to worry about," Heidt assured her with an arch wink. "I'm not hard to please."

No, you're just plain hard.

Heidt led Claudia off the floor and out on deck, clinging to her as if they were superglued together. He seemed very familiar with the yacht's layout.

He's probably been a passenger a dozen times, she reflected, considering how tight he and the Graingers appeared to be.

He guided her as smoothly as if they were still dancing, past life vests and deck chairs, around a small swimming pool and into a dark alcove behind the aft gangway. She could hear his breathing quicken with his mounting excitement. "Okay, Cleopatra, tell me what you're going to do to me. I've been a *very* bad boy."

Claudia pushed him away, playfully tapping his chest. "First things first, Mr. Lincoln . . . tell me about Lindsey."

His jaw tensed. "She's not in the picture anymore. Let's

stop talking and get on with my punishment." Suddenly, he was down on his knees, pressing his face into her crotch, knocking his stovepipe hat askew. "Will you be Mistress Cleopatra when we meet, or is there another name I should use?"

The situation was rapidly spinning out of control. She had to do something, fast.

"Lindsey didn't kill herself, did she?" she blurted, pushing on his shoulders, twisting her body away from him.

Heidt jerked to his feet, crushing the tall hat against the staircase above. "Who *are* you?"

Claudia spoke fast, urgently. "The police have reopened the investigation into her death. They've got a suspect in mind, Senator. I think you know who it is."

He was silent, digesting what she'd said. The waggishness vanished and gave way to a concerned frown. He might be a pervert and he might be a killer, but he hadn't risen to his present political level without brains.

"You're suggesting that I was responsible for her death?" he countered. "That's nothing short of outrageous."

Preston Sommerfield's handsome face popped into Claudia's mind. He had at least as much motive as Heidt to kill Lindsey. "Blackmail is a good motive for murder," she said, throwing out the bait to see what it might produce.

Heidt took a sudden step backward and landed against the cabin wall, his face drained of color. "Who are you with? The police?"

"No."

"The media?"

"I'm not *with* anyone."

An expression of confusion and puzzlement crossed Heidt's face, then cleared. "Wait a second; you're the woman Martin told me about. We *have* met before, haven't we?"

"It doesn't matter, Senator, just tell me about Lindsey."

"We had a business arrangement," he said brusquely. "Nothing illegal."

"But blackmail *is* illegal, and she could have trashed your career."

He was the consummate politician once again, carefully modulating his voice to keep his emotions carefully concealed. "I wasn't anywhere near her the night she died. Check with my office; I was at a fundraiser."

The alcove suddenly felt as tight as a coffin. Without another word, Claudia squeezed around him and out onto the deck.

Bryce Heidt's wife was standing there, arms folded across her pink and white striped Mary Todd Lincoln gown, looking like a playground monitor about to take on the class bully. Claudia pushed past her, leaving Bryce Heidt to explain what they had been doing beneath the gangway.

Chapter 37

Party guests lined both sides of the buffet table. Poached salmon, grilled chicken breasts in cream sauce, steamships of prime rib. A feast of prawns and cracked crab; vegetables sprinkled with pecans and oranges; roasted potatoes. Plates heaped with enough food to feed a third-world country.

After her brush with Heidt, Claudia didn't have much of an appetite. Even though he hadn't physically assaulted her, the encounter had shaken her in a way that Charles Bostwick's attack had not. She now felt unsure of so much that she had come to suspect about Heidt's involvement in Lindsey's death and everything else that had happened over the past weeks.

Dishing a few items onto her plate with little enthusiasm, she went to the table where Zebediah was holding court. He rose with a welcoming smile and drew out a chair for her. "There you are, sweetie," he said, gesturing to a glamorous young woman seated on his left. "Claudia Rose, Jessica St. John."

Lady Godiva in a flesh-colored bodysuit.

She would have been called a starlet in the days of old Hollywood. Long blonde tresses cascaded over a shapely body; strategically arranged but providing precious little cover.

Claudia got a disinterested nod from the young woman, who immediately resumed bragging about her latest film, a less-than-memorable B flick. She clearly wasn't interested in wasting a smile on another woman until Zebediah cleverly inserted himself into the conversation. "Claudia's a famous handwriting expert," he said.

Claudia kicked him under the table, glad she'd connected with a tender spot when he jumped. Predictably, Jessica St. John's attitude did a supersonic one-eighty and she immediately began asking around the table for a pen, pouting when no one could produce one.

The last empty seat at the table was filled by a tall, slender Catwoman whose stealthy movements as she slid into the chair were as feline as her slick black outfit.

Appropriate choice of costume, Claudia thought with a ripple of recognition.

"Good evening, everyone," Catwoman said, and introduced herself as Lillian Grainger's assistant, Yolande Palomino.

Zebediah leaned over and whispered in Claudia's ear. "Maybe you can grill her about Lindsey's boyfriend."

"Exactly what I was thinking."

The meal dragged for Claudia as the woman to her left chattered endlessly about her five wonderful, talented, beautiful grandchildren. She'd heard Zebediah's tales of his days as a prison psychologist before. When it was her turn, she fielded all the standard questions about handwriting analysis: *"Does squeezed writing mean he's a cheapskate?" "What do i-dots the shape of hearts mean?" "Can you tell if a guy loves sex?"* That was Jessica, of course.

Only half of Claudia's attention was focused on the conversation. The other half was divided between her encounter with Senator Heidt, and a longing to know what Jovanic might be learning from Kardosian. He would have had to stop at his apartment to change out of his costume, of course. He wasn't likely to show up at the LA County Jail clad as Marc Antony.

When the chocolate mousse in pastry cups, and the petits fours and traditional pumpkin pie had come and gone, and the coffee and conversation petered out, the guests began drifting back onto the dance floor. The band cranked up and Jessica St. John took the microphone, singing in a husky voice, slightly off-key, "You've got to change your evil ways, baby."

"That song was popular before she was born," Claudia said, making a sour face at Zebediah.

He laughed, and threw a meaningful glance at Yolande Palomino, who was preparing to leave the table. Claudia rose from her chair and moved around the table to sit beside her. "You make a fabulous Catwoman, Yolande," she said.

Behind the black vinyl cat mask , the other woman's smile didn't quite make it to her eyes. Her mouth had the drawn look of a perpetual worrier—one whom life has dealt so many unkind blows that she'd forgotten how to stop waiting for the other shoe to drop. She smiled at Claudia. "Thanks. That's a great look for you, too."

"I wanted to apologize for calling you at work the other day. I didn't mean to upset you."

The tension went out of Yolande's shoulders. "Oh, don't worry about that. You just caught me at a bad moment. One of my kids was home sick and had been calling me all morning. I'm sorry I hung up so abruptly, but it seemed like I was on a personal call every time Mrs. Grainger walked by my desk."

She picked up the leather gauntlets she had left under her chair during dinner and pulled them on. "Would you excuse me? I'm supposed to be making sure everyone's having a good time. It was nice seeing you again, Ms. Rose. Your work is fascinating."

Claudia reached out a restraining hand. "Please wait a moment, Yolande. I wanted to ask you something. Did Lindsey mention anything to you about having a new boyfriend?"

With a look of surprise, Lillian's assistant shook her head. "I didn't really know her all that well. I don't remember her ever mentioning a boyfriend at all."

"Do you remember when the last time was that you spoke to her?"

Yolande's eyes suddenly brimmed with tears. She dabbed carefully at her eyes with the napkin she had left on the table. "As a matter of fact, I do because it was the day she passed away. We'd been talking about *this* party. She was telling me about her costume. She said she was dressing up as a . . . a dominatrix."

Talk about life imitating art.

Claudia got the feeling that if she could have seen under her mask, Yolande might be blushing. Lillian's assistant continued. "If I'd only known . . . maybe . . . maybe I could have done something. But I had no clue that she was suicidal."

Claudia shook her head in understanding. "You couldn't have known. Besides, there's a good chance she didn't kill herself."

Yolande's dark eyes grew round and large. "You really think . . ."

"She may have been murdered by someone she was blackmailing. That's why it's so important that you share anything you know that might shed some light."

"She was a *blackmailer?*"

"She videotaped high-profile men having kinky sex, then threatened to embarrass them if they didn't pay up."

Yolande stared down at her gloved hands, clenching and unclenching them as if fighting the urge to say something. Finally, she spoke in a subdued voice. "She sounded fine when we talked on the phone, then . . ."

"What happened?"

She gusted a resigned sigh and plunged ahead. "A couple of hours after I spoke with her, a letter was hand-delivered from Lindsey addressed to Mrs. Grainger. I knew it was from her because it came in a gas company envelope with a label stuck over the address. You know how she always re-used old envelopes? It was marked *personal,* so I gave it to Mrs. Grainger unopened."

Yolande stole an anxious glance around, making sure nobody was listening, and lowered her voice almost to a whisper. "I . . . I'm sure this has nothing to do with anything, but a few minutes later, Mrs. Grainger came out to my desk. I've never seen her so angry. She said to get Lindsey on the phone. Then she went back into her office and slammed her door. I could hear her yelling."

She stared at her lap, shaking her head a little, as if she couldn't believe what she was saying. "I'd never heard her like that. She *never* raises her voice."

"Did you hear what she was saying?"

"No, but after she'd left for the day, I was putting some papers on her desk for her to sign, and I noticed an envelope on the floor. I picked it up."

"What did it say?" Claudia asked, hardly daring to breathe, for fear that Yolande would bolt like a scared rabbit if she pressed too hard.

"It was Lindsey's envelope. I shouldn't have opened it . . . it wasn't any of my business."

"Yolande, *tell me,* what was it?"

"It was just a few printed words. It said 'It was fun while it lasted.'"

Claudia stared at her. "Lindsey's suicide note?"

"What do you mean?"

"Didn't you know? That's what her suicide note said."

Yolande slowly shook her head, looking bewildered, and Claudia remembered that the contents of the note had not been released to the public.

What did Lindsey's suicide note have to do with Lillian? How did it get to Lindsey's penthouse?

"I never thought he would do such a thing," Yolande was saying. "He always seemed so devoted."

Claudia blinked in confusion, forced her attention back to the other woman. "What? Who seemed devoted?"

"Mr. Grainger . . . Lindsey . . ." She trailed off with a helpless shrug.

"You think Lindsey and Martin Grainger were having an affair and that's what she wrote to Lillian about?" Claudia knew her mouth had dropped open. Such an idea would never have occurred to her, and even now that Yolande was suggesting it, she found it beyond her ability to picture Lindsey Alexander in a personal relationship with Lillian's husband. As a client, maybe, but as the mysterious boyfriend Bostwick had told her about? That really stretched the limits of her imagination.

"Did you check out what I mentioned to you?" Yolande's

voice had dropped so low that Claudia had to lean in close
to hear her.

"You mean about Mexico? I found out that Lindsey used
to visit a condo in Ixtapa-Zihuatanejo . . ." Claudia broke
off as she felt someone come up behind her. Both she and
Yolande turned at the same time.

"What's going on here?" Lillian Grainger smiled at
Claudia, but her voice was cold. "You two look as guilty
as sin."

Yolande leapt out of her chair with a face as shocked
as if she'd been seated on Old Sparky and someone had
flipped on the juice. "Mrs. Grainger! I was just . . . Ms.
Rose was just . . . she was telling me, uh, about a . . . a trip
she wants to . . . uh . . . excuse me . . . I have to go . . . to . . .
to the ladies' room."

Claudia stared after Yolande, who took off like a rocket,
then at Lillian in her elaborate Elizabethan gown. She
forced a smile and tried to fill the gap left by Yolande's
hasty departure.

"I was just asking Yolande, have you ever been to
Ixtapa-Zihuatanejo?"

Lillian stared at her as if she were speaking in tongues.

Chapter 38

"Are you all right, Lillian?" Claudia asked, watching the blood rise in Lillian Grainger's cheeks.

"I feel a little faint." Lillian picked up the napkin Yolande had dropped, and fanned herself. "It's the corset under this dress, it's . . . it's a little tight."

"Sit down, let me get you some water."

"No, don't trouble yourself, I'll be fine. Marty told me your date had to leave, so I came to offer you a ride home."

From the upper deck, the harbor lights twinkled in the distance, gradually growing larger as the yacht turned into the breakwater and the engines throttled back to cut the wake. The party was still in full swing, the music louder, the laughter more shrill with every hour the bar remained open.

Few other vessels were out so late in the evening, and the *Lilliana* cruised into Fisherman's Village around midnight at a leisurely pace, tying up at the dock with a gentle bump against the stanchions.

Along with a handful of other guests, Claudia made her way off the yacht, hurrying past a family of brown pelicans, heads tucked under their wings, brooding on wooden pilings alongside the dock. The air reeked of saltwater and fish.

She hurried past the line of waiting limousines with their dozing drivers, and made a beeline for the south end of Fisherman's Village, past the strip of stores and restaurants, to the area next to Shanghai Red's. The restaurant had already shut down for the night; the valets had closed and locked their key cabinet; the kitchen help had cleaned up and gone home an hour earlier.

Lillian's black Lexus stood alone in a corner of the lot, flanked by oleander bushes on the front and passenger sides. No mistaking whose car it was—the vanity plate read *DimndLil*.

Most of the party guests had parked their vehicles closer to the gangway. Waiting for Lillian under a street lamp in the moonless night, Claudia was acutely aware of how alone she was at that end of the parking lot. She darted a quick look around, her nerves jumping. Saw no one; heard nothing.

The thin fabric of the linen dress afforded little protection from the sharp nip in the air. Yet, the chill Claudia felt wasn't entirely due to the weather. She rubbed her arms against the chill, rehashing the conversation with Yolande Palomino.

Yolande's suspicion of a relationship between Martin Grainger and Lindsey was a stunner. Martin just didn't seem Lindsey's type. But then, who knew what Lindsey's type really was? More to the point, did the information relate to Lindsey's death?

A movement near the shops caught her attention.

Lillian was headed her way at a trot, a small, dark figure in a black nylon Prada slack suit.

"What a relief to get out of that costume," Lillian said, pointing her alarm key at the Lexus and climbing behind the wheel. "Which way do we turn on Lincoln?"

"Take a right to Jefferson and head west, toward the beach," Claudia said, getting into the passenger seat. "You can be back in fifteen minutes."

Lillian threw her a sidelong glance and accelerated out of the lot. "Do you have any booze at home? I have a feeling we're gonna need it. We've got things to talk about, you and I."

At twelve thirty A.M. Bishop Street was all shadows and silence. The last television had been switched off, books dog-eared and placed on bedside tables; goodnight kisses exchanged; lights out.

Lillian braked in Claudia's driveway and killed the engine. As they got out of the Lexus, Flare's bark broke the silence.

Claudia shushed the big Shepherd chained in Marcia Collins' front yard and led Lillian to the redwood staircase. The dog bounded across the yard toward them, whining until it ran out of chain and was yanked backward by the tether.

"What kind of person leaves a dog outside at this time of night?" Lillian exclaimed, scrambling to get around Claudia's other side.

"My neighbor works down at Cowboys until the bar closes at two," Claudia explained as she led Lillian up the stairs. "After everything that's happened to me lately, she feels safer leaving Flare in the front yard while she's not home."

"She'd be just as safe with a dog like that inside the house."

Claudia unlocked the front door and deactivated the alarm.

"Is that floor teak?" Lillian asked admiringly, giving the living room the once-over, like a buyer on a shopping trip.

"Yes, it came from an old ship's deck."

"*Very* nice."

"What would you like to drink, Lillian? I have wine and vodka. That's about it for alcohol."

"I'd love a vodka martini."

Claudia left her on the couch and fixed their drinks.

"Bless you, honey," Lillian said when she brought them back to the living room. "You must be freezing. Why don't you put something warmer on."

Wearing a pair of fleece sweat pants and a sweatshirt, Claudia crossed her bedroom, catching sight of her image in the mirror. Without the black wig, the heavy eyeliner and pale makeup gave her face an eerie look. *Ghostly*.

She removed the bobby pins and was shaking out her hair when the fax machine rang in the office.

*   *   *

"There you are," Lillian said, her smile pure southern comfort. "Like I said, we've got a lot to talk about. Sit down, dear, and drink up." As if she were the gracious host and Claudia the guest.

Settling into one of the wicker armchairs across from the couch where Lillian was nursing her drink, Claudia sipped her drink and waited.

"I've worked hard to create what I have," Lillian said. A startling look of pain filled her eyes. "I started with nothing. Nothing at all. Alcoholic daddy; mama ran off when I was ten. I built my own little empire. That's why I chose to be Elizabeth I tonight." She raised her glass. "Let's make a toast. To Lindsey, may she rest in peace."

"That seems a little odd under the circumstances," Claudia said, leaning across the coffee table to touch Lillian's glass.

Without warning, southern charm evaporated and Lillian's eyes burned like twin bonfires. "Okay, let's get down to brass tacks," she said in a voice as cold as a glacial wind sweeping through the room, clearing away every trace of amiability. "I want to know *exactly* what Yolande told you."

Claudia stared at her in amazement. She swallowed some of her martini, wondering how to respond.

"What's the problem, Lillian? I was just telling Yolande about a little trip I'm planning." Her ability to lie on demand was improving.

Lillian's gaze had a depth of anger that went far beyond a reaction to a breach of confidentiality. "Don't take me for stupid, I heard enough to figure it out. Yolande knows better than to talk about what goes on in my office."

"Look, I don't know what you're talking about. If she said something she shouldn't have, it went over my head."

Lillian sighed deeply and sat back, examining her manicure. Short, squared-off nails on small, practical hands. "I'm disappointed in you. You're lying."

Claudia put her glass down on the coffee table, rose from her chair and started for the front door. "Thanks for the ride, Lillian. This conversation is over. Now, I'd like you to leave."

But Lillian remained where she was. "Don't you want to know what *really* happened to Lindsey?" she asked in a teasing voice, casually swinging one knee over the other.

Claudia paused, hand on the doorknob. She stared at Lillian's leg, which was bouncing back and forth with a metronome beat. "How would *you* know what *'really happened'*?"

"Because I was there the night she died."

"*You* were at her apartment?"

"That's right."

The wicker creaked as Claudia sat back down, feeling like the rodent in a life-sized cat and mouse game. "Okay, I'll bite. What happened?"

"Oh, come on, ask some more questions. You're very good at asking questions."

Claudia narrowed her eyes. "Was she alive when you saw her?"

"Yes."

"Was anyone else there?"

"No."

A spurt of white-hot anger shot up Claudia's spine, and all the stress and tension that had been building seemed to explode in her head. "To hell with your little game and to hell with you, Lillian. Either tell me what happened or . . ."

The naked hatred that poisoned Lillian's face shocked her into silence. "You just couldn't let it go, could you? The police believed she killed herself. Everyone else was happy with that, but it wasn't good enough for *you*. You just had to keep on probing."

"You know that Ivan hired me to . . ."

"But even after Ivan was dead, you couldn't drop it." Lillian snorted inelegantly. "Oh, for pity's sake, don't look at me like that. I don't know anything about *Ivan*'s death."

Claudia thrust her hand into her pocket and took out the pages Jovanic had just faxed to her. She held them out. "Why don't *you* tell *me* the truth, Lillian?"

Lillian took the papers and stared at them for a long

time, the color draining from her face, leaving it pasty-white. Finally, she said in a flat tone, "I never guessed she would save that."

Her hand fell to her side, clutching a faxed copy of a greeting card, with a scribbled note from Jovanic, asking whether Claudia could identify the unsigned handwriting.

The bloated letter *f* bursting out in an otherwise perfectly school-model script immediately identified it as Lillian's handwriting. The text was another shocker:

" 'A wild, wicked, weekend! I never would have believed that kind of ecstasy was possible.' "

The second sheet was a letter from American Airlines, which detailed the items Jovanic had subpoenaed from the passenger manifests.

"You went to her place in Mexico."

Lillian's gaze slid over Claudia's shoulder, refusing to meet her eyes. "I knew you'd put it together sooner or later."

"I'm surprised you'd take that kind of chance with your career over a lover."

"We all make stupid mistakes. This was mine. Where did you get this?"

"Detective Jovanic just faxed it to me. They opened her safety deposit box today. So, she was blackmailing you, too?"

"*Blackmailing* me?" Lillian gave a contemptuous snort and dropped the papers on the coffee table. "She introduced me to many things, but *blackmail* certainly wasn't one of them."

"Then, why would she keep your letter in her lockbox?"

"Sentimental reasons, maybe. Assuming Lindsey had a sentimental bone in her egotistical body."

"Sentimental?" Something wasn't adding up, but Claudia was having trouble grasping just what it was. "So, she arranged for you to go to Mexico . . . with whom? Bryce Heidt?"

The look Lillian gave her was incredulous. "Go to Mexico with *Bryce?* What, for pity's sake are you talking about?"

Claudia was beginning to feel like Alice tumbling down the rabbit hole. "He was her client. She was a dominatrix."

"Lindsey was a . . . a . . . wait a minute. You're saying that Bryce paid her for . . . for . . . ?"

"Kinky sex," Claudia supplied. "Bondage. The video-tapes I told you about that day in your office. I thought he had Lindsey killed to put a stop to the blackmail, but after tonight . . . were you his lover?"

Lillian threw back her head, and laughed without humor. "Oh, Claudia dear, I thought you were so clever." Her mouth twisted into a grotesque smile. "We've both made a very *big* mistake. And that's the only time you'll ever hear me admit it."

Confused, Claudia recalled Yolande's words. "Then, was Martin having an affair with her?"

"Martin?" Lillian gaped at her. "My husband? Martin couldn't get it up with a box of Viagra! Besides, Lindsey scared the bejesus out of him."

In a blinding flash of clarity, it all became crystal clear. *Oh, my God! Why didn't I see it before?*

"Not Heidt . . . not Martin . . . *you* and Lindsey were lovers."

Lillian gave a delicate shudder. "That's exactly what I can't have people saying. It would ruin me privately, socially, financially, politically . . . *especially* politically."

Claudia blinked. Lillian Grainger, the devoted wife. Lillian, the church-going, oh-so-righteous Christian. Lillian, whose employees were required to live up to the rigid moral standards she had set for them. Lillian, the squeaky-clean political hopeful. *Lillian, in a lesbian relationship with Lindsey?* The idea almost made her laugh. Except that Lindsey was dead.

Another realization rolled over her with sledgehammer force. "*You* killed her!"

Lillian laughed again, unbearably smug. "She was much bigger than me, like you are. But she was already halfway to oblivion when I arrived . . . she did love her drugs, that girl. That made it easy. I just slipped a little something extra in her glass." She spoke proudly, as if she had done something praiseworthy. "Then I got her into the Jacuzzi and held her under. It took a little longer than I expected, but not all that long."

A wave of nausea swept over Claudia and she closed her eyes. "The note . . . I knew it was her handwriting."

" 'It was fun while it lasted,' " Lillian quoted, mocking. "How dare she think she could blow me off that way? *I* decide when it's over. Making it look like a suicide note was such a nice touch, don't you think? She would have told everyone, you know. I couldn't take that chance."

Lillian picked up the glasses and carried them into the kitchen. Claudia sat there immobilized with shock, listening to the faucet running, the crystal clinking musically as Lillian washed the glasses and replaced them inside the cabinet.

"We wouldn't want your boyfriend noticing you'd had company, would we, dear?" she said in a friendly tone when she reemerged from the kitchen. She walked behind Claudia's chair.

Then, a sudden, sharp pain at the back of her head; her vision dimmed.

Claudia opened her eyes with effort. Lillian was leaning over her, peering at her. Where had the little pistol in her hand come from?

Claudia reached up and touched the back of her head. Lillian must have hit her with the gun. She tried to push herself out of the chair, but her head felt stuffed with cotton candy, her arms and legs rubbery.

"Get up, Miss Claudia. I want you easy to control, not unconscious."

"You—won't—get—away—with—it."

"I got away with killing Lindsey, and I *will* get away with killing you, too. If they want to believe Bryce did it, that's fine with me. That note I wrote her doesn't prove anything, even if it *was* in her safety deposit box."

Claudia fell back in the armchair. Lillian tugged at her. "Come on, honey, you're going for a midnight swim. Just like Lindsey, only you'll have a much *bigger* pool."

Lillian jammed the gun hard against Claudia's neck,

the barrel connecting painfully behind her ear. She jerked
Claudia to her feet, surprisingly strong for her size.

"With all the attacks you've been yammering on about,
one more won't seem so strange. Everyone knows you were
being followed. That's so convenient for me. You foolishly
went for a walk on the beach . . . someone followed you
again . . .." She cocked the hammer. "This pistol may be
small, but believe me, it's big enough to kill you. Get up
and get outside, now. Before you pass out, you stupid damn
bitch."

Claudia swayed as a wave of vertigo nearly felled her.
The pain in her head was excruciating. Lillian grabbed her
arm and half-pushed, half-dragged her to the front door.
They headed down the steps, the business end of the little
gun pressing into Claudia's side.

On the last step Claudia stumbled, instinctively grabbed
at the railing. A thick splinter of wood stabbed her palm
and sent a lighting bolt of pain up her arm, making her
cry out. A reviving rush of adrenaline gave her a second
wind.

In the yard next door, Flare barked.

"Flare, come!" Claudia shouted. At least, she had intended to shout, but only a thin whisper sounded on the
cold salt air. Still, the dog heard. The barking grew louder,
more insistent.

Lillian slammed Claudia's head into the wall of the house.
"Shut up!"

Barking, snarling, the German Shepherd came bounding
across the grass until she ran out of chain.

"Get in the car," Lillian ordered. "Hurry up!"

One clear thought slid into Claudia's consciousness and
remained there: *If I have to die tonight, it won't be in the
cold surf.* Marshaling every shred of strength she had, she
twisted away and shoved Lillian to the ground.

The gun flew out of Lillian's hand and landed with a
soft thud under one of the hydrangea bushes that edged the
side of the house. She scrambled to her feet, cursing, and
headed for the bush.

Flare hurled herself forward. Once, twice, three times,

she leapt, jerking her chain each time. Claudia stumbled over to the Shepherd. "Flare, come!"

The earth erupted. The post that held her chain broke free and the big dog vaulted across the lawn, dragging the chain behind her.

Rearing on hind legs, the dog knocked Lillian to the ground. Yellow fangs bared, centimeters above her throat. Lillian's features twisted in terror as saliva dripped from the snapping jaws.

Claudia fell to her hands and knees. The gun—she had to find the gun. She inched her way across the grass, her sweat-pants soaked with dew. There it was—no bigger than a toy, but with the stopping power of a much larger weapon.

Surely, someone must have called the cops by now. But no one came outside to see what Lillian's panicked screams were about.

Welcome to LA.

A vehicle swung around the corner, tires screeching, and stopped behind Lillian's Lexus. The glare of headlights turned Claudia's front yard into a grim tableau.

The car door opened and a familiar voice shouted, "Claudia!" Then, Jovanic was running toward them, his weapon drawn. "*Claudia!*"

"She killed Lindsey," Claudia blurted, just before she puked on the grass.

Chapter 39

The blow to her head left Claudia with a major hangover, but the paramedic who checked her said he didn't think there was any concussion. She awoke on Saturday afternoon with only a hazy memory of the frightening events of Friday night.

Jovanic, sitting at her bedside, folded the newspaper he was reading. "So you've decided to rejoin us?" He dropped a kiss on the top of her head.

"Excedrin, please, extra strength." She yawned and stretched. "What happened? All I remember is Flare barking like a maniac and Lillian screaming her head off."

"You heaved your guts up and told me she'd tried to kill you, so I took your word for it and had her prissy ass hauled downtown. Your pal Lillian now has her very own accommodations at county jail," he said. "Not as plush as she's used to."

"Martin will bail her out, won't he?"

"You don't get bail so easily for murder one and attempted. Even with the biggest lawyer money can buy, she's going to be sitting there a while."

Claudia's face creased into a broad smile as she closed her eyes again and dropped back into a peaceful slumber.

Two days later they sat at the kitchen table early in the morning, going over everything for the twenty-fifth time.

"Your fax got me on the right track," Claudia said, glancing at Jovanic over the rim of a mug of strong black coffee.

"I recognized Lillian's handwriting on that note as soon as I saw it. I didn't know what it meant, but I knew it was a big red flag that Lindsey had put it in her lockbox."

"Did the handwriting tell you she was a stone cold killer?"

"No, it couldn't do that. But it did show that she had a lot to hide. I don't know what would have happened if you hadn't shown up when you did."

"Flare might've taken out her windpipe," he said. "I'd like to have seen that."

"What happened with Kardosian?"

"The D.A. made an offer he couldn't refuse. You were right all along that Heidt was behind everything that happened to you ... the break-in here; the shooting. Ivan's death, Earl Nelson's. Everything *except* Lindsey's death. That was a bizarre coincidence.

"When Lindsey was no longer on the scene, Heidt decided to take advantage and retrieve the tape she'd used to blackmail him; but when Kardosian went to the apartment on the flower delivery pretext, expecting it to be empty, Ivan was there."

"He was just packing up Lindsey's belongings. Poor Ivan. Wrong place, wrong time."

"Kardosian claims he didn't mean to kill him. And, as you know, Earl Nelson was attempting to continue the blackmail, and Heidt wasn't having any of that."

"He fingered Heidt?"

"No, but he did give us the middle man, and when we squeezed him hard enough, he copped to making the connection. Once our pal, Kardosian, started talking, he couldn't spill information fast enough."

A slow smile spread over Claudia's face. "So, is Heidt in jail, too?"

"The arrest warrant is being prepared. I'd say his political career is about over."

"And what about Brandi?"

"We got her into a program. She's a tough little chick, but I think she'll be okay." He pushed back his chair, stood, and came around the table. Drawing her into his arms, he loosened her robe and slipped his hands inside. "Let's think of something more pleasant."

The insistent heat of his hands burned through the silk of her nightgown. Her arms went around his neck and she pressed her body into his. It felt right. Was she falling in love with him? Maybe. And for now, anyway, she had neither the strength nor the desire to resist.

The telephone rang, party-crashing the moment.

"Don't answer it," Jovanic mumbled, his lips warm against her ear.

She pulled away smiling, answered in her business voice, "Good morning, Claudia Rose."

"Ms. Rose," the caller said. "I'm an attorney in Washington, DC. I've got some handwriting here that I'd like you to analyze. It's a case of spousal abuse . . ." He started giving her the details.

She listened intently to the caller and picked up a pen to make notes. Glancing at Jovanic, she read the disappointed resignation on his face. Turned back to the phone and spoke to the would-be client. "Let me take your number. I'll have to get back to you."

Read on for a sneak peek
at the next Claudia Rose mystery
from Sheila Lowe

WRITTEN IN BLOOD

Available September 2009 wherever books
are sold or at penguin.com

The man heaved himself off the driver's seat of a Mercedes sedan, holding on to the door frame until his feet were settled on the asphalt. The unbuttoned suit had an expensive cut, but it was snug in the shoulders and the belt disappeared under his belly. Thick, wiry hair cut short was just starting to gray. A salt-and-pepper beard hid his jaw.

Despite the cool fall afternoon, his forehead was damp with perspiration as he lugged a briefcase up the wooden stairs, his breathing too labored for a man in his forties.

Claudia Rose stood at her front door waiting for him, thinking he looked like a heart attack waiting to happen. Then her attention was drawn back to the Mercedes.

A woman stepped out with a wriggling bichon frise clamped under one arm. She wore a plum-colored Akris Punto fitted jacket and short pleated skirt on the kind of figure most women would kill to have. A phone pressed to her ear with the hand that wasn't holding the dog, she bumped the door shut with a curvy hip and followed her huffing companion to the staircase.

The stylish woman was Claudia's new client, Paige Sorensen.

The man reached the porch and proffered a sweaty handshake, trying to hide the fact that he was winded. "Bert Falkenberg," he said. "I—I'm helping Mrs. Sorensen with this matter."

As she considered how to wipe her hand on her pants without his noticing, Claudia smiled and let him precede her into the house. She waited on the porch until Paige Sorensen ended her phone call a few moments later and ran up the stairs.

"You must be Ms. Rose," Paige said, flashing a smile that had probably charmed the pants off more than one admirer. She cuddled the bichon frise to her cheek. "I hope you don't mind that I brought Mikki. I take him everywhere. He's very good."

When she'd phoned for the appointment, Paige had sounded young and vulnerable. This well turned-out woman made Claudia wonder whether her first impression had been a bit hasty. She reached over and gave the squirming dog a scratch behind the ear and invited her client inside.

Paige Sorensen was a recent widow and the headmistress of the Sorensen Academy, a Bel-Air school for girls. She had already explained that her late husband's will was being challenged and she needed a handwriting expert to authenticate his signature. Her attorney had recommended Claudia Rose.

"His children are accusing me—"

Before she could finish, Paige was interrupted by the sound of a ring from her Gucci handbag. She gave Claudia a wry smile and apology as she got the phone out and answered.

Bert Falkenberg sighed, and Claudia wondered why Paige didn't turn the damn thing off. A high-pitched voice, talking fast, carried through the phone.

Paige listened for about thirty seconds. "Okay, Annabelle, stop! Tell Brenda to send the other girls to their rooms. You go to my office and stay there till we get back."

She rang off and turned to Falkenberg. "I told you you should have stayed behind, Bert. *Somebody* needs to be in charge."

He gave her a look. "It'll keep." He turned to Claudia. "Now, here's the situation with Mr. Sorensen's will. . . ."

The touch of Paige's hand on his sleeve halted him midsentence. "I'll handle this."

A flash of annoyance lit Falkenberg's eyes, but he leaned back against the sofa cushions without another word.

"My husband passed away a month ago," Paige began, reiterating what she'd told Claudia over the phone. She gently urged the bichon's haunches into a seated position on her lap. The little dog fidgeted for a moment before he laid his head on a miniature forepaw and closed his eyes.

"He—" She faltered. "He had a stroke—a series of strokes. He left nearly everything to me. His kids accused me of forging his signature on the will." Her eyes filled with tears and her pouty mouth trembled. "It's just crazy. I would never do something like that!"

"Insane," Falkenberg echoed. "Utterly absurd."

Claudia gave them her best sympathetic professional face, adjusting her impression of Paige a little more. If the husband's children were old enough to accuse her of forgery, he must have been significantly older than Paige.

"I'm very sorry for your loss, Mrs. Sorensen," Claudia said. "It's unfortunate, but this sort of thing is common in families." An important question: "Who is your lawyer?"

"Stuart Parsons in Beverly Hills. He said you're the best handwriting expert around."

The compliment pleased Claudia. She liked Parsons because he knew how to protect his expert witnesses from the sometimes vicious attacks that opposing counsels liked to launch.

She said, "Why don't you show me what you've brought. Did you find examples of your husband's genuine signature for me to compare to the questioned one?"

Paige turned to Falkenberg. "You've got the files, Bert?" Returning her gaze to Claudia, she said, "I'm a nice person and they're calling me a liar. I need you to prove it's his signature. There's too much at stake—my reputation."

Millions of dollars, too, Claudia thought. Paige had let that slip when she'd made the appointment. She glanced at Bert Falkenberg, taking note of his broad hands as he snapped open the briefcase and set it on the coffee table between them. Workman's hands with poorly manicured fingernails that seemed more fit for outdoor work. An affront to the Italian silk suit and tie. *He hasn't always worn Armani,* she thought.

Falkenberg removed several file folders from his briefcase and fanned them out on the table. He eased his large
frame back against the cushions and let his eyes roam the
room. His gaze traveled to the family photos on the fireplace mantel, fixing on a snapshot of Claudia standing in
the arms of a tall man. The man was leaning down so they
were cheek to cheek, a rare grin replacing his usual cop's
deadpan expression. Falkenberg stared a long time at that
photograph but his face gave nothing away and Claudia was
left wondering what he was thinking.

Paige repositioned the little dog on her lap so she could
reach the folders Falkenberg had placed on the table. As
she leaned forward, a thick rope of hair the color of clover
honey fell over her shoulder. "These are some checks and
other papers that he—that Torg, my husband—" Fat tears
welled up in each outrageously blue eye and spilled down
her cheeks. Sniffling, she dug in her purse with a trembling
hand and brought out a lacy handkerchief to dab away the
tears. "It was a complete shock when I found out he'd left
everything to me."

Falkenberg shifted his bulk, fidgety. Claudia glanced
over at him, sensing that the abrupt movement was intended
to extinguish some internal reaction to Paige's words. She
murmured something vague and spread open the folder
Paige had handed to her, leafing through the documents
she found inside.

Every signature on the checks, trust deeds and business
contracts had been executed in a bold, firm hand. Extralarge
capital letters, elaborate, written with a flourish.

Flipping over one of the checks, Claudia ran her fingertips across the back, noting that Torg Sorensen had exerted
pressure on the pen strong enough to emboss the paper. To
a handwriting analyst, it all added up to one thing: an in-
flated ego and an aggressive need for power. Torg had been
the type of man you couldn't push around. Paige's husband
could not have been easy to live with.

Returning the items to their folder, Claudia placed it
on the table with a sharp reminder to herself to stay out of
Sorensen's personality.

A major area of her handwriting analysis practice consisted of personality assessment and forensic behavioral profiling. But in cases like this one, her job would be to verify the authorship of a document.

Sometimes it was tempting to blur the lines. Sitting in her living room, no one could prevent Claudia from privately visualizing the man who had penned that showy signature. But in the courtroom her two specialties had to be kept separate.

If she accepted this case her task would be to compare the true, known signatures of Torg Sorensen with the one on his will, and offer an opinion as to its authenticity. Period.

Inside the next file she found three checks, a grant deed and a power of attorney. The signatures on these documents bore little resemblance to the first group. The letter forms had deteriorated to little more than a shaky line, and the writing stroke exposed the tremor of an unsteady hand.

Claudia picked out a grant deed and studied the signature. The name rose at an extreme angle above the printed signature line, the final letters fading into a feeble trail of ink. The state of this signature seemed even more weakened than the others, begging the question of why someone in such obvious poor physical, and possibly mental, condition was signing legal documents.

"Is there any question about his competency to sign?" Claudia asked.

"None," Falkenberg put in before Paige could respond. "I'll testify that he was completely lucid when he signed it. There was no mental impairment. The children wouldn't have a leg to stand on if they tried to use that argument."

"So, you're certain that all the documents in this folder were signed *after* the stroke?"

"Yes," Paige confirmed, still looking as if she might break into tears. "He *insisted* on signing those papers himself."

The third and final folder remained on the table between them. This was the crux of the case, the reason why Paige had sought the help of a handwriting expert: the key document containing the signature contested by her stepchildren.

This folder contained a certified copy of Torg Sorensen's

will. A probate court stamp on the first page indicated that the original was on file in the County of Los Angeles Superior Court.

Claudia viewed the shaky scrawl with a practiced eye. A decline in writing quality was to be expected after a major assault to the brain such as a stroke. It could also make proving authenticity tougher. Before she would form an opinion about the signature she would take measurements and view the documents through her stereo microscope. Already her mind had begun taking inventory of the writing style, the alignment, the master patterns.

"How old was Mr. Sorensen when he died?" she asked.

"Uh, he was, uh . . . seventy-three."

Claudia did a quick mental calculation. That meant Torg Sorensen was at least twice Paige's age.

As if reading her mind, color flooded her client's face. "I know people think I'm just some bimbo who married an old man for his money, but it's not true! And I didn't forge his signature, either! I *loved* him."

Sensing his mistress's distress, Mikki the dog jumped up with a sharp yip. He pressed his front paws against her breast, licking her chin and doing a little cha-cha on her lap.

Bert Falkenberg frowned and cleared his throat, antsy again.

He doesn't know what to do with her.

"I know it's got to be upsetting to be accused," Claudia said gently. "If I take this on, I'm going to need a list of his medications."

Paige frowned. "Why would you need that?"

"Some drugs affect handwriting, so I have to know what he was taking. I'll also want to see his medical records so I'll know exactly what his physical condition was at the time he signed the will."

"He had a stroke, he—"

"Did he sign on his own or was someone guiding his hand? Was he lying down or sitting up? Was he wearing corrective lenses? What kind of writing surface did he use? What time did he take his meds?" Claudia met Paige's bemused expression with a smile. "It's important for me to know these things, especially in a case like this, where there's such a major change in the handwriting. I'll give you a list of questions that I'll need answers to."

Paige looked as if she were exhausted. Her hand moved rhythmically over the little dog's fur, but her eyes were glued to the paper in Claudia's hand. "At first, he couldn't use his right hand at all. Then he started working with a physical therapist, and after they released him from the hospital we hired a private therapist. When was that, Bert?"

"Two and a half weeks after he had the first stroke."

"He was pretty impatient and difficult to deal with." Paige's lips twisted in a cheerless smile and her next words confirmed what Claudia had seen in Torg Sorensen's handwriting. "The truth is, he was *always* difficult, he —" She seemed to catch herself. "About a week after he came home from the hospital, he had me call his secretary over to the house. They were locked up in his room together all afternoon. That must be when he changed his will. It was a couple days later the second stroke hit him and he went into a coma. He never came out of it."

Claudia noted that the will had been witnessed but not notarized, which she thought was surprising, given the size of the Sorensen estate. A mobile notary could have been called in. Why had that not been done?

Two witness signatures appeared under the name of Torg Sorensen, testator. Bert Falkenberg was one of them. He'd written a small, illegible signature that slanted to the left. His handwriting told Claudia that he would not be forthcoming unless there was something in it for him. Left-slanted writers were particularly hard to get to know. The illegibility added another layer of emotional distance and said that he guarded his emotions well.

The second witness signature was larger, more conventional. The name Roberta Miller was penned in the Palmer model common to older women who'd had religious school training, and was typical of many who worked in administrative jobs.

"Is Roberta Miller the secretary?" Claudia asked.

Paige said that she was. The question was more out of

curiosity than a need to know. Paige's attorney would undoubtedly question the witnesses, but unless they were accused of forging the signature on the will, Claudia wouldn't need to interview them herself.

The bleat of a cell phone interrupted again. This time it was Falkenberg who dug out his phone and checked the screen.

"Damn it. Annabelle." He hauled himself off the sofa, excused himself, and headed for the front door as he flipped open the phone.

Claudia watched him go, curious about who Annabelle might be and why she had called so many times.

Paige cleared her throat before offering some explanation. "She's new at the Sorensen Academy," she said. "She's finding it difficult to settle in."

"Oh, is it a residential school?"

"A few of the girls live on-site. Annabelle's one of them. The trouble is, the other girls are constantly picking on her because she's . . . different from them. She doesn't even *try* to fit in."

"Different how?"

Paige looked uncomfortable, looking as though she was sorry she had opened that line of conversation. She leaned forward. "This is confidential, right?"

Getting Claudia's assurance, she continued. "Annabelle tried to kill herself a couple months ago. She came to us right out of the hospital. That's why we can't ignore her phone calls. She's still pretty fragile."

The front door opened and Bert returned. "I'll talk to her when we get back," he said, lowering himself onto the sofa beside Paige.

"She's really taken a liking to Bert," Paige said. "He's become kind of a father figure for some of the girls."

Claudia felt a stirring of interest about Annabelle, who had been so unhappy that she had attempted suicide, yet she felt comfortable calling this bear of a man for . . . what? Support? He did have that big cuddly look. Maybe she saw him as a teddy bear. A young girl might be drawn to that kind of man.

An image of her own father, loving but ineffectual in the face of her mother's vitriol, reached out from the past. She firmly pushed the image away.

"Do you work at the school, Mr. Falkenberg?"

He nodded. "I help Mrs. Sorensen with the business end of running the Sorensen Academy. The administration of a private school is quite different from a public one."

"I'm sure it must be." Returning her attention to the case, Claudia indicated the file folders on the table. "I have to be frank, Mrs. Sorensen. Because of the physiological effects of the stroke on your husband's handwriting, this is a difficult case. I'll do my examination and let you know whether I think I can help."

Paige visibly sagged with disappointment. "But Bert *saw* him sign it, didn't you, Bert?"

"Yes, yes, that's right, I did."

Paige's body strained toward Claudia, something like desperation showing in her eyes. "You *have* to testify that his signature is genuine—that's what I'm paying for!"

"What you're paying for is my objective opinion, and that's all I can promise you." Stacking the folders together in a neat pile, Claudia slid them back across the coffee table with an apologetic shrug. "I'm not your lawyer, Mrs. Sorensen, I'm an advocate of the court, and that means I deal with the truth, *whatever* it may be."

"But I'm *telling* you the truth. He signed the will."

For a moment, no one spoke. The sudden roar of a leaf blower outside shattered the silence, startling them. The sound rose and fell under the window, amplifying the tension in the room as the gardener walked the noisy machine up the pathway. The return to quiet when he switched it off was as jarring as the racket it had made.

Bert Falkenberg abruptly snatched the file folders from the table and tossed them into his briefcase, giving Claudia an icy glance. "If you can't handle this case, maybe you'll refer us to someone who can."